COFFEESHOP INFO CENTRE AMSTERDAM

'Get Smart Before You Get High'

Free Information
Coffeshop information & Directions

CBD Supplements
Oil, Melt Tablets, Edibles, CBD E-liquids & more

Amsterdam Genetics
Cannabis Seeds, Merchandise & Smoke Gear

3 Minutes From Amsterdam Central Station
Prins Hendrikkade 10 | 1012 TK Amsterdam

coffeeshop-info-centre-amsterdam.com

CONNOISSEUR GUIDE

Amsterdam
COFFEESHOPS

Photography
William Llewellyn
Krzysztof Kadynski
Tomas Cotter
Ava Llewellyn
Craig Canna

Written By
William Llewellyn

*Information gathering and review were a team effort.

Layout Design
Catherine Llewellyn

Cover Design
Andrea Ho

Editors
Catherine Llewellyn
Tim Zakowski

Digital
Diana Pinkett
Nick Karpenko

FIRST EDITION

Published by Weedful, LLC.
Copyright © 2019. All Rights Reserved.

visit:

www.connoisseurguide.com
www.amsterdamcoffeeshops.com

Disclaimer: This book features content about marijuana and related products, which may be illegal. All content is for educational and entertainment purposes only. This book is intended for readers over the age of 18 years, and is not intended to condone or encourage the use of marijuana. No part of this book may be reproduced, stored in a retrieval system or transmitted in any form or means electronic, mechanical, photocopying, recording, or otherwise, without the express written permission of WEEDFUL, LLC. Fort Collins, CO 80525. Brief text quotations with use of photographs are exempted for book review purposes only. The opinions and presented herein is believed reliable, but its accuracy and completeness are not guaranteed by the publisher. All rights reserved.

SINCE 1992 THE BORDER OFFERS THE BEST PRODUCTS AND WELCOMES YOU WITH A WARM SMILE.

The Border opened its doors in 1992 on the border between Amsterdam and Amstelveen. Since that time it became a benchmark. The Border only sells the best premium products and is easily accessible. Not just for those coming from Amsterdam, but from the surrounding municipalities as well.

THINK GREEN
THE BORDER

Our close-knit, enthusiastic team, comprised of twenty staff, have enjoyed working at The Border for years. We try to give every customer our utmost attention and provide them with as much information about the products as possible. All our bar staff has an official budtender diploma, a certificate for good hospitality, and confirmation that the holder has the proper cannabinoids expertise.

WWW.THEBORDER.NL

ABOUT THIS GUIDE

The Connoisseur Guide series by WEEDFUL aims to help readers discover the exceptional products and experiences that can be found in today's legal cannabis markets around the world. We highlight the craft cultivators, the artisan producers, and the innovators that are taking the market to new heights of excellence. Our motto is "Smoke like a Local" because we know it takes time and experience to find the most exceptional products in any given area.

We could not have chosen any other city except Amsterdam for our inaugural edition. In the history of cannabis, this city will always have a special place. Amsterdam had stood alone for decades, as the only city in the world where you could buy and consume cannabis openly. It was a place cannabis users felt free to just be themselves. Even with all of the progress made in other countries, there is still no place like Amsterdam when it comes to embracing the culture of cannabis.

Inside this edition we review ALL 168 coffeeshops in Amsterdam. Some are extremely serious about cultivation. You can find some truly outstanding flower here if you know where to look. Other shops specialize in fine hashish, or gourmet edibles. Then there are the places we really like to hang out; some of the most comfortable, chill, and unpretentious establishments. Others still stand out for their history, or elaborate décor and amenities. We review all of the city coffeeshops in this book, but do highlight our favorites in a variety of categories.

This guide was created by colleagues from The Netherlands, UK, and the United States, who all share a love for this city. We spend a lot of time in the coffeeshops here, and enjoy sharing our experiences with others.

We hope you enjoy Connoisseur Guide: Amsterdam Coffeeshops edition.

How to Use this Guide
This book has been organized into three sections.

- **General Information:** The first section includes general information on the coffeeshops, the law, and the products you will find here. We also provide some tips for spotting connoisseur quality items, and cover some important unwritten rules on shop etiquette.
- **Coffeeshop Directory:** The second, and largest, section of this book, is where we explore all 168 coffeeshops in Amsterdam in detail. This includes descriptions, photos, addresses, hours, and shop amenities.
- **Our Favorite Shops:** The third section is at the back of the book for quick referencing. Here we highlight the shops we feel are the most noteworthy establishments in Amsterdam. This includes our favorite hangout shops, and go-to spots for connoisseur weed (flower), hashish, and edibles.

Table of Contents

Part I: General Information

Cannabis and the Law 11
Coffeeshop Etiquette 15
Connoisseur Flower (Weed) 19
Hashish Guide 23
Extracts (Concentrates) 27
Moon Rocks (Caviar) 31

Part II: Coffeeshop Directory

Abraxas 34
Amnesia 36
Amsterdamned 38
Atlas 39
Baba 40
Babylon 42
Bagheera 44
Balou 46
Barney's 48
Barney's Lounge 50
Barraka 52
Basjoe 54
Best Friends Centrum 56
Best Friends Oost 58
Best Friends Zuid 60
Betty Boop 62
Black Star 64
Blue Lagoon 66
Blue Sea 67
Bluebird 68
Boerejongens Bij 70
Boerejongens Centre 72
Boerejongens Sloterdijk 74
Boerejongens West 76
Bronx 78
Bulldog 90 80
Bulldog Energy 82
Bulldog Harbour (formerly Port 26) 84
Bulldog Palace/Ex-policestation 86
Bulldog Rock Shop 88
Bullwackie 90
Bushdocter 91
Carmona 92

Catch 33 94
Central 96
Chapiteau 98
Cheech and Chong's 100
City Hall 102
Club Media 104
CoffeeshopAmsterdam 106
Crash Light 108
Crush 110
D&L 112
Dampkring 114
De Bommel 116
De Kade 118
De Keeper 120
De Kroon 122
De Overkant 124
De Prijs 125
De Republiek 126
De Supermarkt 128
De Watersnip 130
DNA 132
Dolphins 134
Eastwood 136
Easy Times 138
El Guapo 140
El Marssa 142
Family First 144
Feels Good 146
Flashback 147
Flower Power 148
Free 1 150
Freedom 152
Funky Munkey 154
Funny People 156
Get Down To It 158
Goa 160
Green House Centrum 162
Green House Namaste 164
Green House Pijp 166
Green House United 168
Green Place 170
Green Planet 172
Greenhouse Effect 174
Grey Area 176
Happy Days 178
Happy Feelings 180
Happy People 182
Het Ballonnetje 184
Het Gelderse 186
Hugo 188

Hunter's	190
Hunter's Bros	191
Hunter's Filiaal	192
Hunter's Mercator	193
Ibiza	194
Johnny	196
Jolly Joker	198
Kadinsky 1	200
Kadinsky 2	202
Kadinsky 3	204
Kashmir	206
Katsu	208
Kooi	210
La Tertulia	212
LoFt	214
Los Angeles	216
Massawa	218
Mediterrané	220
Millennium	221
Mr. K and Co	222
Nachtegaal	224
New Times	225
Nice Place	226
Nieuw Amsterdam	228
Nogal Wiedes	230
Pacific	231
Papillon	232
Paradox	234
Popeye	236
Prix d'Ami	238
Reefer	240
Relax	242
Relax Zuid	244
Resin	246
Rick's Coffeeshop	248
Risky Business	249
Rock It	250
Rockland	252
Rookies	254
Roots	256
Roxy	258
Rusland	260
Ruthless	262
Sensemillia	263
Sensemillia Osdorp	264
Siberië	266
Smoke Palace	268
Smokey	270
Softland	271
Solo	272

Speakeasy 274
Stone's 276
Super Skunk 278
Super Skunk De Pijp 280
'T Keteltje 281
'T Ooievaartje 282
Terminator 284
The Border 285
The Dream 286
The Noon 288
The Old Church 290
The Otherside 291
The Plug 292
The Point 294
The Saint 296
The Spirit 298
The Store 300
The Stud 302
Topweazle 304
Trefpunt 306
Tweede Kamer 308
Vondel 310
Voyagers 312
Warda 1 314
Warda 2 315
Wauw Shop 316
Yin-Yang 317
Yo-Yo 318
1e Hulp 320
3 Floors Lounge 322
96 324
137 325
156 326
420 Café 327
420 Coffeeshop 328

Part III: Our Favorite Shops

Best Coffeeshops 333
Best Weed Spots 339
Best Hashish 345
Best Edibles 351
Best Vapor Lounges 357
Special Interest 363
Map 366

GENERAL

CANNABIS AND THE LAW

In 1976, the Netherlands officially amended its drug laws to make a distinction between hard and soft drugs. Soft drugs are those considered to be less harmful to your health than hard drugs, such as cocaine or heroin. This began what is referred to as the gedoogbeleid, or Dutch toleration policy. Essentially, for the sake of reducing harm, improving the use environment, and separating drug markets, certain criminal activities are tolerated in the country. Cannabis use is among them; considered a soft drug under this framework. Though it was never officially made legal in the Netherlands, certain laws pertaining to cannabis possession, cultivation, and sale are not enforced, provided a strict set of circumstances are met. If you understand these laws and follow some basic rules, you should find your visit to Amsterdam to be a wonderful experience.

Possession:

In the Netherlands, possession of up to 5 grams of cannabis product (marijuana, hashish) is tolerated. There is no criminal punishment for having up to this amount on your person. Larger quantities, however, are not tolerated. It is not a great idea to walk around with your pockets full of marijuana. Though random search is highly unlikely in the Netherlands, coffeeshops are open to police inspection. We were there once when police locked the doors at a cannabis-related event, and searched attendees inside to see if they had more than 5 grams. Typically, if you have more than 5 grams the police will confiscate it, though technically you could be fined or otherwise punished.

Sale in Coffeeshops:

The sale of cannabis is tolerated in the Netherlands, provided it takes place in specifically licensed coffeeshops. The main reasoning behind this is that it separates soft and hard drug markets. As the logic goes, if cannabis users are permitted to buy their product in these licensed businesses, they are less likely to be exposed to hard drugs when purchasing on the black market. These coffeeshops, however, must adhere to a strict set of regulations. They are also open to frequent random inspections, and can have their licenses suspended or revoked if found to be violating any of the rules. These rules include:

- No sale of cannabis to minors (<18 yrs old).
- No advertising the sale of cannabis.
- No sales larger than 5 grams.
- Must not cause any nuisance.
- No use or sale of hard drugs.
- Cannot hold >500 grams of inventory.

Cultivation:

Cannabis cultivation laws are not enforced in the Netherlands when growing 5 plants or less for personal use. However, the police often do confiscate the plants if they are found. Commercial cultivation is not permitted in Amsterdam. There is no regulatory or legal framework in place for it at this time, though we are beginning to see some steps in that direction. For now, what is known as the "backdoor" problem persists. Simply put, cannabis is tolerated when it leaves the "front door" of the coffeeshop, but the inventory is produced through illegal channels. Getting it into the coffeeshop (through the "backdoor") remains a crime. Dutch tolerance has created a strange middle ground. Imagine if alcohol was legally sold in bars and restaurants, but all brewing was illegal, and all bar

CONNOISSEUR GUIDE: AMSTERDAM

and restaurant owners had to buy from the black market as if we were still in the alcohol prohibition era. The current policy does address some problems, but unfortunately ignores others.

Extracts:

Not all forms of cannabis are permitted in the Netherlands. Flower is fine. Traditional resin (hashish) is fine. So is Nederhash (Isolator). Hash oil, however, is not permitted. It is classified as a hard drug under the nation's Opium Act. According to a recent legal case, the defining characteristic is that the former types contain plant matter. The latter is highly concentrated and principally devoid of plant material. As such, any product that is very high in THC and free of botanical residue, such as is the case with items like BHO, wax, and shatter, risks being classified like hash-oil under these laws... a hard drug.

Edibles:

Edible cannabis products are permitted in the Netherlands provided they use crushed cannabis as the psychoactive ingredient. The taste of cannabis flower can be hard to mask, however. This makes edibles preparation a bit tricky. In the U.S., marijuana companies rarely use flower for edibles. Extracts are utilized almost exclusively, as the taste can be more neutral and far easier to mask. But hash oil is banned in the Netherlands, along with other highly concentrated extracts. Thus, they cannot be used in food preparation.

Right now, only products that are cake-based like brownies and muffins seem to be allowed in Amsterdam. This is probably due to the fact that they could easily be made with crushed flower. Items such as cereal bars, gummy bears, and infused drinks are all illegal, as the main ingredient in each instance would have to be some form of purified extract. Authorities have been pretty active about enforcing this as of late.

Cannabis Smoking:

Cannabis smoking doesn't fall under the same prohibitions as tobacco smoking in the Netherlands. Though officially banned in certain areas like near schools and playgrounds, technically speaking, one could still smoke cannabis in a wide range of other public places without violating anti-tobacco smoking laws. In 2018, Den Hague was the first Dutch city to specifically ban public cannabis consumption in many areas of the city center. Amsterdam and other municipalities are sure to follow suit. We've long held that regardless of what you could technically get away with in this city, Amsterdam has close to two hundred coffeeshops. Most of them have an ample smoking lounge for your use. Marijuana remains technically illegal in this country. It is best to be a polite visitor, and limit smoking to the coffeeshops, private residences, or open spaces where you are unlikely to offend others.

Tobacco Smoking:

Recent years have brought fourth expanded prohibitions on the public consumption of tobacco in the Netherlands. Smoking is now banned at work and in enclosed public spaces including shopping centres, bars, cafés and restaurants. Note that this ban specifically effects tobacco, not cannabis. Coffeeshops (and other businesses) are exempt from the tobacco consumption ban provided they install a separate room specifically for smoking tobacco products. This room must be closed off from the rest of the establishment, such that smoke does not readily escape into other areas. Employees are also not permitted in the smoking room during open hours, so this area is to be unserviced. If these requirements are not met, than only pure cannabis products may be consumed on premises. No mixed joints!

It is not uncommon to find visitors of coffeeshops unaware of, or simply ignoring, these laws. Some feel that is it acceptable to smoke mixed joints in any coffeeshop so long as nobody is complaining. You'll often receive advice about just keeping tobacco "off the table." We highly discourage this practice. Coffeeshops are subject to random inspections by Dutch authorities. We've seen a shop temporarily lose its license during such inspection, because a single customer was found to be smoking tobacco. If you really want to make yourself unwelcome at a coffeeshop, be the sole reason they have to close down for 2 weeks. There are plenty of coffee shops with special tobacco rooms, which you'll find noted in this guide. Stick to them if mixed joints are your thing.

Wietpas/Residents Only:

In 2013, the Netherlands passed a law that only residents of the country are permitted to visit coffeeshops and purchase cannabis. However, local municipalities may opt out of this requirement. Amsterdam was first among them. All visitors to the city with proper identification showing they are over the age of 18 are still allowed in the coffeeshops. If you venture outside the city, however, don't just automatically expect entry into the local scene. You may be refused. Neighboring Haarlem is an exception. They remain very open there, as well.

Wietpas (Weed Pass) was to be a national membership requirement for coffeeshops. To gain entry to these businesses, not only would you have to be a resident of the country, but you would also have to apply for access to specific establishment(s), and then be granted a club card. This would obviously be a much more restrictive form of the current law. However, the Wietpas was dropped in 2012.

Anyone over the age of 18 can still enter the coffeeshops in Amsterdam.

COFFEESHOP ETIQUETTE

First time to the coffeeshops? You are in for a treat. Amsterdam is among Europe's most welcoming and fun cities. And frankly, the coffeeshops can be some of the coolest, most friendly, and chill places on the planet to visit. After all, the scene here is that of a hub for consumers from around the world who come to enjoy cannabis and mingle among fellow enthusiasts. You will not find many uptight people. Even so, there are some things to consider when it comes to local etiquette. Written and unwritten rules exist here. Violating them will quickly make you stand out as a "newbie". Do not worry; we are not talking anything too serious. Still, it is not all that hard to fit in like an Amsterdam regular if you know what to expect. In this section, we review some of the more important aspects of proper coffeeshop etiquette.

#1: Buy Something

Would you walk into a restaurant with your own food, and expect a table so you can hang out and eat? Of course not. Yet some visitors to Amsterdam get quite upset when they are expected to buy weed and/or drinks at every coffeeshop they visit. Remember, these are businesses so you should buy something. It would be recommended to purchase some smoke if you find product you like, and grab a coffee or drink if you plan to stay. If you are going to be there a while, get a refill. Do not nurse one coffee for four hours.

#2: Don't Touch the Weed

When the budtender shows you a bin of fresh bud, the recommended etiquette is to let the staff handle it. Fight the urge to reach out and grab the product. Cannabis buds are fragile. They are coated with fine hair-like structures called trichomes, which hold the precious cannabinoids like THC and CBD. These trichomes rupture easily. You know when you break up weed with your fingers, and they get all stinky and sticky? Those are busted-open trichomes oozing resin all over your hands. For some, grabbing the product is a major faux pas. So it is "look but do not touch", unless you are specifically prompted to. If you are, handle the product gently, ideally by holding the stem only.

#3: No Sunglasses, Hats, or Hoods

If you walk into a coffeeshop wearing a hat, hood, or sunglasses, you may be asked to remove it. The explanation is simple: security. These accessories all disguise your identity to varying degrees. Remember, these businesses are handling a lot of weed and cash on a constant basis. It should be understandable that they are guarded. These shops are not immune to crime. Many owners and staff have been robbed over the years, some even harmed in the process.

And on the other hand, let's be frank - sunglasses indoors?

GENERAL

#4: No Tobacco in Most Shops

Tobacco smoking is now prohibited in public buildings in Amsterdam, including all restaurants, hotels, and cafés. Coffeeshops have a specific exemption, but only if they have on premises a separate tobacco lounge. This lounge will be closed off from the rest of the shop, and staff cannot enter during business hours (do not expect table service). You will usually find the tobacco lounge in a second room somewhere in the back, behind a glass door. Given the limited size of most shops, a separate closed off tobacco room is not widely feasible. Only some shops have them. For the rest, only pure cannabis smoking is permitted.

This next bit is important. Some coffeeshops might not notice what every customer is smoking, or choose not to chase down every customer in violation. As such, you are likely to see some mixed joint smoking during your travels, where it is not allowed. Please, do not join in and ignore the rule. Shops have been given suspensions (temporary closures) for not enforcing the tobacco ban. Not only will other travelers be denied the opportunity to visit the establishment but a closure means no revenue, and lost wages for staff. It is just not good for anybody. There are coffeeshops in Amsterdam that have invested in a tobacco room. Patronize them, and hold off on tobacco use in the others.

#5: Ask Before Taking Pictures

The coffeeshop business is still a quasi-legal industry in Holland. The advertising of cannabis is not allowed in Amsterdam. There is also a lot of illegal activity that goes on to support these shops, and perhaps some stigma about working in them. With these things in mind, some owners are very "old school". They shun digital attention. If you pull out your camera in one of these shops and start snapping away, you may get yelled at, or worse, thrown out. Other shop owners are remarkably open with their customers taking pictures. Many even encourage social media sharing, as they understand this form of "free advertising" drives a lot of their business and creates customer connections with the shop. How will you know what kind of shop you are in? Simply ask. They will likely appreciate the courtesy regardless of how they feel.

#6: Tip a Helpful Budtender

Did you have a positive experience with your budtender? Did they help you find the perfect strain? If so, consider leaving a tip. How much? In our experience, the Dutch are very practical with tipping. At restaurants, most patrons will leave a couple of euros per person extra, five if the service was exceptional. Coffeeshops are similar. A couple of euros with your order would no doubt be appreciated. Remember, this is a service job so like any other, reward it if it is good.

CONNOISSEUR FLOWER (WEED)

GENERAL

There is no question about it. Amsterdam has a stellar reputation for cannabis. After all, this city has long been a global center for the development and trade of new strain genetics. The varieties you can find here are seemingly endless. The quality of many options, truly world class. However, things are not perfect. Amsterdam has never had a legal market for cannabis cultivation. Operators are forced to rely entirely on an illicit supply chain. This presents some challenges for both those in the coffeeshop business, as well as consumers. Principle among them; consistency. Not every product in every shop is equally impressive.

Having become so involved in the coffeeshop scene here in Amsterdam, we have come to appreciate some things about the local market. One of them; the underground supply chain is highly competitive. That is, there are not enough top quality grow operations to supply every coffeeshop. Supply is a constant challenge - the more selective the shopkeeper wants to be, the more difficulty they may face in meeting inventory demands. In fact, the better shops often have to compete with each other to lock in the best growers with long-term commitments.

Generally speaking, product quality is very high here in Amsterdam. Still, the highest quality product, what we consider to be of connoisseur grade, is not going to be found in every shop in the city. It is hit or miss. However, with a little guidance and a selective eye, there is an ample supply of world class cannabis to be discovered here. In this section, we offer some tips to help you identify what we would rate as connoisseur-grade product. Later on, some of our favorite shops for finding it.

How to Spot Connoisseur Flower

COLOR: Top quality flower generally grows from healthy, meticulously cared for plants. Though the physical appearance of strains may vary greatly from one another, one of the ways this care is often reflected is in the vibrant expression of the plant's natural color(s). If the plant has a mix of greens and oranges or purples, we generally want these to all look rich and well-defined.

TRIM: High quality cannabis should be carefully hand-trimmed. This process removes leaf material on the outside of the bud, leaving clean, exposed flower. It should, however, not be over-trimmed. Cuts into the flower itself can damage trichomes and expose cannabinoids and terpenes to oxidation. The bud should also be clear of unnecessary stem. The only visible part of the main stem should be at the bottom of the flower, and should only be enough to hold.

TRICHOMES: High THC content is usually a big focus with connoisseur cannabis. The best producing plants will usually look almost frosted over with a dense covering of shiny trichomes. With low potency/quality cannabis, you might still see the trichomes, but the density may

GENERAL

be too low to be noteworthy. Also know that potency is not always the main focus with connoisseur cannabis. Some plants may be grown for their rare flavor or unique effects.

TOUCH: With high resin production, cannabis buds should be tacky or sticky to the touch. As this reaches extreme levels (25%+ THC), we may even find the flower to be hard and crunchy. Tighter, denser buds are also generally safer than looser or "more open" flower, which might be a reflection of less-than-optimal growing conditions. Connoisseur bud is also usually dried to a point where the stem snaps, but the flower retains some moisture. It will not burst into powder when broken up. There are some exceptions to this when growing in drier climates.

SMELL: This is a key aspect in which the best weed reveals itself. Connoisseur cannabis should be carefully dried for maximum aroma. Look for strong, appealing odors such as cheese, citrus, pine, fruit, diesel, etc. This smell should be immediately noticeable upon opening the jar. When producers dry plants too quickly, it can rob it of aroma and flavor, which might otherwise better develop during a proper cure. Avoid bud that does not smell or smells weakly, or worse, seems "off" with scents of mold, hay, or wet grass.

TASTE: The flavor of cannabis flower can be diminished if the plant is not flushed (the nutrients withheld before harvest) or dried properly. Flower that has been rushed to market might still have a strong psychoactive effect, but could be lacking when it comes to taste. Connoisseur cannabis must be carefully cultivated and prepared if you want the best flavor from it. It should also smoke smoothly, and not be harsh on the throat.

SEEDS: Commercial and connoisseur grade cannabis alike should not have seeds. When a female flower (bud) producing plant has been fertilized by a male, it enters a phase of seed production. With this, it produces far less THC. In today's quality-driven market, seeded cannabis is not worth much. Occasionally, one or two seeds slips in. That might not be a big deal, but you never want to accept cannabis bud that is visibly seeded.

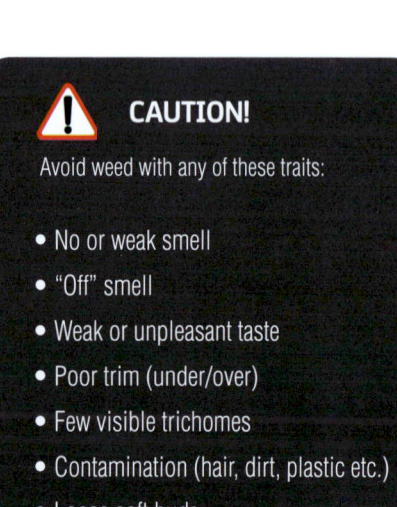

⚠ CAUTION!

Avoid weed with any of these traits:

- No or weak smell
- "Off" smell
- Weak or unpleasant taste
- Poor trim (under/over)
- Few visible trichomes
- Contamination (hair, dirt, plastic etc.)
- Loose soft buds
- Seeds

CONNOISSEUR GUIDE: AMSTERDAM

INDICA VS. SATIVA

You will often find the cannabis flower (weed) sold as **Indica** or **Sativa**, or even a **Hybrid** mix of the two. Sometimes, the same can also be said for other cannabis products like hashish and edibles. These titles are based on a classification system that dates back many decades, and suggests there are three subspecies of the cannabis plant, each with distinct physical and psychological effects. With this general classification system, the consumer is presented with different options depending on the type of high that is desired. The generally accepted cannabis subspecies are as follows.

Sativa

Originally identified in central Asia. Sativa plants are characterized as being tall (may exceed 10 ft. in height), with more widely spaced branches and thin leaf structure. These plants usually express high THC (tetrahydrocannabinol) concentrations, which is the primary psychoactive component of cannabis. The high from this type of cannabis is usually said to have pronounced energy and creative properties.

Indica

This subspecies of cannabis was first identified in India. Indica is described as a short and bushy plant, often reaching only 3-4 ft. in height. It also has a thick leaf structure, with a more pronounced density of branches and flowers (buds). Resin production may also be higher. Indicas are high in THC, which is often accompanied by a notable concentration of CBD (cannabidiol). The high from the Indica plant is usually described as being sedating, with more distinct pain-relieving and appetite-stimulating effects.

Ruderalis

There is also a third type of cannabis according to this classification system. Ruderalis is a wild (uncultivated) subspecies, which is said to originate in Europe. This is a short plant with minimal resin production. Very low in THC, ruderalis is only interbred with other species of cannabis for its potential autoflowering properties. Such hybrids may flower under longer light conditions.

As science delves more deeply into the genetics and physiological effects of cannabis, our traditional classification system is being called into question. Some researchers suggest there are actually 2-3 distinct species of the plant. Others view the original subspecies system to be overly simplistic and lacking. It does appear that the psychoactive effects of this plant are much more complex than originally thought. There are hundreds of different cannabinoids, terpenoids, and flavonoids in cannabis. Many of these may turn out to play a role in dictating how a particular strain affects the user. As science continues to explore this subject, it is likely that our original Sativa and Indica product classifications will give way to a robust system, which is based more on chemistry than lineage.

For now though, the traditional Indica/Sativa/Hybrid labels remain widely accepted. It is important to understand that even if oversimplified, these are honest attempts by the cannabis shops and growers to describe the effects of various cannabis products for users. Though empirical, the general associations between certain plants and effects may still be strong. With this in mind, we can generally rely on these labels for determining some general traits about a product. Cannabis that produces a more sedating high, the classic "couch lock" effect, is likely to be described as an Indica. If it produces a more energetic and "heady" high, it will probably be listed as a Sativa. Products described as Hybrid might fall somewhere in the middle; the effects perhaps not as clearly defined by one of these two labels.

HASHISH GUIDE

Hashish (in Dutch, "Hasj") is a cannabis product made by extracting and concentrating the plant's resins. Within these sticky resins we find a majority of the cannabinoid, essential oil, and terpene content of cannabis, and thus much of its psychoactive and therapeutic activity. By isolating these resins from other inert plant materials, we can make products with a much higher percentage of THC than the unprocessed flower (bud) itself. Hashish is also more easily transported and stored than cannabis flower, which can be quite helpful in markets such as Amsterdam, where cultivation and bulk supply remain illegal.

You will find two primary categories of hashish in the coffeeshops - imported and domestic. These two categories of hash are often quite distinct from one another in makeup and potency. Further, they tend to sell at notably different price points. This section will serve as a general guide to both types of hashish, and how to spot the best connoisseur-grade products in each.

Imported Hashish (15-45% THC):

Traditional hashish is one of the oldest cannabis resin products known, having been widely circulated throughout Asia and Europe for many centuries. This form of hashish is made by collecting and pressing the resin-producing trichomes that grow on the outer surface of the cannabis plant. This is generally accomplished by dry-sifting the plant against fine screens. With this, the bulk of other plant materials are discarded, and the THC-rich kief powder collected. The smaller the holes in the screens, the finer the kief retrieved, and generally the higher quality the product. After collection, this kief is pressed into the hard blocks we recognize as hashish.

You can find imported hashish in all of the city's coffeeshops. This is (by far) the most popular form of cannabis resin available in Amsterdam. A majority of the hashish sold here has been imported from Morocco, though you can commonly find products from Afghanistan, Pakistan, India, and Lebanon here as well. In this unregulated supply market, quality can vary greatly. As such, personal inspection of any hashish you buy is going to be much more useful than purchasing a product based on its country of origin. This inspection should involve a close review of its appearance, texture, aroma, and effect. Here are some things to consider when shopping.

Black and Brown Hash (Above) Blonde Hash (Below)

COLOR: The color of hashish usually ranges from tan (blonde) to black. These products are often sold in light and dark varieties given this difference. Color is not nec-

CONNOISSEUR GUIDE: AMSTERDAM

essarily an indicator of potency or quality, though. The same kief powder is often made into both light and dark varieties, depending on how much pressure and heat are used when pressing the blocks (heat and pressure tend to produce darker products). Generally though, avoid greener hash, as it reflects a great deal of plant material, and lean towards darker varieties, which tend to be darker due to a high percentage of resins.

A pocket microscope can be very useful with sample evaluation. The attached photo set shows a piece of Moroccan hashish, both at no zoom and under 100x magnification. You can see that the hash is a pressed mass of clean trichomes. We do not see any notable content of extraneous plant fiber.

Moroccan hashish chunk (Above). 100x Magnification (Below)

TEXTURE: High quality imported hashish is usually softer. Again, pressure and heat play a role in determining the physical properties of the final product, so there are always going to be exceptions. Still, it is generally good when a hash is pliable in your hand. It suggests that a high concentration of oily resins/terpenes should be found in it. Alternately, very hard hashish might have a lot of unwanted plant fiber. It can still be a decent product, but if you are looking for the best quality, we recommend opting for a softer variety.

SMELL: Smell can be very useful in identifying connoisseur-quality hashish. If the product is fresh and well crafted, it should be highly aromatic due to the high concentration of plant terpenes. Similarly, it should be notably flavorful when smoked. Like cannabis in general, the smells and flavors of hashish can vary a lot from one product to another given the diversity of the plants used to make it. But it should be flavorful. That is arguably one of the great things about connoisseur-quality hashish. The tastes, smells, and effects can be as diverse as cannabis itself; a richly enjoyed experience on many levels.

POTENCY: With regard to potency, random testing of samples in Dutch coffeeshops (Rigter en Niesink, 2017) found the median THC percentage of imported hashish to be 20%. The THC level was as low as 1.9% in some samples, however, and as high as 45.8%. Most products fell between 17-26% THC. Perhaps contributing to some very low numbers is the fact that hashish is sometimes adulterated with sawdust, dirt, or other materials. Again, the market is unregulated. The good news is the quality has been trending up, with significantly higher potencies noted in recent years. Connoisseur quality hashish generally has a high percentage of THC because it is made from more refined kief powder. With this in mind, it is generally better to opt for the stronger product, even if you have to use less of it.

🔥 Hashish is best for smoking, either mixed in a joint or as a bowl topper.

Nederhasj (30-66% THC):

The second general type of hashish, domestic, is widely known in the local market as Nederhasj, or simply "Dutch Hash". This is typically made via a more modern water extraction process. This involves submerging cannabis in ice water, and using fine mesh bags to separate the plant's trichomes from other materials. These products are often also called isolator, water hash, bubble hash, or full melt. The latter term actually refers to one of the highest purity water-hash products, which melts completely when smoked due to the very high portion of plant oils.

COLOR: Like imported hashish, Nederhasj comes in a range of light and dark colors. Again, color is not necessarily an indicator of quality, though you do want to avoid products that are greener as they will contain more plant matter. Lighter products in general could reflect less plant material and higher potency, but again, there can be many exceptions based on the method of processing.

APPEARANCE: Compared to imported hashes, many high quality Nederhasj products do look more "sugary." This is due to the high concentration of tiny resinous trichome heads. These can provide a bit of shine and grit when isolated away from the other plant materials. Upon close visual examination, many look beautiful and obviously quite pure. If high heat and pressure are used in the pressing though, this sugary appearance may be lost, and a darker, more tar-like mass formed.

SMELL: While the water extraction process used to make Nederhasj may be better at extracting THC, it does have its drawbacks. For one, it is more open to the loss of terpenes, especially if not followed carefully and gently. As such, bubble hash or water hash concentrates are sometimes slightly less aromatic and flavorful than imported hashish, at least if the imported product is fresh and of high quality. The yield with Nederhasj is also fairly low for producers. This leads to much higher costs in the shops. Be cautious of cheap Nederhasj for this reason. It could just be a relabeled import.

POTENCY: Water extraction can produce a much more refined product than traditional dry sifting. The technology is better at isolating the resinous head of the trichome, and excluding other inert plant materials. Combine this with the higher THC concentrations found in domestic cannabis in general, and you can have a very potent form of hashish. Random testing of samples in Dutch coffeeshops (Rigter en Niesink, 2017) found the median THC percentage of Nederhasj to be 32.6%, which is more than 50% higher than the imports. The THC range during these tests was as low as 8.9%, and as high as 66% THC. Most products fell between 25-45% THC, again, quite above the imported counterparts.

🔥 Nederhasj is best for smoking, though full melt hash may also be amenable to dabbing.

Kief / Dry Sift (20-60% THC):

Kief is also occasionally sold in Amsterdam. The term "crystals" is sometimes used for this product. Normally used in the making of hashish, this is simply un-pressed material. Note that higher purity kief is usually lighter in color. Similarly, dark or greenish kief may reflect the intrusion of significant plant material.

One of the advantages of this type of concentrate is that it is not made with solvents or high temperatures. As such, a significant portion of the plant's original terpenes are preserved. This means that kief can be quite aromatic and flavorful. However, air also easily penetrates the loose powder. This can oxidize (damage) and evaporate volatile components. As such, kief does not make for the most shelf-stable product. This type of concentrate is fairly rare in Amsterdam, though located on occasion.

🔥 Kief is best for smoking, either mixed in a joint or as a bowl topper.

EXTRACTS (CONCENTRATES)

Imported hashish and Nederhasj dominate the scene in Amsterdam for cannabis resin products. The market is not quite as diverse as the United States, where you now find a wide range of potent cannabis extracts such as shatter, wax, oil, live resin, sauce, and crystalline THC. This is due to an old Opium Law in the Netherlands, which defines "hash oil" as a hard drug. It appears the presence of plant matter in the end-product is the legal consideration here, though there is some grey area as to where this line is drawn. As such, you may still find some extracts on occasion. This section explains some of the basic types.

Wax / Budder (60-85%+ THC):

Wax is a modern form of concentrate that was made popular by cannabis dispensaries in the United States. It is usually made with a solvent such as butane or propane. With a bit of filtering, the solvent can be used very effectively to strip resins from the plant. These are collected in a gooey mass rich in cannabinoids and terpenes, which may be whipped into a waxy consistency. Compressed ("supercritical") CO_2 gas may also be used for extraction. This is a natural solvent, though requires the application of a much more technically challenging process. Less common in Amsterdam, you may find "CO2 wax" in a small number of coffeeshops.

Wax is usually light tan or yellow in color, and is whipped into a thick and creamy consistency similar to peanut butter. Some forms may be dry and crumbly, though. Wax is usually highly potent, often exceeding 80% THC by weight. It also contains a high portion of plant terpenes, and as such can be highly aromatic and flavorful. This extraction technique, however, remains in legal question. As such, connoisseur-grade wax is scarce in Amsterdam, and generally sells for a high price when located.

🔥 Wax is best for vaping and dabbing.

Rosin (50-75% THC)

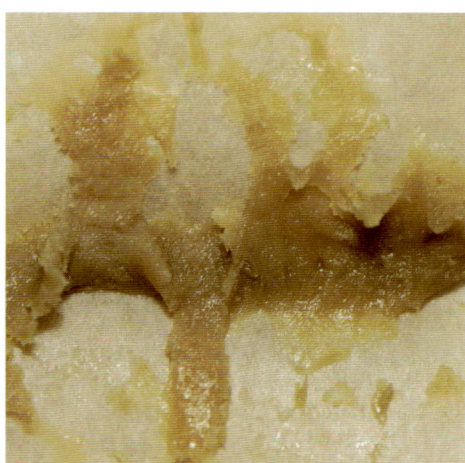

This form of cannabis concentrate is made via a simple mechanical process. Here, the cannabis plant is placed under heat and high pressure. This forces the resins out, where they may be collected. Rosin is usually gray to light brown in appearance, and has a consistency similar to that of a wax or budder (thick and creamy like peanut butter). While the method of extraction allows for significant terpene content, the amount retained is still generally lower than waxes. As such, rosin may be slightly less flavorful. Rosin extraction does have the advantage of offering a high potency concentrate without the use of solvents, though.

🔥 Rosin is best for vaping and dabbing.

Shatter (70-90% THC)

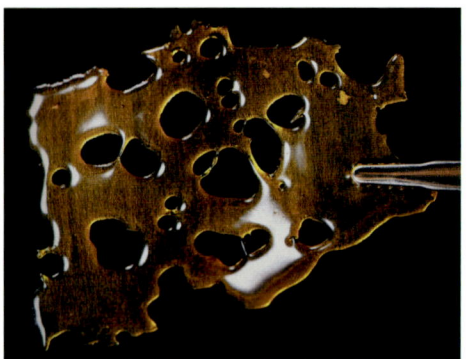

CO2 Distillate (95%+ THC)

Like Wax, Shatter is also made with a solvent-based extraction method, usually butane or propane. The final product in this case, however, is not whipped, and has less wax/fat content in comparison. Shatter usually turns out as a translucent semi-solid, with a texture and stiffness that range from brittle candy (hence the name) to sticky taffy. Terpenes and residual solvents can both soften the material, and thus will influence the final rigidity of the extract.

The difference between shatter and wax goes beyond basic aesthetics. First, even though this concentrate is vacuum purged, it does tend to hold residual solvents more than whipped products like waxes. While in most cases the residual levels are low, they are still often toxic. As such, some consumers prefer wax to shatter for this reason. Otherwise, shatter can be more flavorful. The lack of agitation better preserves the volatile plant terpenes, which can be damaged by oxidation.

Shatter is a highly valued extract among connoisseurs for its potency, often beautiful aesthetics, and high flavor. High quality shatter is translucent and lighter in color, often a shade of tan or yellow. It should also be very aromatic and flavorful.

💧 Shatter is best for vaping and dabbing.

Distillate extraction takes a standard product such as CO_2 oil or budder (BHO/PHO), and processes it further to separate and isolate specific cannabinoids (usually THC or CBD). This is accomplished by running it through a molecular distillation chamber, which takes advantage of heat and boiling point differences to separate the various constituents. The end product is typically a clear light yellow or orange syrup, almost pure in its cannabinoid content.

Given the high level of purification, the terpene content of CO_2 distillate extracts tends to be negligible. As such, it usually lacks aroma and flavor. In the United States, CO_2 distillate is widely used in the preparation of edibles, specifically because of its neutral taste. It can make masking the taste of cannabis, which can be quite strong and difficult with flower and hashish, quite easy.

Distillate is also widely used in smoking products. While some suppliers directly sell the high potency oils for vaping, most process them further to add flavor. This is typically accomplished by adding in terpenes, which have been extracted from cannabis separately. Given the free-flowing properties of CO_2 distillate + terpene mixtures, as well as the consistent nature in which they can be flavored, they are widely used to manufacture vaporizer pen cartridges. While uncommon in Amsterdam given the legal issues with high potency extracts, this form can still be found on occasion.

💧 CO2 Distillate is best for vaping and preparing edibles.

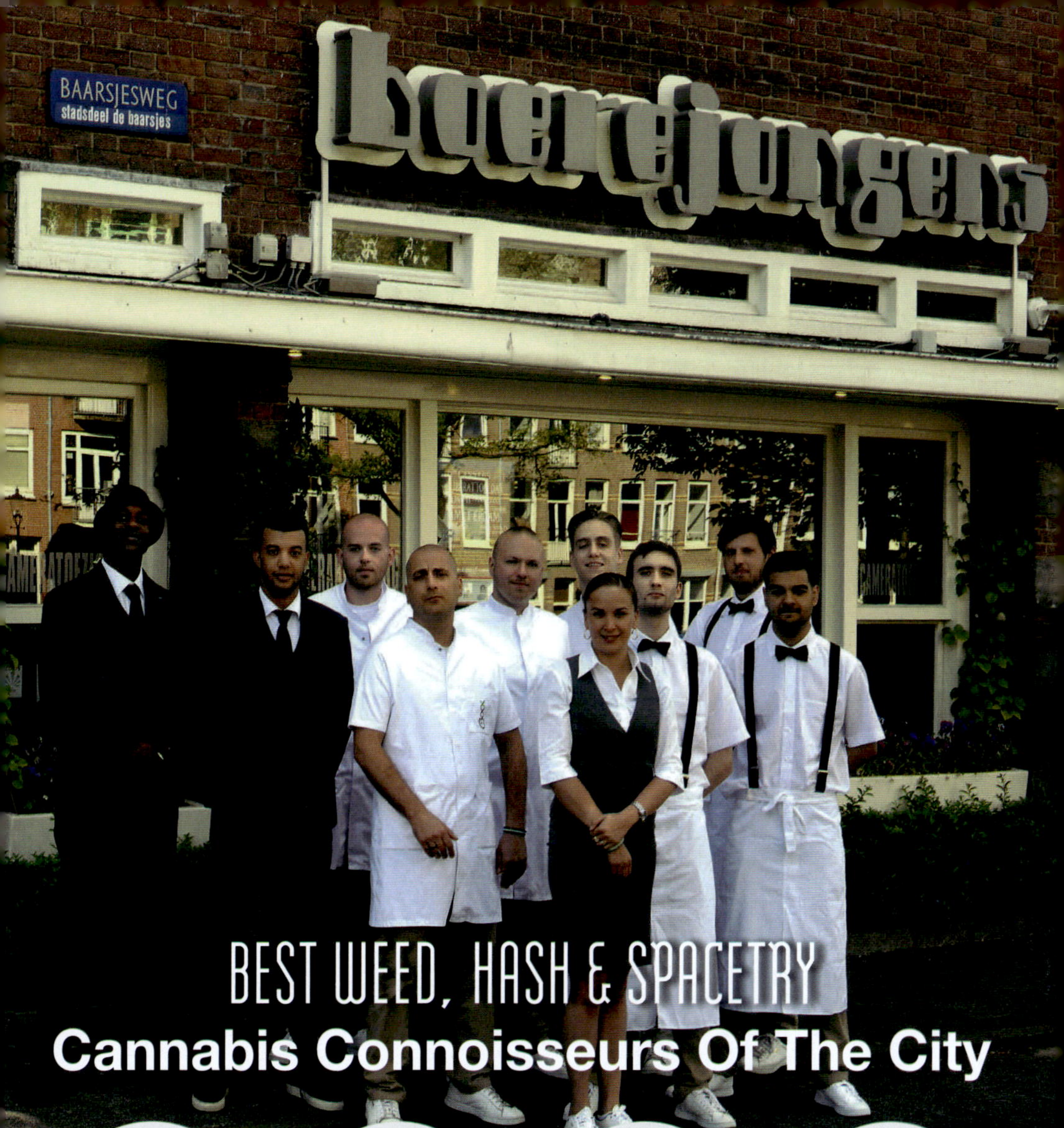
BAARSJESWEG
stadsdeel de baarsjes
boerejongens
BEST WEED, HASH & SPACETRY
Cannabis Connoisseurs Of The City

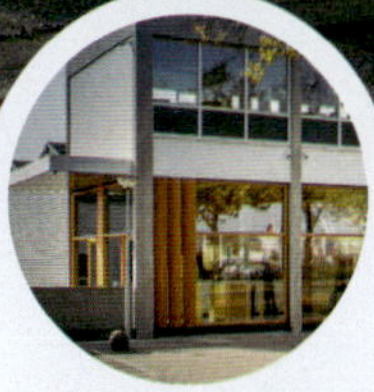

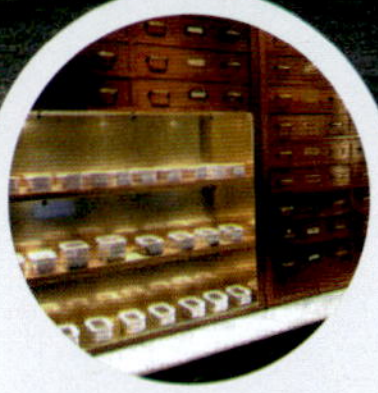

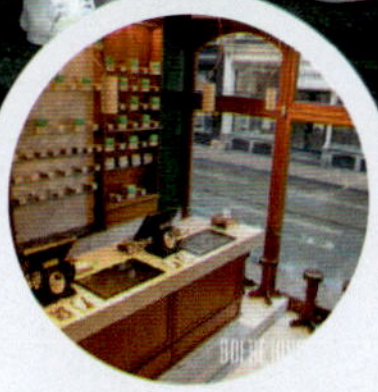

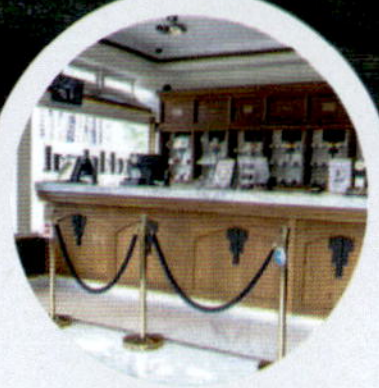

Flagship Store
Boerejongens Sloterdijk
Humberweg 2

Boerejongens BIJ
Bonairestraat 78

Boerejongens Center
Utrechtsestraat 21

Boerejongens West
Baarsjesweg 239

amsterdamgenetics.com

Moon Rock
1e Hulp (Centrum)

MOON ROCKS (CAVIAR)

Betty Boop

When you take marijuana buds, drizzle melted rosin, wax/budder, or hash oil on them, and roll them in raw kief, you get what many lovingly refer to as caviar. Also called moon rocks, this combination cannabis product usually looks like a fuzzy bonbon... with a thick outer coating of kief covering a gooey oil-logged flower inside. When made with high quality ingredients, the aesthetics of connoisseur-grade moon rocks can be stunning. It should also be a highly flavorful product. Provided everything is fresh, moon rocks will usually contain a high portion of aromatic terpenes, often from multiple plant sources.

Potency (50-60%+ THC):

Moon rocks are generally quite strong. The exact potency will, of course, be based on the quality of the individual ingredients. Connoisseur-grade moon rocks will generally make use of cannabis bud that exceeds 20% THC, some form of concentrate above 70% THC, and kief above 40%. The average potency usually exceeds 50-60% THC by weight. However, there are also low quality forms available in some shops. In the worst case, making moon rocks could be a way of salvaging crappy bud. Consumers should always use their judgment, and look for those products with a beautiful appearance and pungent aroma.

Green Place

Legality

Cannabis extracts of high purity, which do not contain appreciable plant material, are technically not allowed under tolerance policies in the Netherlands. As such, the legality of moon rocks is sometimes called into question. This product should be permitted under existing Dutch law if an acceptable form of extract were used, perhaps rosin. In such case, all components (weed, hash, extract) should be legal. Further, we aren't even clear if the extract can even be (legally) considered separately from the final product. At the core of every moon rock is still a cannabis bud. The availability of this type of product in Amsterdam might change, for the better or worse, in the future. For now, moon rocks can be found with a little bit of searching.

🔥 Moon Rocks are best for smoking; generally rolled in a joint.

Mr. K & Co.

CONNOISSEUR GUIDE: AMSTERDAM

COFFEESHOP
DIRECTORY

SHOP FEATURES

 Smoking Lounge (Cannabis)

 Smoking Lounge (Tobacco)

 Vaporizer(s)

 Outdoor Seating

 Hot Food

 WiFi

 Games

 Television

 Wheelchair Accessible

 Billiards

COFFEESHOPS

SHOP FEATURES

SHOP HOURS:
Daily:
8:00am-1:00am

ABRAXAS

ADDRESS: Jonge Roelensteeg 12-14, Amsterdam (Centrum)

MAP IT

Abraxas Coffeeshop is located on a very narrow alleyway named Jonge Roelensteeg, which sits directly south of Dam Square. It is just off the upscale shopping street of Kalverstraat, which is bustling with tourists most afternoons. With all of the distraction to be found here, the alleyway that hosts Abraxas can easily go unnoticed. Many also overlook it simply because of its unassuming appearance. If you do pass this street by, it would be a shame, because you would have missed one of the most interesting coffeeshops in the city.

The Shop

Abraxas is a theme coffeeshop. It takes its name from the children's book "The Little Witch". The main characters in this classic story are a young witch and her talking raven companion, Abraxas. The Little Witch is a tale of magic and adventure. Likewise, Abraxas Coffeeshop is mystical in its style of décor. There are beautifully colorful spiraling tile mosaics on the walls. Intricate woodcarvings can be found throughout, which make the counters, stools, and tables appear as if they were grown directly out of trees. A myriad of tiny lights shine from overhead, reminiscent of a starry-night sky. In a more contemporary sense, the Abraxas Coffeeshop theme might be compared to Harry Potter or Lord of the Rings.

The shop itself is on two levels. One of the first things you will notice as you enter on the ground floor is the cannabis counter, which will sit directly in front of you. Here you are presented with a (quite artistic) digital menu of their weed and hashish offerings. A little further inside is a larger counter, where you can purchase hot and cold beverages, snacks, and the odd souvenir (they also have a large souvenir shop next door). There is bench and stool seating found throughout this level, perfect for chilling with a joint and cappuccino, and soaking up the ambiance. If you prefer vaporizing to smoking, a pair of Volcano units can be found near the main counter.

On both ends of the shop are also tight spiral staircases. These lead up to the second floor, where you will find additional seating in two connected rooms. Long wooden benches wrap around the back walls of both. There are plenty of tables, and ample stool seating. There are also semi-transparent panels in the floors, which were at one time see-through, providing a visual connection between levels. Although time may have worn these down a bit, it has not had this effect on the luster of the shop itself. Abraxas is a work of art.

The Menu

The cannabis menu at Abraxas is fairly large. There are usually just shy of a dozen selections on the weed side. Strains tend to be recognized old-school city favorites (think White Widow, Amnesia, and Haze). There are fewer options on the hash side, but still a nice spread of imported varieties from regions such as India, Nepal, Lebanon, and Morocco. There may even be a domestic option or two. Purchases are provided in pre-weighed and labeled bags. They also sell pre-rolled mixed and pure joints.

COFFEESHOPS

CONNOISSEUR GUIDE: AMSTERDAM

COFFEESHOPS

SHOP FEATURES

SHOP HOURS:

Daily:
9:30am-1:00am

AMNESIA

ADDRESS: Herengracht 133, Amsterdam (Centrum)

MAP IT

Amnesia Coffeeshop is a trendy establishment in the heart of Amsterdam Centrum's canal ring. This shop is located on Herengracht, which runs alongside a beautiful canal of the same name. Amnesia is not an especially large shop, existing on one level. Although only one long room, it certainly makes for a big enough shop to draw in a crowd. Given the popularity and reputation of this shop, it should come as no surprise that it may be difficult to find seating on the weekends.

The Shop

While Amnesia Coffeeshop may not be the largest shop in the city, it does stand out amongst its contemporaries for its character. Its décor is polished and tastefully detailed. The shop has somewhat of a nightclub feel, with lots of black and rich purples throughout. A shelf with stool-seating runs along some of the walls, while tables, chairs, and cushioned leather benches provide room for groups. Also great are the wooden benches and chairs out front for relaxing and taking in the canal on sunny afternoons, which is heavily trafficked by boats in the summer.

One thing Amnesia Coffeeshop is noted for are the snacks. You will probably not go hungry looking for something to munch on here. Going well beyond the basic chips and bits, they often have a variety of bakery-style cakes and pastries on the menu. Further, they make arguably some of the best milkshakes among the city coffeeshops. We highly recommend one if you are in the mood.

Vaporizer aficionados will also find comfort here. This shop hosts a trio of Volcano Digit units along the right side wall. Vaporization appears to be something widely appreciated by the management, who include similar units in all of their coffeeshops. They keep the bags and filling chambers behind the counter, along with alcohol wipes. Just ask, and they provide everything you need to get started.

The Menu

This coffeeshop is involved with the owner(s) of Barney's and Barney's Lounge, the famous pair of high-end coffee shops (also, some related businesses). Similar to Barney's, the menu here is generally noted for its quality cannabis offerings. The owner(s) have often entered Dutch cannabis competitions in the past, and you are likely to find a few competition-winning strains on its menu. They are also fairly big on contemporary strains. You will likely recognize some genetics that have been imported from the USA, which are often crossed with local varieties. Barney's has its own established strains, which it also sells through its Barney's Farm seedbank.

CONNOISSEUR GUIDE: AMSTERDAM

COFFEESHOPS

CONNOISSEUR GUIDE: AMSTERDAM

COFFEESHOPS

SHOP FEATURES

SHOP HOURS:
Daily:
7:00am-1:00am

AMSTERDAMNED

ADDRESS: Haarlemmerstraat 6, Amsterdam (Centrum)

MAP IT

Amsterdamned was previously known as the Picasso Coffeeshop, a name the shop held for many years. It has since undergone rebranding. This coffeeshop is located on Haarlemmerstraat, a bustling area of the city packed with restaurants and small trendy boutiques. This shop too has somewhat of a trendy feel, fitting in quite nicely with the surrounding neighborhood.

Inside, you will find a clean and very contemporary décor. You can still find some reprints of Picasso's work in here; maintaining some connection to the old shop. The ambiance of the place is a mix of artsy and modern; the type of shop that could easily fit in as a café or bakery. While that may be the case, we would never suggest Amsterdamned trade in its role of cannabis coffeeshop.

The Shop

This coffeeshop is on two levels. Downstairs is the counter along with a seating area. The shop has a large window so the front room gets a lot of natural light during the day. For its size, it has a very open feel. There are a couple of prime seats at the front window, providing occupants an excellent opportunity to "people watch". Come here during peak hours, and you'll see an endless stream of people walk by during your visit. If the downstairs fills up, or you're looking for a change of pace, perhaps you should try the second seating room upstairs. The décor is equally enjoyable on this level along with sizable windows and a bit more room for seating than downstairs.

The Menu

The cannabis menu here is fairly traditional for a Dutch coffeeshop. The selection is not large, but does include a decent mix of weed and hashish items. The weed strains tend to be old-school Amsterdam favorites. Think Amnesia, Haze, Cheese etc. On the hashish side, there are several standard hard hashes imported from places like Morocco, Lebanon, Afghanistan, and India. While the selection may represent the latest strain trends, value here is fairly high, especially when you consider the neighborhood. Haarlemmerstraat is home to some of the pricier establishments in the city. The basic menu prices here are significantly lower in comparison, plus they usually run specials. They also sell in both gram and price (10€ and 20€) increments. This shop is popular among the locals which is usually a sign that there is more to a place than just marketing or a catchy décor.

Amsterdamned opens at 7:00AM, and is just a short walk from Centraal Station. It makes this coffeeshop a great place to go grab a smoke (if you are looking) and coffee if you are traveling to or from Amsterdam in the early morning hours. There is also no shortage of excellent café and restaurant options in this neighborhood if you work up an appetite in the process.

SHOP FEATURES

SHOP HOURS:
Daily:
10:00am-12:00am

COFFEESHOPS

MAP IT

ATLAS
Parlevinker 8, Amsterdam (Noord) **:ADDRESS**

Atlas Coffeeshop is in the Buiksloot neighborhood, at the very northern border of Amsterdam-Noord. The surrounding area is largely residential, and generally one of the more peaceful corners of the city. Atlas is close to several parks and many beautiful canals. A short stroll to the north is the expansive Ilperveld Natural Reserve. If you like fresh air and nature, you will appreciate this section of Amsterdam. There is no shortage of beautiful places to take a walk, have a smoke, and enjoy the outdoors.

The Shop
Outside, Atlas may remind you of a neighborhood recreational center or local bar. Inside, you will find an unpretentious and comfortable establishment for a Dutch coffeeshop. There are tiles lining the floors, detailed trim on the walls, and a good number of tables and chairs. Most customers are local. Given the relative popularity of the practice, most likely have a preference for mixed smoking (weed or hash plus tobacco). As such, Atlas Coffeeshop has a large dedicated tobacco smoking room to the right as you walk in. In there you will find several tables and more than a dozen chairs. There is also a table football game (foosball) and Photo Play machine if you are looking for something to pass the time. If you prefer pure cannabis and wish to stay away from tobacco smoke, you will find table and bench seating in the front room, near the cannabis counter.

The Menu
Atlas Coffeeshop has a small cannabis menu displayed on a digital screen. You will find just several types of weed and a couple selections of hash. The tight selection here does not indicate a disinterest in cannabis strains or quality, however. To the contrary, we find Atlas Coffeeshop to be highly focused on the quality of its offerings. It appeared to us the management is more interested in finding a few of the best items they can find to offer its customers, than just filling up a big menu for tourists, who rarely make it to this part of the city. This place is indeed quite popular among the locals, which is perhaps a testament to the quality of the cannabis.

COFFEESHOPS

SHOP FEATURES

SHOP HOURS:

Daily:
9:00am-1:00am

BABA

ADDRESS: Barentszstraat 130, Amsterdam (Oost)

MAP IT

Baba Coffeeshop is located on Barentszstraat, in the Zeeheldenbuurt neighborhood of Amsterdam-West. It is close to Westerpark in one of Amsterdam's more rapidly developing areas. This location was formerly the De Barentsz coffeeshop which was closed some time ago. Before occupying this space, Baba was on Warmoesstraat, in the very heart of the city center. In 2015, it was forced to close due to changes in zoning regulations which forced its relocation. This move was a significant change for Baba because the original location was frequented by mostly tourists and the new location primarily serves locals.

The Shop

Baba extensively renovated this space when they took it over. The new shop has an upscale restaurant or city tea house feel. It is beautiful, quite contemporary, and polished. This is quite different from the décor at its original location which was more urban and progressive. By the looks of it, no expense had been spared to ensure customers feel relaxed and comfortable while they enjoy their favorite bud.

The standout feature in the center of the shop is a six foot statue of Ghanesha, the Lord of Good Fortune, who provides prosperity, fortune and success. He is the Lord of Beginnings and the Remover of Obstacles of both material and spiritual kinds. His presence may perhaps be the reason the atmosphere is welcoming and friendly.

Given the investments, it should come as no surprise that Baba is not short on amenities. Patrons have free WiFi access, with password displayed for easy use. At the back of the coffeeshop there is a tobacco smoking room, for those who prefer mixed joints. Otherwise, herbal "tobacco mix" is readily available for use in the main part of the shop. This shop also has bongs available for its visitors, as well as a Verdamper vaporizer, which is a cross between a bong and a traditional vape.

The Menu

While there are a few contemporary items, the offerings at Baba coffeeshop are generally considered traditional old-school weed strains and imported pressed hashes. In addition, they have pre-rolled joints and space cakes on the menu. The pricing appears to be a bit more reasonable, likely given that it needs to be more competitive for the business of local residents who make up more of their revenue than the tourists. Although a bit out of the way in comparison to the original city center location, it is still worth the journey; just a 20 minute walk or via public transportation.

COFFEESHOPS

COFFEESHOPS

SHOP FEATURES

SHOP HOURS:
Daily:
10:00am-1:00am

BABYLON

ADDRESS: Beursstraat 27, Amsterdam (Centrum)

MAP IT

Babylon Coffeeshop is a reggae-themed establishment. It sits on a small side street parallel to the Damrak, just behind the Beurs van Berlage. A beautiful example of modern Dutch architecture, the Beurs van Berlage once served as the location of the Dutch Stock Exchange. It now functions as a venue for concerts, conferences, and other events. Babylon sits on a fairly quiet street behind it, directly next to a Police (Politie) station, off all things. In most cities, purchasing cannabis so close to a building full of police officers would be anxiety-filled. In Amsterdam, one may say it is oddly comforting. That is the beauty of Dutch tolerance.

The Shop

Babylon Coffeeshop sits on one level. As you walk in the front door, there is a long counter to the left. Here you can review the menu and purchase cannabis products, as well as hot and cold beverages. As you walk in further, you will find a doorway and glass partition against the back wall. Behind it is the shop's smoking lounge. The room décor is contemporary and moderate in size. There is comfortable black leather bench seating lining the walls, along with several small wooden tables and stools. There is also a flat screen television. It will likely to be playing something on low volume, so as to not drown out the chill or reggae ambient music.

The Menu

The cannabis menu at Babylon is considerable in size. On the weed side you will find about a dozen strains or so. Expect to find a mix of old school favorites, along with some newer varieties. The hashish options are typically imported, much of it (though not exclusively) from Morocco. While most are traditional pressed varieties, you are likely to also find some high quality imported isolator hash here.

Babylon is perhaps most well known for its modest prices. For a shop that is in the tourist-packed city center, it is considered a more reasonable option. The hashish tends to be of especially good value, as well as quality. If you find something you really like, ask about offers for discounts on 5 gram purchases.

COLORADO!

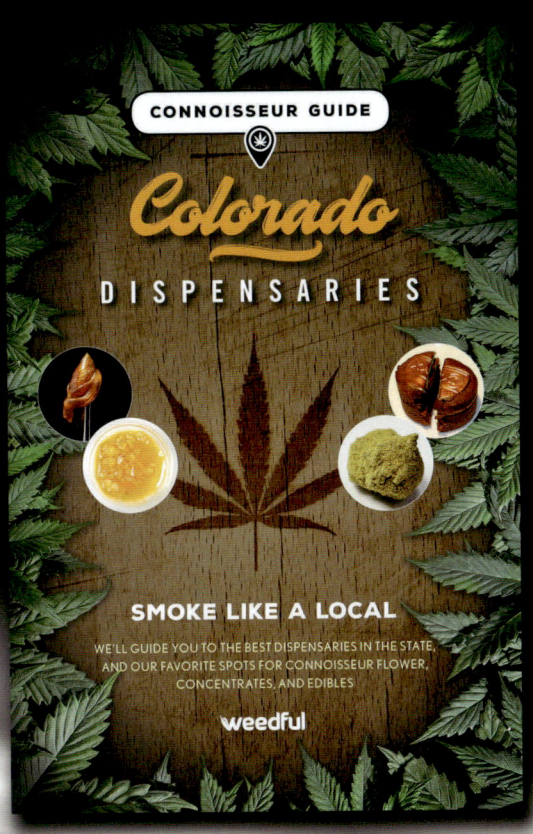

The next stop for the CONNOISSEUR GUIDE series is the United States. Beginning in Colorado, with many cities to follow, we're seeking out the best of the best in these mega legal markets. Join us as we explore the local craft cultivators, top shelf concentrates, gourmet edibles, and innovative new technologies. If you are looking for a connoisseur experience in the USA, you won't want to miss the full series.

www.connoisseurguide.com

COFFEESHOPS

SHOP FEATURES

SHOP HOURS:

Daily:
7:00am-1:00am

BAGHEERA

ADDRESS: Kloveniersburgwal 60, Amsterdam (Centrum)

MAP IT

Bagheera Coffeeshop is a small establishment found in the Nieuwmarktbuurt, the area surrounding Neuwmarkt ("New Market") Square. It sits just to the south of the square, along the Kloveniersburgwal canal. The shop gets its name from Bagheera, the black Indian leopard from the famous children's novel The Jungle Book. An interpretation of this character is found in the logo, which depicts the image of a teeth-baring Black Panther. In contrast to the aggressive tone of its logo, Bagheera Coffeeshop has a relaxing and welcoming vibe.

The Shop

The front room would be best described as having the appearance of a small café or juice bar. It is clean, well lit, and hosts a counter for ordering drinks and fresh smoothies, as well as cannabis products. You will probably notice a lot of fresh fruit like oranges and bananas here. There are a couple of seats near the front window, and for those who prefer al fresco, there are some tables out front. This is a great place to sit and smoke if you enjoy people watching, as this area of the city is trafficked heavily.

Further on into Bagheera Coffeeshop you will find a closed smoking room, which allows mixed cannabis/tobacco smoking on the premises. The inside décor is very reminiscent of a modern café. Long leather bench seating lines the walls, and in front, small white mica tables. Pull up small leather stools are found on the other side of the tables. The seating, walls, and floors in this room are largely gray, contrasted with splashes of lime green as the accent color. There are a couple of flat screen televisions mounted on the walls for anyone needing visual entertainment.

The Menu

The cannabis menu at Bagheera is fairly large. There are more than a dozen different strains of weed. These is a fairly even mix of old-school favorites (think White Widow, Amnesia) and more contemporary strains. There is also about half a dozen types of hashish. These are generally imported varieties, mainly from Bab Berred and the Riff mountains of Morocco. From time to time, you will also find higher potency "isolator" varieties on the menu. Bagheera Coffeeshop also serves space cakes, marijuana infused tea, and pre-rolled joints. The pricing ranges from the "quite reasonable" to "consistent with city center." Additionally, this shop offers free WiFi for its visitors, and a Volcano vaporizer.

COFFEESHOPS

CONNOISSEUR GUIDE: AMSTERDAM

COFFEESHOPS

SHOP FEATURES

SHOP HOURS:
Daily:
9:00am-1:00am

BALOU

ADDRESS: Halvemaansteeg 5, Amsterdam (Centrum)

MAP IT

Balou Coffeeshop sits among a cluster of establishments surrounding the Rembrandtplein (Rembrandt Square), a popular tourist hangout. It sits just to the north, on a small street adjacent to the Amstel. This particular shop takes its name from the famous children's story The Jungle Book. Specifically, the lovable talking bear named Baloo (Balou, in Dutch). One might say the shop's mascot appears a bit happier than its famous storybook cousin, for you will see it is dancing with a lit spliff in its mouth. Since Rudyard Kipling's famous book was published in 1894, this means his work exists in the public domain. As such, Balou joins a small collection of iconic characters that have been legally adopted by Dutch coffeeshops.

The Shop

Balou is a fairly traditional for a Dutch coffeeshop. While it would not be considered "polished", the interior is comfortable for visitors. There is interesting "trippy" mural art on the walls. The atmosphere of the shop is very relaxed and welcoming. It is split between two levels. Downstairs is a small counter for ordering cannabis, drinks, and snacks. There are also several tables here, though most people prefer to park themselves with their purchases in the upstairs lounge. There is more seating in this room, including a long fixed table in front of the shop's large second floor windows. The walls are also adorned with murals and a flurry of rolling papers that have been inscribed with short messages by visitors. This feature is reminiscent of Grey Area Coffeeshop, just with less foot traffic.

The Menu

The cannabis menu at Balou Coffeeshop is traditional for a Dutch shop. On the weed side, expect to find about a dozen options consisting mostly of old-school Amsterdam favorites like Amnesia and Silver Haze. You may find a contemporary strain or two on the menu as well as a less potent imported weed option, such as Jamaican outdoor. These are always nice for visitors new to smoking. The hash menu is also very traditional. Expect to find a list exclusively of imported pressed varieties from placed like Nepal, India, and Morocco. Pricing on both sides of the menu tends to be reasonable, which is a big bonus for a shop in the city center. Balou also carries a selection of space cakes and pre-rolled joints.

CONNOISSEUR GUIDE: AMSTERDAM

EESHOP
Gratis wifi
COFFEE SHOP
FLO

Coffeeshop

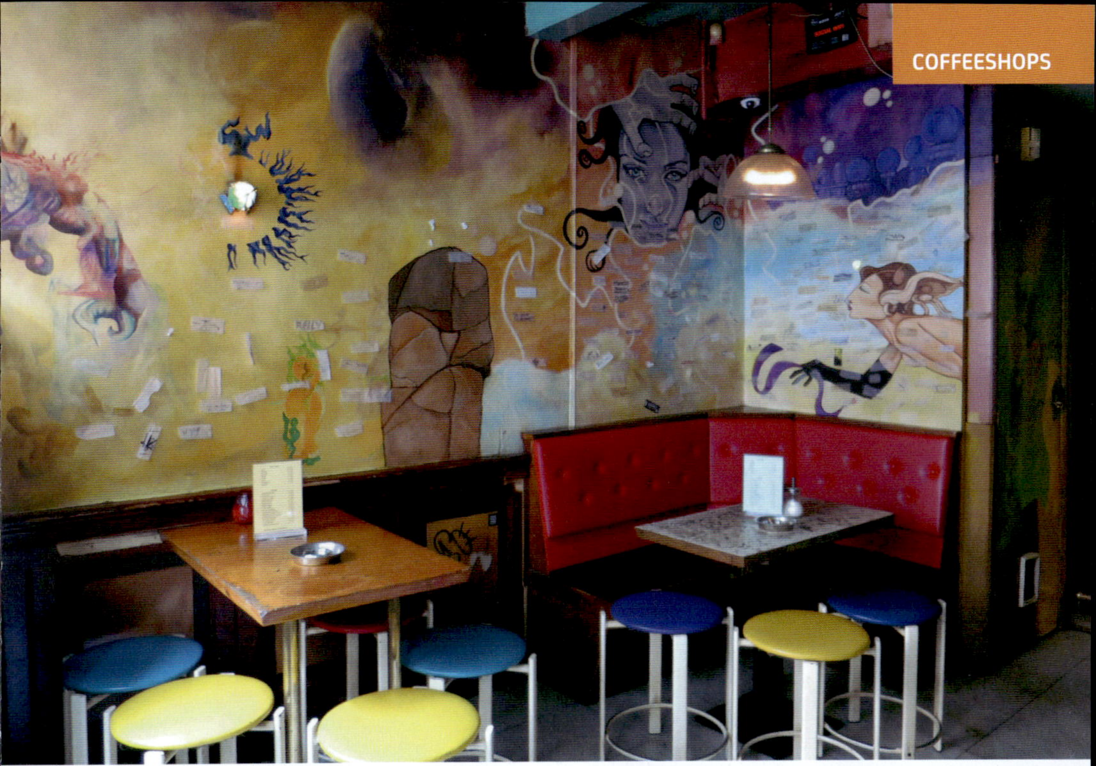

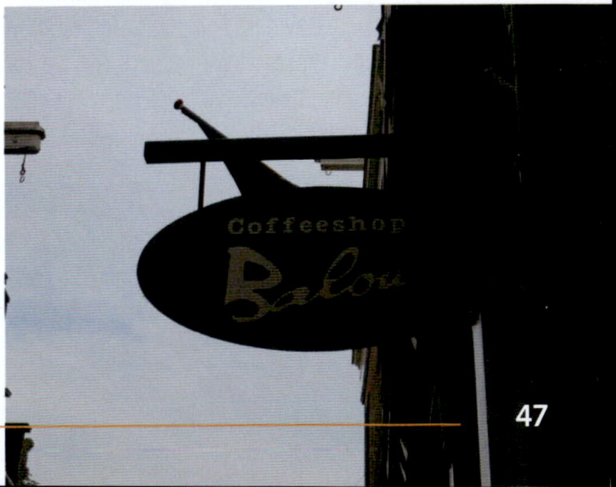

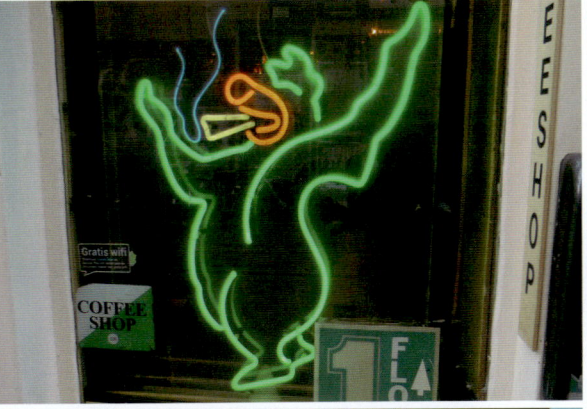

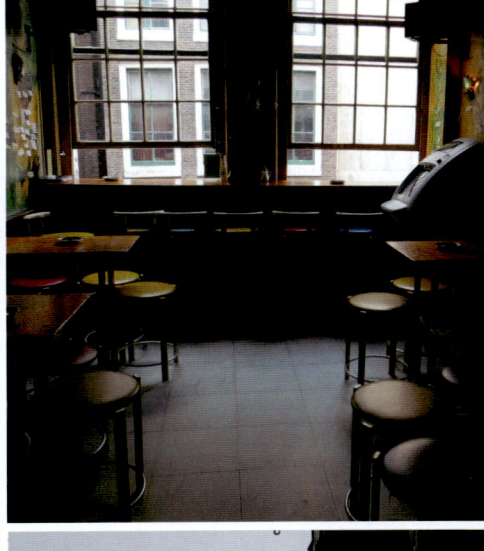

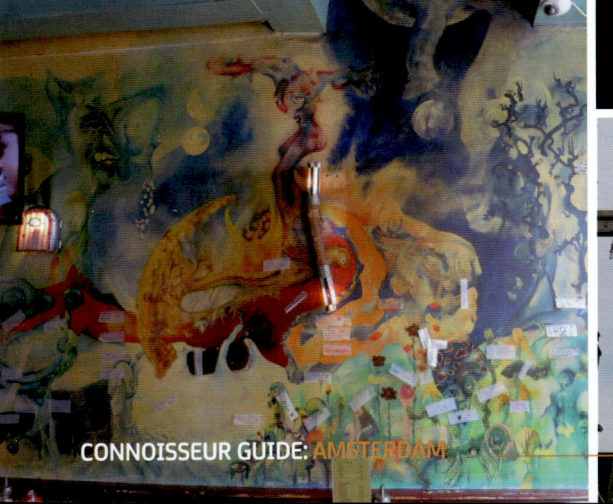

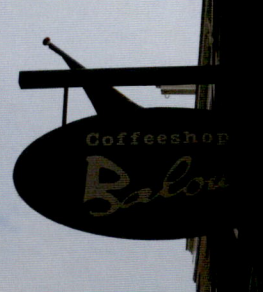

COFFEESHOPS

SHOP FEATURES

SHOP HOURS:

Daily:
9:00am-1:00am

BARNEY'S

ADDRESS: Haarlemmerstraat 102, Amsterdam (Centrum)

MAP IT

Barney's Coffeeshop is located on Haarlemmerstraat, a trendy section of the city just to the west of Centraal Station. Typical for businesses in the area, this shop is not especially spacious. As you proceed through the door, you step down to enter the one long room that is the coffeeshop. Inside you will find a shop with a decidedly upmarket feel. The décor is modern, warm and intimate with polished wood, and ample mood lighting throughout. There is not a lot of room for standing around so if you plan on staying, grab a seat at one of the bar height tables along the wall.

The Shop

Be sure to take a look around the shop. Note that above the tables are display cases that hold the shop's many cannabis awards. There are also flat screens at each table. But frankly, we are at a loss for the programming so for us, not the place to sit and watch TV. Barney's has long fostered an atmosphere where travelers feel comfortable pulling up a stool, light a joint, and chat with others (we do recommend the large tables toward the front for conversation). This is the vibe we find at this coffeeshop and what has made Barney's special.

This coffeeshop grew to fame during the 1990s, while in its earlier iteration of "Barney's Breakfast Bar." As one might guess from the name, it was a combination coffee-shop and restaurant. Throngs of bleary-eyed tourists would pack the place in the morning, most there to feast on an English or American breakfast (eggs, sausage, bacon, pancakes etc.). That is, with a side of fine cannabis, of course.

Barney's operated their "hash and eggs" style establishment for years, all the while competing in cannabis competitions like the High Times Cannabis Cup. Eventually, their reputation for both good food and good herb grew too much for the small shop to bear. It was becoming crowded…bursting at capacity. Something had to be done to address the popularity. Today, Barney's is simply Barney's Coffeeshop. The restaurant was moved across the street, to a cannabis-friendly establishment called Barney's Uptown. Barney's Coffeeshop is regarded as a connoisseur establishment.

The Menu

This shop is popular with cannabis connoisseurs. This is probably owing to the fact that Barney's has a long history of entering cannabis competitions, with many trophies to their name. You should find some of their award winning weed and hashish on the menu. The genetics are largely contemporary, often with Barney's own unique hybridizations.

CONNOISSEUR GUIDE: AMSTERDAM

BARNEY'S LOUNGE

ADDRESS: Reguliersgracht 27, Amsterdam (Centrum)

MAP IT

Barney's Lounge Coffeeshop is found on Reguliersgracht (Regulator's Canal) in the southern part of the canal ring. This section of the city is known for its picturesque bridges and waterways. Particularly famous here are the "Seven Arches of Reguliersgracht", a series of arching brick bridges that date back hundreds of years. These are among the most photographed landmarks in the city, so it is likely you are looking at one of them when you see a picture of Amsterdam's scenic waterways.

The Shop

This coffee shop sits on one level, and is thin and long in its dimensions. Though it does reside in an old brick building architecturally in line with its historic neighborhood, one will find a modern establishment inside Barney's Lounge. The décor is contemporary; a bit of a mix between nightclub and a upscale coffee lounge. The colors are dark, but the room is well lit with overhead and accent lightning. There are plush leather seats all around, along with artistic photographs and framed paintings hung on the walls. Something "chill" is usually playing on the radio. There is undoubtedly a lounge atmosphere in here, which makes you just want to melt into a comfy seat, relax, and enjoy yourself.

Barney's Lounge is also highly accommodating to "vaporists". That is, those who prefer using a vaporizer to smoking cannabis. To that end they have multiple Volcano vaporizer units at this place. We have been keeping track, and at present they are near the top of the list for most number of Volcano units in an Amsterdam coffeeshop. In fact, they are second only to Barney's own flagship location on Haarlemmerstraat. Combine that with its chill, funky vibe, and you can see why we rate this one of the best vapor lounges in the city.

The Menu

Barney's Lounge is, of course, part of the famous Barney's brand of Amsterdam. This also includes Barney's Coffeeshop, Barney's Uptown restaurant, Barney's Farm, and Amnesia. The owners are known for their contemporary establishments and upscale service, which cater to the more sophisticated connoisseur crowd. To that end they boast a menu with many entries (and winning varieties) from cannabis competitions. The genetics tend to be quite contemporary. Expect to find some of Barney's own hybridizations using modern West Coast USA strains.

COFFEESHOPS

SHOP FEATURES

SHOP HOURS:
Daily:
9:00am-1:00am

BARRAKA

ADDRESS: Gravenstraat 9, Amsterdam (Centrum)

MAP IT

Barraka Coffeeshop is located on Gravenstraat (Grave Street), a small side street near Dam Square. The street is closed to automobiles, though it is heavy in foot traffic given its proximity to key Amsterdam attractions. One end of this street leads to De Nieuwe Kerk. This translates as The New Church. Contrary to its name, this is a famous and old church-turned-museum, concert, and exhibition hall. At the other end of this street is Nieuwendijk (New Dike), a busy section of the city's most popular shopping district.

The Shop

Barraka is a small shop on one floor, with much less grandeur than this neighboring architectural marvel. Its décor is still quite impressive though; we'd say reminiscent of an upscale bar or café. There is a lot of dark wood inside, and a beautiful, polished bar where you place your order. It feels familiar; comfortable. As a bonus on warm days, you will find a couple of small café tables outside. The street is not what one would describe as picturesque, though a fairly quiet place to relax and escape the madness of Dam Square.

The Menu

The cannabis menu at Barraka Coffeeshop is representative of the feeling they cultivate in this establishment. It is presented in a red leather folder with gold lettering on the outside. You know, the type of over-the-top presentation you expect to find at an upscale steakhouse. The selection here is extensive. On the weed side you might find roughly two dozen (yep) strains, almost exclusively old-school favorites. They are categorized by potency, medium, medium/strong, and strong. More than a dozen types of hash are sold at Barraka as well, listed under the categories Moroccan hashes, dark hashes, and very special hash. Mostly pressed imports, though they do carry an isolator variety or two. They also sell pre-rolled joints, space cakes, and hash infused tea.

Alien Visitors (Centrum)

COFFEESHOPS

SHOP FEATURES

SHOP HOURS:
Daily:
10:00am-1:00am

BASJOE

ADDRESS: Kloveniersburgwal 62, Amsterdam (Centrum)

MAP IT

Basjoe Coffeeshop is located on the Kloveniersburgwal canal. This was one of the outer canals in the old city, which takes its name from the old civic guards called the Kloveniers. A bit of history, during World War II this canal was also one of the borders of the Jewish quarter. Today, it is a beautiful and vibrant part of Amsterdam centrum. Basjoe is just a bit north of the University Von Amsterdam (University of Amsterdam) campus. It is also several blocks south of the Nieuwmarkt. This is a popular section of the city and is a host to a lot of visitors.

The Shop

From the outside, Basjoe has the appearance that feels a bit like a nightclub. Perhaps it is the dark trim around the doors and windows or the entrance with its large glass door and polished silver trim - hard to pinpoint exactly what it is. It is a bit more posh than what you get at most coffeeshops.

Inside, the atmosphere at Basjoe is down to earth, frankly, quite different than what you would expect from the upscale façade. First, we would say it is much more reminiscent of a city café or bakery than a nightclub. There is a lot of wood, and the room is bright and open. You are likely to find a delicious selection of desserts displayed on the counter, many infused with cannabis products. In fact, Basjoe is well known for its selection of marijuana edibles. You will notice a large chalkboard behind the counter, which displays their extensive offerings. This shop is also known for its gourmet coffee and tea selections, far superior to the average coffeeshop in Amsterdam, which frankly, are not always the best places for coffee. They also provide tables outside, perfect for enjoying the canal view on a sunny afternoon.

The Menu

The cannabis menu at Basjoe Coffeeshop is fairly large. On the weed side, you will usually find a little over a dozen options. There is a pretty even split of contemporary and old school strains, which means something like Kush and Sour D sitting side-by-side with White Widow and Amnesia. The hash selection is also large; maybe 10 or so options. These are imported pressed varieties from the usual exporters including Morocco, Afghanistan, Nepal, and India. Pricing is reasonable for both weed and hash, though everything is listed with a minimum purchase of two grams, except the pre-rolled joints. They do have a Volcano here for those that prefer vaporizing to smoking.

COFFEESHOPS

CONNOISSEUR GUIDE: AMSTERDAM

COFFEESHOPS

SHOP FEATURES

SHOP HOURS:

Mon-Fri:
8:30am-1:00am

BEST FRIENDS CENTRUM

ADDRESS: Huidenstraat 13a, Amsterdam (Centrum)

MAP IT

Best Friends Centrum Coffeeshop is found in the De Negen Straatjes section of Amsterdam, which translates in English to "The Nine Streets" or "9 Streets". This small neighborhood resides in the inner city's canal belt, and is known for its selection of trendy independent stores, fashion boutiques, and cafés. In recent years, the Nine Streets has become an increasingly popular destination for travelers, who often rank it to be among one of the most beautiful areas of the city. Best Friends Centrum is a small coffee shop with a contemporary feel, and fits in seemingly well with its neighbors.

The Shop

The Best Friends Centrum coffeeshop is located on the lower floor of its building. You step down to enter. Inside you'll first notice a counter, where you purchase cannabis products and other basics (coffee, tea, drinks, snacks). Further on is a closed smoking room, which allows the consumption of tobacco products on premises. Inside you'll find two long wooden wrap-around benches against the walls, a large table in the center of the room, and plenty of soft pull-up stools spread around. There are also two flat screen TV's, and chill music playing. This room is quite comfortable, making Best Friends Centrum an easy place to relax if you want to take a break from shopping or sightseeing.

The Menu

Best Friends Centrum has a fairly large cannabis menu. The weed side is broken up into three sections, which are Best Offers, Regular, and Import. As you might expect, these are generally listed from strongest to weakest in potency (and also highest to lowest price). You'll find more than a dozen items under their Best Offers, including many traditional and contemporary strains. Their Regular offerings are local outdoor varieties, and typically a nice balance between strength and economy. The Imports are weak and seeded buds, recommended only for inexperienced or occasional smokers.

On the hashish side of the menu, offerings are broken into Best and Black types. These include common pressed varieties from popular places such as Morocco, Lebanon, Pakistan, and India. Quality is generally very good here. Additionally, they sell a wide variety of pre-rolled joints, space cakes, and something they call a "THC Tube", which is two grams of unpressed kief. Kief is not widely sold in Amsterdam, likely because it is more difficult to transport, store, and source vs. pressed hashish. We think it makes a nice addition to the menu.

COFFEESHOPS

CONNOISSEUR GUIDE: AMSTERDAM

COFFEESHOPS

SHOP FEATURES

SHOP HOURS:

Mon-Fri:
7:00am-1:00am

BEST FRIENDS OOST

ADDRESS: Niasstraat 1, Amsterdam (Oost)

MAP IT

Best Friends Coffeeshop is located in the Indische Buurt section of Amsterdam. In English, this translates into "Indies Neighborhood". This is a largely residential community in the Eastern part of the city, known for being a diverse cultural center. It attracts young professionals and families from many different parts of the world. In recent years, this area has been the subject of rapid revitalization, making it an even more trendy and desirable place to live. Even so, this part of the city remains much quieter than the center. It can serve as a nice change of pace for visitors.

The Shop

Walking up, you will notice that Best Friends is quite a large place. With three large windows and a corner entrance, it takes up much of the lower level of its building. Inside, you will find a large room that serves as the waiting area. It feels like the lobby of a small boutique hotel. It is well appointed, with dark tile floors, and a display featured in the center (behind railings) featuring a fountain and artificial blossom tree. On the back wall are two counters where you can quickly make your cannabis purchase.

If you want to stay a while, there is a smoking lounge behind glass on one side of Best Friends. Inside are a couple of tables, as well as a wooden bar counter with several pull-up stools. Here you can also order from a selection of basic drinks and snacks. Though the room is small, the area is modern, clean, well lit, and comfortable. Tobacco smoking is also allowed here, by making use of the smaller glass-enclosed area found in the back.

The Menu

Best Friends coffeeshop offers a wide variety of both flower (weed) and hashish items. Further, their pricing tends to be more reasonable than those you will find at many shops in Amsterdam. While this is common outside the city center, as these establishments must cater to a more local clientele, we find their sister shop in the centre (Best Friends Centrum) to also have a price-focused menu. As such, consumer value, variety, and friendly service seem to be the hallmarks of this brand.

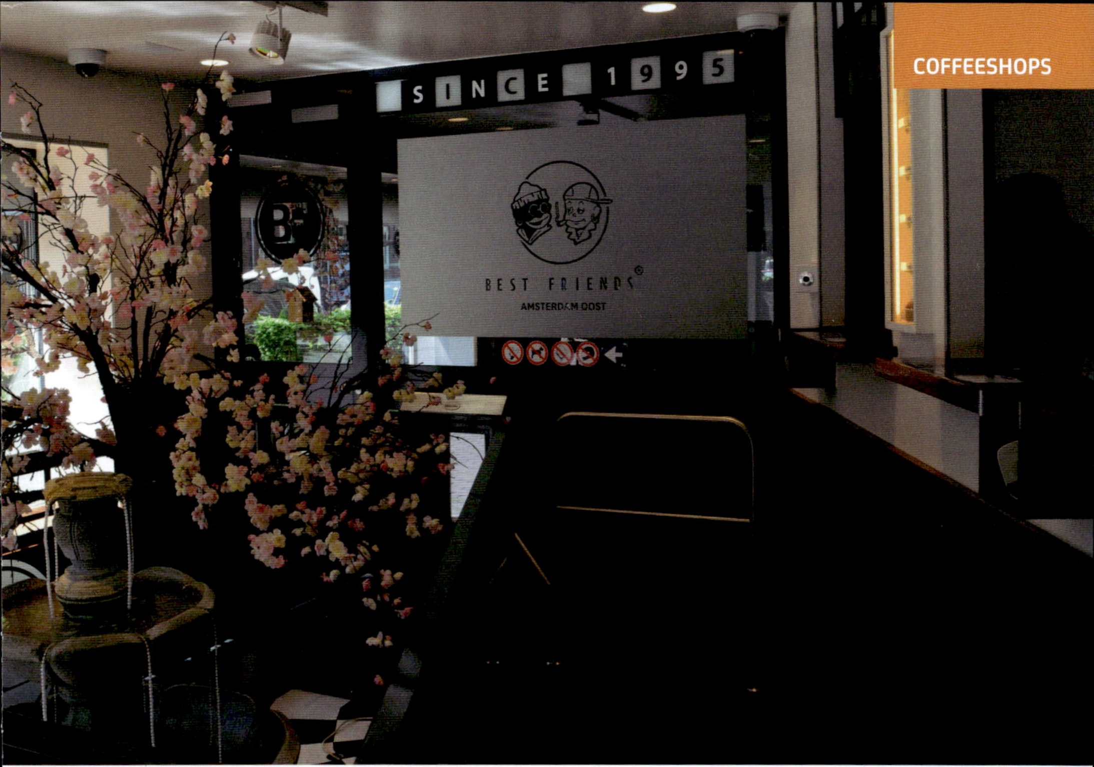
SINCE 1995
BEST FRIENDS
AMSTERDAM OOST

APPY
AMSTERDAM

CINNAMON SURPRISE
VANILLA CHOCO
TRIPLE CHOCO

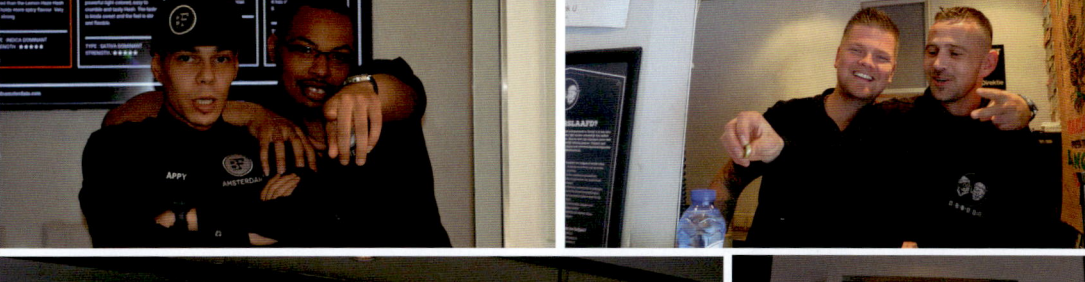

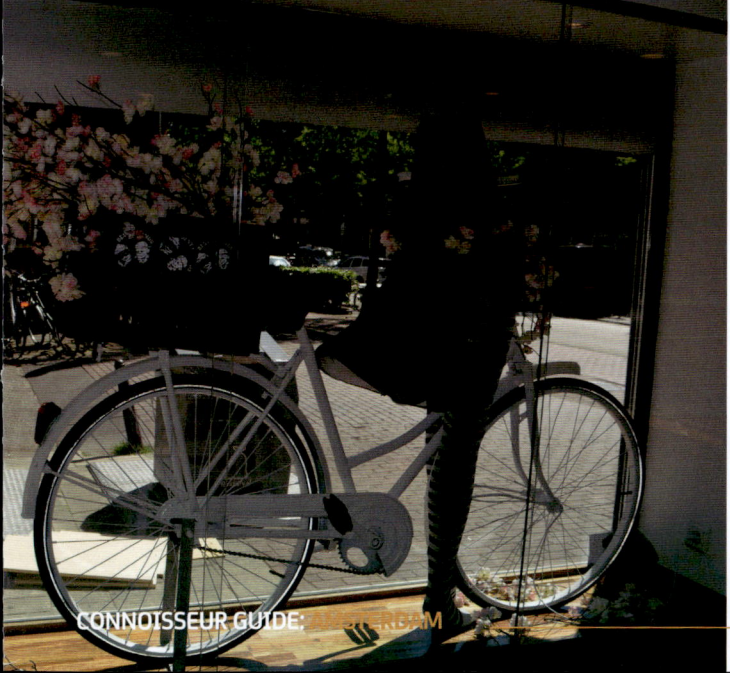

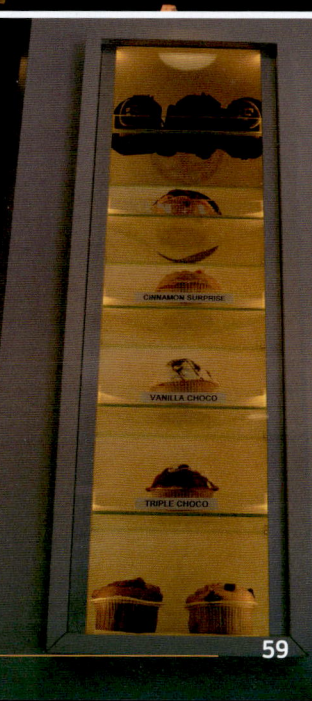

COFFEESHOPS

SHOP FEATURES

SHOP HOURS:

Daily:
7:00am-1:00am

BEST FRIENDS OUD ZUID

ADDRESS: Amstelveenseweg 61II, Amsterdam (Zuid)

MAP IT

Best Friends Zuid (South) coffeeshop is located in the Oud Zuid (Old South) section of Amsterdam, just outside the entrance to Vondelpark. This is one of the city's most beautiful green areas. A trip to Vondel is mandatory if you are visiting during the warmer months. This is generally a more residential part of the city. As such, there are more trees, less businesses, and fewer people overall traveling around here. We would not go so far as to say it is quiet though. Rather, just a little less hectic, and perhaps a bit more beautiful, at least from a nature perspective.

The Shop

This is the third Best Friends shop. The Oud Zuid branch joined the brand in mid-2018. This also makes this among the newest coffeeshops in Amsterdam, at least from an ownership perspective.

Inside, one will find a counter in the center-front of the room. Here you review the weed/hash menu and make your purchase. The interior is still undergoing renovations. The décor of the new place is artistic and contemporary. Light colored wood and soft hanging lights seem to compliment the black leather seats and trim quite well. You feel like you are in a small city nightclub. It is hip, yet cozy. Red velvet ropes out front only add to the vibe. While Best Friends Zuid looks like it is going to be a very chill hangout place, during our recent visits it was take and go only. This is likely to change any time, once the remodel is complete.

The Menu

The cannabis menu at Best Friends is fairly large. The weed side is the most robust, with typically over a dozen selections. The strains are largely made up of traditional Amsterdam genetics. Think items like White Widow… Haze hybrids. The hashish side of the menu is a bit smaller, but still tends to have a nice variety on most days. You'll usually find a decent mix of different Moroccan imports, along with a few others from Pakistan and India. They have a special selection for dark hashes here; many quite soft and potent. If you come on the right day they may have some quality Temple Ball, which isn't all that common. Though not many options, they do also make some delicious edibles here. We definitely recommend the gooey chocolate cupcakes if they are available.

COFFEESHOPS

CONNOISSEUR GUIDE: AMSTERDAM

COFFEESHOPS

SHOP FEATURES

SHOP HOURS:
Daily:
9:00am-1:00am

BETTY BOOP

ADDRESS: Reguliersdwarsstraat 29, Amsterdam (Centrum)

MAP IT

Betty Boop Coffeeshop is located just behind Amsterdam's famous Flowermarkt (flower market), close to where the Singel canal meets up with the Amstel. This location was once the sister to the original Betty Boop coffeeshop, adjacent to the red light district. That shop was famously known as one of the places in Amsterdam that Quentin Tarantino wrote much of Pulp Fiction. Sadly, the original Betty Boop was forced to move to a new location. In the interim, this shop, Betty Boop Too (as it was called), was renamed to simply Betty Boop. Some of the staff, menu, and furnishings from the original location can be found here.

The Shop

On the outside, Betty Boop Coffeeshop features a modern façade, with three large sections of floor-to-ceiling glass. Management also places a couple sets of outdoor chairs and tables here, which are perfect for enjoying a sunny afternoon. On the inside, you will find the shop spread out over two levels. Recent renovations have erased much of the old Betty Boop branding in here, which used to be quite prominent. The newly revamped décor is much subtler in this regard, instead boasting a more updated contemporary appearance.

The first floor has a few tables, along with a narrow wall counter if you want to roll a quick one for your walk. These provide you options for both quick and extended visits. While comfortable, we feel it would be a mistake not to venture upstairs. This is the shop's main smoking lounge. Here, you will find a long comfortable bench along one wall, and several tables spread about. Many of the chairs are leather, and quite plush. There is one table, though, in particular that is regarded as "prime seating." It sits just in front of the second floor's large floor-to-ceiling windows. On a warm day, the staff will open these windows up. After doing so, this table will sit right in front of a balcony-style railing. It will provide the occupants plenty of fresh air, and an incredible vantage point to watch the crowds below.

The Menu

Betty Boop Coffeeshop's cannabis menu is fairly large, at least on the weed-side. There are more than a dozen choices here, ranging from the hot items of the day such as the Kush strains, to Amsterdam's most traditional varieties. The hash menu is about half the size, though still carries a decent variety. These are usually pressed hashes from the popular exporting countries. In addition, the shop also carries space cakes and pre-rolled joints. Pricing here tends to be reasonable for the city center, though expect to see a few "premium cost" options.

COFFEESHOPS

COFFEESHOPS

SHOP FEATURES

SHOP HOURS:

Sun-Thurs:
11:00am-12:00am

Fri-Sat:
11:00am-1:00am

BLACK STAR

ADDRESS: Rozengracht 1-A, Amsterdam (Centrum)

MAP IT

Black Star Coffeeshop is located on Rozengracht (Roses Canal), in the Jordaan district. This is a famous upscale neighborhood, with many galleries, restaurants, and boutique shops. There is an energetic vibe in this part of the city. The street that Black Star is found on is particularly busy, and highly trafficked by both cars and tourists. This establishment is hard to miss. It resides in the lower two levels of a very distinct cream and red colored building. Outside is a large neon "Coffeeshop" sign. There is also a smaller second sign with their logo, which depicts lips smoking a joint on a bright red, yellow, and green background.

The Shop

You will find inside Black Star an African-themed coffee shop. The décor presents mainly continental-focused colors and artwork. The full name of this shop is actually "African Black Star Coffeeshop", though it tends to be known as just Black Star. The fact that the sign just reads "Coffeeshop Black Star" probably has something to do with it. This shop has a separate ordering area to the front. The budtender will buzz you in after purchasing your smokeable of choice, and/or a snack or beverage.

Once inside, you will see a standard fare of wooden seating and tables. The room is basic, but welcoming at the same time. You will notice a closed glass room to the side. This is the shop's tobacco smoking area. Look a little farther on and you will also see a rainbow painted staircase, which leads to a second, smaller seating area below. The basement room is popular, especially when the main smoking room gets busy, and among those who prefer a more relaxed vibe or private conversation.

The Menu

The cannabis menu at Black Star offers a fairly large assortment of both flower (weed) and hashish. The genetics on the weed side tend to be traditional; the old-school strain types long established as Amsterdam favorites. The hashish side is also traditional, a selection of pressed imports from Morocco and other common source countries. There is also a small selection of edibles (space cakes) offered here.

Amsterdam is a city for cycling.
There are four times more bikes than cars.

COFFEESHOPS

SHOP FEATURES

SHOP HOURS:

Mon-Sat:
9:00am-1:00am

Fri-Sat:
9:00am-12:00am

BLUE LAGOON

ADDRESS: Overtoom 342, Amsterdam (Oost)

MAP IT

Blue Lagoon Coffeeshop is found on Overtoom, in the Helmersbuurt neighborhood of Amsterdam West. It is just to the north of Vondelpark, which happens to be a wonderful place to stroll on a warm sunny afternoon. We highly recommend a visit when the weather is nice. This part of the city is largely residential, and has a more urban feel to it given that many of its buildings were constructed in the 1900's.

The Shop

The décor of Blue Lagoon coffeeshop is contemporary. There is polished hardwood floors, colored accent lights, dark trim, and a lot of overhead recessed lighting. The atmosphere is chill and comfortable. It feels somewhat like a neighborhood coffeeshop.

In this shop one will find a large closed-off tobacco smoking lounge. Inside, ample table and stool seating, as well as a full-size pool table can be found. Outside, there is additional seating along with a bar, where one can purchase cannabis products, coffees, teas, others drinks, and snacks. There are also several large screen TV's found throughout. Though Blue Lagoon is popular with local residents, the vibe of this establishment seems quite welcoming of visitors.

The Menu

The cannabis menu at Blue Lagoon is modest in size, as expected of a shop that caters more to locals than tourists. As for the selection, it is best described as traditional. On the weed-side, the strains are typically old school. Think genetics such as White Widow, Haze, and Bubblegum. They probably have less than a half dozen options on the hashish (hasj) side. The hash gets listed first on the menu, however, which likely reflects a more prominent focus for this shop. Expect to find some quality imports here.

SHOP FEATURES

SHOP HOURS:

Sun-Thurs:
10:00am-12:00am

Fri-Sat:
10:00am-1:00am

COFFEESHOPS

MAP IT

BLUE SEA

Van Woustraat 87, Amsterdam (Zuid) **:ADDRESS**

Blue Sea Coffeeshop is located on the eastern edge of the Nieuwe Pijp (The New Pipe) neighborhood. Though this is a busy part of the city, Blue Sea is just far enough from the hustle and bustle to be a bit more of a locals' shop. Worry not if you are a city visitor though. They do seem to be welcoming of tourists here.

The Shop

The outside of the shop is representative of its name. There is a clear "ocean oasis" theme on the sign, and the brick is painted blue. Aside from the blue paint, the theme does not seem to carry over into the interior. As you step in, you will find a Moroccan/Dutch vibe, not beach-like. The shop is unpretentious and simple, but very chill and cozy.

Blue Sea is divided into two rooms. The front room is modest in size, with four wooden tables and some chairs. This room is closed off from the rest of the shop, and serves as a tobacco smoking area. If you prefer mixed joints, you will be accommodated here. The main room to the back is more comfortable and a bit larger. Here you will find some cushy couches to rest on. There are also a few tables and stools available by the counter. Though this establishment is not heavy on amenities, they do have pinball and a vending machine.

The Menu

For a small and mainly locals' coffeeshop, Blue Sea boasts a fairly large menu. At last check there were more than a dozen strains on the weed-side, and roughly as many different types of hash. The genetics are mixed here. Expect to find both old-school strains, and some contemporary West Coast USA varieties. They also have several options for pre-rolled weed or hash joints, as well as space cakes, if you prefer an edible.

CONNOISSEUR GUIDE: AMSTERDAM

BLUEBIRD

ADDRESS: Sint Antoniesbreestraat 71, Amsterdam (Centrum)

MAP IT

SHOP HOURS:
Daily:
9:30am-1:00am

Bluebird coffeeshop is located in the Nieuwmarkt district of Amsterdam. It is right near Rembrandthuis, once the home-turned-museum of the famous painter. Bluebird is an unpretentious shop. You will not find metallic silver floor tiles or a disco ball here. Instead, it is a down-to-earth coffeeshop. That is not to say it is boring. To the contrary, it is quite interesting. The windows and architecture are fairly open and modern, and the shop is inviting. There is cool artwork hanging on the walls, ample seating, and even a comfortable couch. We would best describe Bluebird Coffeeshop as a "chill" location.

The Shop

This shop is moderate in size, and split into two levels. The ground floor hosts a couple of outdoor tables, a small amount of indoor seating, and a counter for borrowing bongs and other smoking supplies. You have to walk upstairs to find the main area of the shop. Once here, you will notice a counter for ordering snacks, coffees, teas and others drinks, as well as cannabis to the right. To the left, a closed smoking room for those that prefer mixed joints (with tobacco). Seating can be found around the rest of the floor. Bluebird Coffeeshop has plenty of interesting corners and nooks, so you should not have much trouble finding a spot that is right for you to hang out for a while. Though be warned, this place is popular.

The Menu

Bluebird Coffeeshop has long been known for its cannabis menu, and has entered competitions on occasion. They typically have an extensive and diverse list of offerings. When everything is in stock, the weed menu will usually list nearly two dozen strains. These range from low potency (economical) imports for beginners, to the high THC contemporary varieties coveted by connoisseurs.

Their hash menu is arguably more impressive. As far as diversity, again they will stock nearly two dozen items on this side of the menu. These range from traditional sieved and pressed imports from places like Morocco, India, Nepal, and Afghanistan, to high potency Dutch Isolator hash, to what they have dubbed "Super Ice-o-lators". The quality, in our experience, is quite consistent and seems to earn this shop a fair amount of regular business.

They also serve some of the other requisite items, such as pre-rolled joints and edibles. The latter come in the form of THC infused space cakes and muffins. Additionally, this shop has a pair of Volcano vaporizers available for use. This makes it one of the better Vapor Lounges in the city.

COFFEESHOPS

CONNOISSEUR GUIDE: AMSTERDAM

COFFEESHOPS

SHOP FEATURES

SHOP HOURS:

Daily:
10:00am-10:45pm

BOEREJONGENS BIJ

ADDRESS: Bonairestraat 78, Amsterdam (Oost)

MAP IT

Boerejongens Bij (formerly De Bij) is the third of four locations in the Boerejongens chain. The Dutch name De Bij translates into "The Event" in English. This shop is found on a neighborhood corner in Amsterdam West. The area is largely residential, with tall apartment buildings and narrow tree-lined streets. Around here you can expect to see more bikes than cars, and far fewer tourists than you will in the city centrum.

The Shop

Like its sister shops, the Bij is quite different from the old-school vibe of many other coffeeshops in the city. It has the feel of a pharmacy (apotheek) or Colorado cannabis dispensary. The décor inside is very clean and clinical. All the budtenders wear white coats, and look like pharmacists. In some ways, it is perhaps even a bit more clinical than the average USA dispensary.

At the same time, this place is a classic. Check out the large wall of wooden specimen drawers behind the counter, which came from an old archaeology closet. Or how about the polished wood trim, velvet ropes, marble floors, and artistic carvings found throughout the shop. These antique features contrast with the fully interactive digital menus, which are embedded into the counter. Information can be found about which strains might help with which issue or produce a desired effect.

Boerejongens Bij is a take-and-go establishment. While there is an open room to the right of the shop, it is not meant to be a seating area with a single elevated table in the center of the room. This is meant to be used for rolling a joint, or taking a pause before lighting up elsewhere. There is also a modern display about cannabis along the far wall, along with a large selection of souvenirs.

The Menu

The cannabis menu at Boerejongens is usually ample in size. Further, this shop has a well-deserved reputation for quality. This extends to the full menu. Many of their items are award winning. For weed, they tend to favor contemporary genetics. Think West Coast strains from the USA, sometimes carrying a unique local twist. The hashish is both domestic nederhasj and imported. Though the former is more potent, this shop is perhaps better known for its imports, particularly its highly flavorful Moroccan "Block" hash. Lastly, they have some world-class edibles here. The various cakes, muffins, and brownies are delectable - far exceeding most shops with selection and creativity.

CONNOISSEUR GUIDE: AMSTERDAM

COFFEESHOPS

COFFEESHOPS

SHOP FEATURES

SHOP HOURS:
Mon-Fri:
7:00am-12:45am
Sat-Sun:
9:00am-12:45am

BOEREJONGENS CENTER

ADDRESS: Utrechtsestraat 21, Amsterdam (Centrum)

MAP IT

Boerejongens Center coffeeshop is primarily a takeaway establishment located on Utrechtsestraat, to the south of Rembrandtplein. This is a busy part of Amsterdam, with small boutique shops and restaurants lining the streets. The Dutch word "boerenjongen" translates into "farmer boy". This is one of the four Farmer Boy's shops.

The Shop

Like its sister shops, the vibe at Boerejongens Center coffeeshop is quite different from most Dutch establishments. It is a modern take on the long-standing part of this city's culture. The best way to describe it would be to compare it to a medical marijuana dispensary in the USA. Inside, the atmosphere is clinical, with budtenders in white coats greeting visitors from behind a large wood and marble counter.

Boerejongens Center is primarily a take-and-go establishment. However, this shop actually has a HORECA license (hotel/restaurant/café). For this, they also serve coffee and snacks, and maintain a separate smoking area. Do you see that staircase in the back? It leads up to Boerejongens' small but very comfortable smoking lounge. This room is furnished with plush leather chairs, and beautiful wood trim. Enough people know about this room though, so it is often full.

The Menu

As far as cannabis goes, Boerejongens Center Coffeeshop is connected with Amsterdam Genetics. They have been providing modern strains to a good number of the city's connoisseur coffeeshops. Likewise, this coffeeshop is also regarded as a connoisseur establishment. They have entered many cannabis competitions, and have multiple awards to their credit. The staff is well trained and educated about cannabis, which is really helpful if you have specific requests.

The cannabis menu itself is quite robust. First, the weed selection is top notch. You will recognize many of the genetics originating from the USA, which are often embodied in Amsterdam Genetics' own hybridizations. For hash, they are well known for their "block hashes". No, we are not taking about brick hash here. Block is a growing technique where the weed used for making hash is grown in sections or blocks. These blocks are strain specific, which allows for a much more refined and controlled end-product. The edibles are also really good here. What is best of all about this shop though is perhaps the pricing. It tends to be reasonable for a connoisseur shop located in the city center.

COFFEESHOPS

CONNOISSEUR GUIDE: AMSTERDAM

COFFEESHOPS

SHOP FEATURES

SHOP HOURS:

Daily:
10:00am-1:00am

BOEREJONGENS SLOTERDIJK
ADDRESS: Humberweg 5, Amsterdam (West)

MAP IT

Boerejongens Sloterdijk is named after the local neighborhood. The Sloterdijk is found in the Northwest corner of Amsterdam, near the harbor. There is a lot of commercial activity here. As such, the neighborhood around Boerejongens has a very industrial feel to it. The construction is often quite modern as well, owing to the fact that a lot of the business expansion occurred in the latter part of the 20th century. Whereas the center is packed with historic canal homes, here you will find heavily glassed high-rises and office parks. Lately though, the Sloterdijk has been in transition. Residential properties are increasing; more people are moving here.

The Shop

This Boerejongens location has a similar feel to their other shops. The vibe inside is elegant and clinical. If we were to define it, we would say it feels like a cross between a bank and an American cannabis dispensary. You will also notice that the budtenders wear lab coats, and are highly educated about the products. The white marble floors and wide counter give the large open room an air of opulence. The clean wooden shelving, gold trim, and glass display cases only accentuate it. If you are looking for an experience comparable to visiting a high-end dispensary in Denver, check out a Boerejongens shop. It is probably as close as you will find in Amsterdam.

Like the other Boerejongens locations (barring the Center, which does have a small smoking lounge upstairs), this is a take-and-go location. The management of this chain focuses intently on product and presentation. This has probably helped facilitate their rapid expansion in Amsterdam. It is worth noting that there is ample parking outside. This is a great shop if you are driving through Amsterdam.

The Menu

Boerejongens is considered a connoisseur establishment. The products they offer on all fronts, be it weed, hashish, or edibles, is known for consistency…consistently high quality. On the weed side, expect to find some unique strains. They like hybrids, often mixing old school city favorites and contemporary USA genetics. For hashish, they have exceptional imports. Check out their potent and highly flavorful block hashes from Morocco. As for the edibles, they have set the bar here in Amsterdam. The ornately decorated and designed products are simply stunning.

COFFEESHOPS

CONNOISSEUR GUIDE: AMSTERDAM

COFFEESHOPS

SHOP FEATURES

SHOP HOURS:
Daily:
7:00am-12:45am

BOEREJONGENS WEST

ADDRESS: Baarsjesweg 239, Amsterdam (Oost)

MAP IT

Boerejongens West is a takeaway coffeeshop found on Baarsjesweg, in the De Baarsjes neighborhood of Amsterdam West. This part of the city is newer than most sections of Amsterdam. It is also a largely residential neighborhood, with a high density of more modern-style block apartment buildings. De Baarsjes is not heavily trafficked by tourists, and is a bit less hectic than the city center. Rembrandt Park is also to the west, if you want to visit one of the city's nicest green areas.

The Shop

The Dutch word Boerenjongen translates into "Farmer Boy" in English. This is one of four "Farmer Boys" locations. The décor of this shop (like all three locations) is quite distinct from most Dutch cannabis establishments. Instead of being austere, it is elegant. When you walk in you will find a room that resembles an early 20th century city pharmacy or bank. Giant marble tiles make up the flooring. There is a long wooden counter with a marble top in the rear half of the shop. Behind the counter is a full wall of old wooden cabinets and shelves. The place is simply beautiful.

Though this coffeeshop has en elegant early 20th century appearance on the inside, there is a modern edge to it. The operations of Boerejongens resemble that of a Colorado medical marijuana dispensary. There is a rope line in the front of the counter, directing customers to queue when busy. The displays include a lot of seeds and genetics references. A visit to this shop is about making a purchase. The environment is clinical. Likewise, one will find the staff to be knowledgable about marijuana strains and pharmacology. In short, this is not your traditional Dutch "weed bar."

The Menu

Boerejongens hosts an interactive computer system for its menu, which helps shoppers sort through their offerings to find the best options for them. And what is on order? This shop has been very active in entering cannabis competitions, and has numerous award-winning products to their credit. You can order some of them right here. On the weed side, expect to find contemporary genetics. Think Kush, Diesel, fruity hybrids. For hashish, they specialize in highly flavorful imported "Block" varieties from Morocco, though you can find some more potent nederhasj as well. And when it comes to edibles, this shop really stands out. We highly recommend a stop here if you are shopping for some.

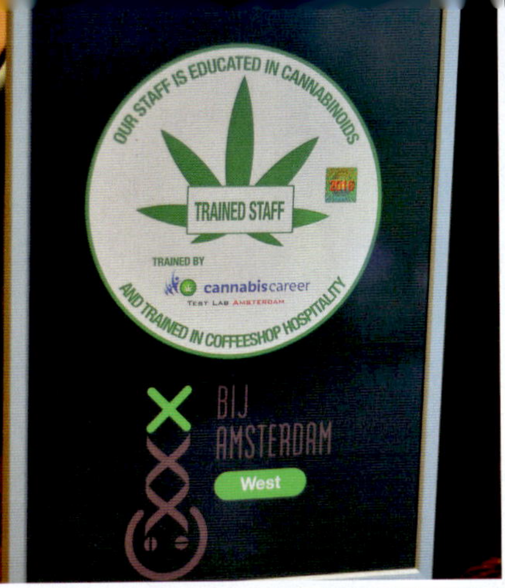
OUR STAFF IS EDUCATED IN CANNABINOIDS
TRAINED STAFF
TRAINED BY
cannabiscareer
TEST LAB AMSTERDAM
AND TRAINED IN COFFEESHOP HOSPITALITY
BIJ AMSTERDAM
West

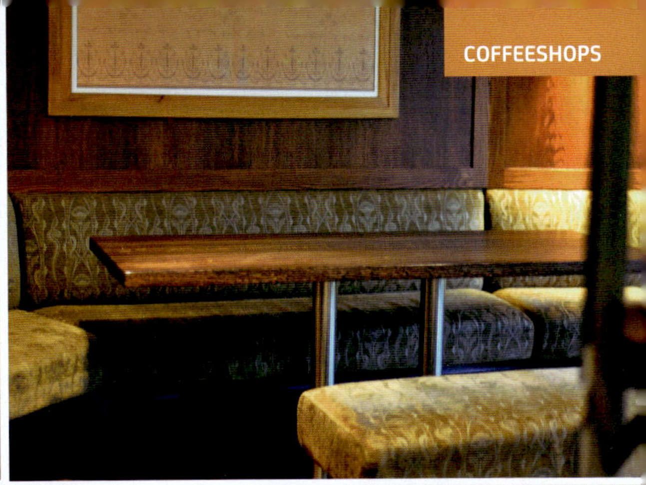

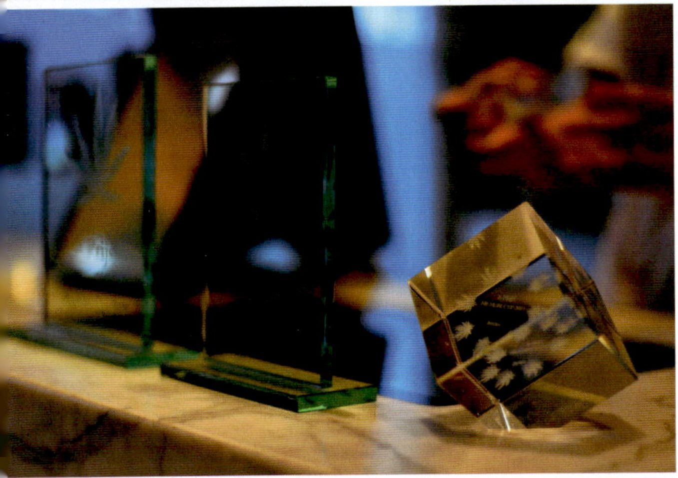

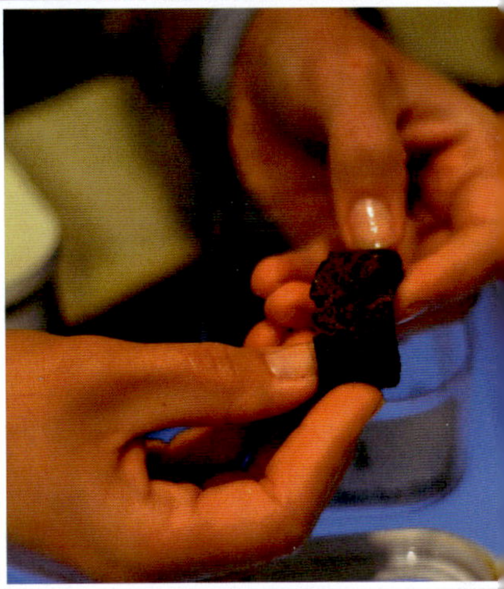

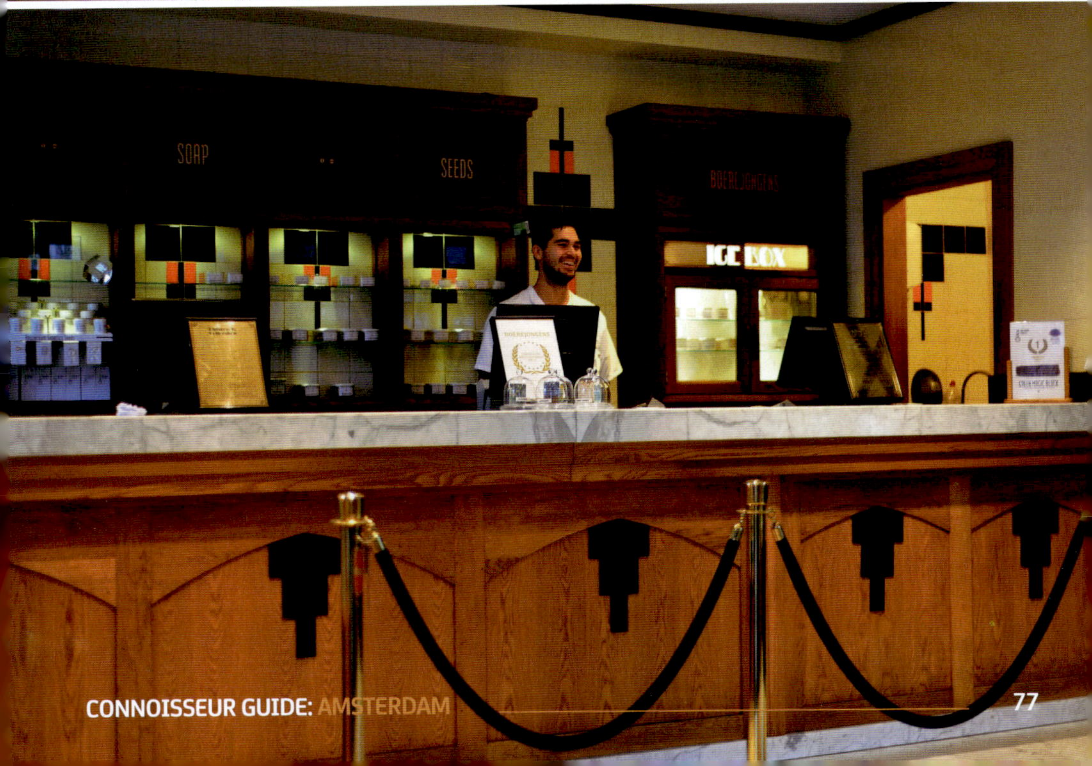
SOAP
SEEDS
ICE BOX

SHOP FEATURES

SHOP HOURS:
Daily:
10:00am-1:00am

BRONX

ADDRESS: Marnixstraat 92, Amsterdam (Centrum)

MAP IT

Coffeeshop Bronx is located on Marnixstraat, at the western edge of Amsterdam Centrum. This road is situated on a thin but busy strip of land between the Jordaan and Frederik Hendrikbuurt, two beautiful and highly desirable residential neighborhoods. While the immediate area around this coffeeshop is perhaps less noteworthy, just a few blocks to the north is the Marnix Bowl. This is a world famous skate park, and central Amsterdam's largest. It is worth a visit even if you do not skate. The park is beautiful, and a great place to see street art.

The Shop

Bronx is modest in size. Similar to many parts of the city, the buildings in this neighborhood do tend to be tall and narrow. The upper floors are mostly residences, with businesses sometimes on the lower levels. This coffeeshop makes use of a split-level floor plan, which does provide enough room to accommodate customers. Likewise, this is not just a take-and-go establishment. It is a neighborhood hangout, catering mainly to local clients.

As you walk in off the street and into the front room of Coffeeshop Bronx, you are presented with the shop's main counter. Here you can purchase cannabis products, along with a basic assortment of coffees, teas, drinks, and snacks. Once you have what you need, you may proceed into the shop's smoking lounge. Just open the door and go down a few steps to the split lower level. There is also a second stairway, which leads to an upper balcony. The seating here is basic, wooden chairs and benches. Since this shop does have a lounge closed off from the main shop, tobacco consumption is permitted on premises.

The Menu

The cannabis menu at The Bronx is limited in size compared to some of the busier shops in the Jordaan. If you are strain hunting and desire a large selection, this may not be the place for you. On the other hand, prices are usually more reasonable in shops that do not have the benefit of a large tourist draw. Further, if the stock is bad these places will risk losing their business from the locals. In our experience, you can often find good value when visiting smaller neighborhood shops like these.

Marnix Bowl Skate Park

COFFEESHOPS

SHOP FEATURES

SHOP HOURS:

Daily:
8:00am-1:00am

BULLDOG 90

ADDRESS: Oudezijds Voorburgwal 90, Amsterdam (Centrum)

MAP IT

Bulldog 90 coffeeshop is located in the Red Light District, close to The Oude Church (The Old Church). This is the heart of Amsterdam, one of the busiest sections of the city center. As such, the area is heavily trafficked by visitors. Expect a lot of activity.

The Shop

Also known as "Bulldog The First", this coffeeshop was officially founded in December 1975. Depending on how you qualify it, this is either the longest or second-longest running coffeeshop in the city. At one time Bulldog 90 was actually an illegal establishment, selling cannabis in violation of Dutch law. They were, unquestionably, pioneers in the cannabis movement. We can see tribute to this controversial history throughout the shop.

One of the most notable features is the "Orange Raid Alarm". The bartender upstairs would drop an orange down a dumbwaiter shaft in the event of a police raid. This would serve as advance warning to everyone in the basement consuming (and selling) cannabis. This usually provided enough time to stash or dispose of the illegal goods before the officers made it down the steep narrow staircase. The shop is filled with historic photos and memoirs like this for modern day visitors to enjoy. And in spite of much expansion, cannabis is still sold in the basement, in a tribute to their roots.

The shop itself is quite impressive in its décor. The interior consists of polished old wood and accent fixtures. It almost has the feel of an upscale bar or steakhouse. In spite of heavy visitor traffic and use for years, the interior of the shop has been beautifully maintained. The outside is no exception. At some point, the shop was even able to add a large area of canal-side seating which offers breathtaking views on sunny days.

Art is a major theme in this coffeeshop. A lot of tourists visit The 90 specifically to see its famous painted façade, created by Harold Thorton. He became well known in Amsterdam in the early 1970s. The mural was painted back in December 1975 and has made The Bulldog Nr.90 impossible to walk past without noticing. Many of Thorton's paintings also adorn the Bulldog Hotel in Amsterdam, and are certainly worthy of a visit.

The Menu

Bulldog moves a lot of cannabis, and has a lot of buying power with growers. Sometimes they get flack for being "too commercial", but in our experience you can usually find quality flower on the menu here. However, by their own admission they are not contemporary strain hunters. If you want 38% THC Gorilla Glue, this is not the place. The stock usually reflects traditional genetics, with a focus more on flavor and experience.

COFFEESHOPS

1975 – 1982
ORANGE RAID ALARM

AN ORANGE WAS DROPPED
DOWN BY THE BARTENDER
IN THE SHOP ABOVE
TO WARN THE DEALER OF
A POLICE RAID

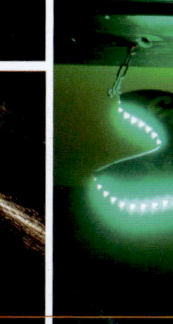

CONNOISSEUR GUIDE: AMSTERDAM

COFFEESHOPS

SHOP FEATURES

SHOP HOURS:
Daily:
8:00am-1:00am

BULLDOG ENERGY

ADDRESS: Oudezijds Voorburgwal 218, Amsterdam (Centrum)

MAP IT

Attached to The Bulldog Hotel is another of the brand's coffeeshops, The Bulldog Energy. This shop is located on the same canal-side street in the Red Light District as the more famous Bulldog 90, just a bit further to the south. Energy used to be the "Smart Shop" for The Bulldog brand. It sold a variety of energy, herbal, and psychedelic products including magic mushrooms. Today, changes in local law mean that no mushrooms are to be found here. Instead, the place has morphed into what would aptly be described as a "trippy" coffeeshop.

The Shop

The décor in Bulldog Energy is hard to put into words. The experience is fantasy-like, a theme along the lines of Harry Potter or Lord of the Rings. Just about everything is custom in here, and quite intricate in detail. It begins with rocks, which are cemented into the walls of the entryway façade and bar. The walls inside curve in a bit, and are painted beige. Decorative spider webs cover many of the light fixtures, which tend to throw off only dim light. The tables look like moss-covered boulders, and the benches appear to be made of old fencing. It all makes for the visitor a feeling of being in a cave or hobbit hole. It is very abstract and trippy!

Fret not if you prefer the light of the outdoors. They do have outdoor seating. Like The Bulldog 90, there is a large sectioned off area that sits canal-side. Here, you will find several large wooden tables with pull-up chairs. On a sunny day, this is a great spot.

The Menu

Aside from the décor, the shop's offerings are consistent with those of The Bulldog brand. There is a digital cannabis menu here, with a formidable list of offerings for both flower (weed) and hashish. On the weed-side, expect to find some of the old-school strains that made Amsterdam famous. The hashish is also traditional; pressed imports from places like Morocco, Afghanistan, and Lebanon. They do not chase the latest high-potency THC strains and extraction techniques at Bulldog. Instead, the focus appears to be more on flavor, and providing an experience consistent with fond old memories.

They offer other things on the menu aside from cannabis, starting with a fairly large selection of coffees, teas, and drinks. If you need to stave off the munchies, they also have some odd snacks and desserts. Further, there is plenty of Bulldog memorabilia available here for purchase if you want to bring something home to remember your visit.

CONNOISSEUR GUIDE: AMSTERDAM

Window Brothel, Red Light District

COFFEESHOPS

SHOP FEATURES

SHOP HOURS:

Daily:
9:00am-10:00pm

BULLDOG HARBOUR

ADDRESS: Coenhavenweg 26, Amsterdam (West)

MAP IT

Bulldog Harbour (formerly Bulldog Port 26) coffeeshop is the newest addition to the Bulldog chain, opening its doors in April 2015. It is located in the Coenhavenweg area of Amsterdam West, one of the city seaport locations. The surrounding area is very industrial. Due to this, the clientele here is mainly local. Some tourists do manage to venture out, more notably during the summer months.

This coffeeshop would probably appeal most to people with an automobile. There is free parking here. As one can imagine, this part of the city sees less hustle and bustle than central Amsterdam. There are a number of hotels in the area, and it is not far for tourists visiting the West side. You can locate the coffeeshop by public transport or by bicycle, with it being only a ten minute cycle ride from Westerpark and Sloterdijk.

The Shop

The décor inside Bulldog Harbour is polished, and a bit classic in appearance. There is a lot of wood and exposed brick. The place has a small local café or restaurant feel. The strong smell of cannabis and Bulldog "accouterment" makes it immediately clear you are in a coffeeshop, though. Like all Bulldog coffeeshops, this place hosts a smoking lounge. The area is modest in size, but relaxed and comfortable. Be sure not to miss the patio seating outside. The port view is something unique this shop offers, and worth checking out, especially on a sunny day. Some additional amenities include a PlayStation, table games, and a wide selection of hot/cold drinks and snacks. They offer something else that is of interest - a loyalty card. It allows you to get 10% back for every purchase. You can cash the value in when you please. This is another indication that they have a lot of locals for customers. If you are looking for something different though, this coffeeshop can definitely be a nice place to chill, away from the bustling metropolis of Amsterdam Centrum.

The Menu

The other Bulldog locations usually have a robust cannabis selection. The same is true here. On the weed-side of the menu, expect to find roughly a dozen items on offer. They specialize in old-school Amsterdam strains here. In doing so, they seem to focus more on flavor and consistency than testing the latest limits of THC production. The hashish-side of the menu is equally traditional. Expect to see pressed imports from places like Morocco, Afghanistan, and Nepal. Purchases are usually pre-weighed, and you can buy anywhere from 0.5g up to 5g. They also stock several types of pre-rolled joints.

COFFEESHOPS

CONNOISSEUR GUIDE: AMSTERDAM

COFFEESHOPS

SHOP FEATURES

SHOP HOURS:

Daily:
8:00am-1:00am

BULLDOG PALACE

ADDRESS: Leidseplein 15, Amsterdam (Centrum)

MAP IT

Bulldog Palace is located at the Leidseplein (Leiden Square). This is one of the busiest sections of the city, packed with restaurants, nightclubs, and various facets of shopping. The Bulldog is far from a business with a minor presence here. In fact, it seems to be a cornerstone of the square. With its large neon signs, three separate businesses (coffeeshop, nightclub, and souvenir shop) on premises, and ample out-front seating, one simply cannot miss it when visiting the area.

There is interesting history behind this particular location, which opened its doors in 1985. The original Bulldog coffeeshop was one of Amsterdam's first, with roots dating back to cannabis prohibition. The owners were notorious for defying Amsterdam's cannabis laws. The original location was raided so many times that the exact number has been lost to history. Once cannabis toleration policies came into effect, however, The Bulldog was poised to thrive. Within a decade they would become the largest chain of coffeeshops in the city, and amass enough resources to buy the location Bulldog Palace now occupies, former police headquarters #14. Is it irony or poetic justice? It all depends on how you want to look at it.

The Shop

First, you should know that the coffeeshop only makes up a small portion of this building. Technically speaking, it is The Bulldog Ex-policestation (formerly The Bulldog Havri), which is found in the old jail below The Palace. Alcohol cannot be served in coffeeshops, so this is considered a separate business. This may be the most interesting part of the whole operation, though. The coffeeshop has preserved a great deal of the old jail. Steel bars are found throughout, and an old cell houses the shop's closed-off smoking room. It is essentially a museum in here now, packed with interesting old photos and artifacts from the years of alcohol prohibition. There is even an original (deactivated) Thompson 1928 machine gun hanging on a back door, arguably one of the most emblematic pieces from this era.

Upstairs is the large Palace bar/restaurant. The décor is modern, perhaps barring the giant classic Wurlitzer jukebox that is actually a DJ booth. It is positioned over the entrance, so you walk below it as you enter. The atmosphere in here is "Grand Café". Think of it as part high-end nightclub, part restaurant. The place is clean, the furniture well maintained, and the atmosphere is lively. While The Bulldog Palace is not the most traditional Dutch coffeeshop, it is one of the most iconic, and its popularity is a clear reflection of that.

COFFEESHOPS

CONNOISSEUR GUIDE: AMSTERDAM

COFFEESHOPS

SHOP FEATURES

SHOP HOURS:

Daily:
7:00am-1:00am

BULLDOG ROCK SHOP

ADDRESS: Singel 12, Amsterdam (Centrum)

MAP IT

Bulldog Rock Shop coffeeshop is located beside the Singel canal, just around the corner from Centraal Station. This shop rests at the very northeast corner of the Grachtengordel, which translates into "the Canal District" in English. This is an area of historic interlocking canals within the center of Amsterdam, lined by many 17th century canal homes. The district is on the UNESCO World Heritage list, and is one of the most picturesque and popular parts of the city. The Rockshop is run by the famous Bulldog brand, and as such is one of the more maintained and polished establishments in the city.

The Shop

As its name suggests, the Bulldog Rock Shop is a themed coffeeshop. It pays tribute to 1970's era rock 'n' roll music. Visitors will find music memorabilia from this era including framed guitars, gold records, and an endless collection of photographs throughout. The décor is upscale and comfortable. Thick dark wooden counters and tables are complimented by plush stools and soft comfortable leather benches. The benches are covered in Bulldog's distinct dark (brown and white) cowhide pattern, which adds an unusual but nice touch to the place.

The inside has the feel of a trendy city bar, not your traditional Dutch weed shop. Of note, there is also some minimalistic bench seating outside, perfect for relaxing in front of the canal on a sunny day. Though 70's theme in theory, in practice this shop has evolved a bit over the years to include a wider scope of music (and audience). You are just as likely to find modern rock music playing on the radio as you are something from the classic era of rock 'n' roll. Likewise, not all of the celebrities featured on The Bulldog Rock Shop's walls are at retirement age just yet. Some are distinctly young. No matter, the cool rock 'n' roll vibe of this place endures.

The Menu

The cannabis menu at the Bulldog Rock Shop is consistent with other Bulldog locations. On the weed-side, expect to find roughly a dozen items. These are made up of mainly old-school Amsterdam genetics, which may include some long recognized strains such as White Widow and Super Silver Haze. For hashish, they favor traditional pressed imports from Morocco and other common source regions. They also stock a selection of pre-rolled joints, with both pure and mixed (with tobacco) varieties.

The Canal Ring

COFFEESHOPS

SHOP FEATURES

SHOP HOURS:
Mon-Thurs:
10:00am-12:00am
Fri-Sat:
10:00am-1:00am
Sun:
11:00am-12:00am

BULLWACKIE

ADDRESS: Woestduinstraat 76, Amsterdam (Oost)

MAP IT

Bullwackie Coffeeshop is found on Woestduinstraat, a relatively quiet residential street in the Hoofddorppleinbuurt section of Amsterdam South. This roughly translates into "the neighborhood around the Main Village Square" in English. This square (Hoofddorpplein) is just a short walk to the east. There is a small park in the center, and it is bordered by a series of small cafés, restaurants, and pubs. This is a lively area during the evenings; quite popular with residents in the neighborhood.

The Shop

The name of this shop pays tribute to Lloyd Barnes, a music producer better known by the name Bullwackie. Originally from Trenchtown Jamaica, Barnes emigrated to New York during the mid-1960s. There, he founded the independent reggae music label "Wackies." During the 1970s and '80s, they were known for their influential music, which melded traditional Jamaican reggae with the urban vibe of the underground New York music scene.

Inside, Bullwackie has a traditional Dutch vibe. The décor is simple, without much by way of amenities or frills. It is a practical shop. They have cannabis. They sell it. There is no pretense. The shop caters mainly to locals, so they are not really trying to impress tourists. Though all are welcome here, the shop is tailored for short visits. There is no smoking lounge. For some time now, Bullwackie has been operating exclusively as a take-and-go location.

The Menu

The cannabis menu at Bullwackie is modest in size. On the weed-side, expect maybe 10 items or so. They do not really chase contemporary genetics much here. Instead, they seem to focus on recognized old-school favorite strains. Though the selection is a little smaller, this shop probably places more emphasis on hashish, specifically Moroccan imports. This is perhaps owing to its higher consumption (vs. weed) by local residents. They also have a decent selection of pre-rolled joints, if preferred. As you might expect, prices tend to be a more favorable here compared to the more tourist-focused shops in the Centrum.

SHOP FEATURES

COFFEESHOPS

SHOP HOURS:

Daily:
9:00am-1:00am

MAP IT

BUSHDOCTER

Thorbeckeplein 28, Amsterdam (Centrum) **:ADDRESS**

The Bushdocter coffeeshop is located on Thorbeckeplein (Thorbecke Square), named after a prominent 19th century Dutch politician. Thorbeckeplein is a small tree-lined square in the southern part of the Canal Ring. It is close to the Rembrandtplein (Rembrandt square), also a very active part of the city for nightlife. Likewise, you will find this square bordered side-by-side with pubs, restaurants, and other eateries. It can be quite a draw on sunny afternoons as well. You will often find the square packed with visitors resting in the shade, or enjoying a bit of al fresco dining under an outdoor canopy.

The Shop

The Bushdocter is fairly large inside. There is ample seating downstairs, and a more expansive room upstairs that hosts some nice views of the square. However, the indoor seating is not the most notable feature of this shop. As a business in Thorbecke Square, Bushdocter coffeeshop has access to a great deal of outdoor seating space. On sunny days, they take full advantage of it. They will place roughly a dozen small tables outside, with enough seating for several times that number. Bushdocter likely has the distinction of having the greatest volume of outdoor seating of any coffeeshop in the city center.

The Menu

This coffeeshop is also known for its cannabis products, hashish in particular. They have entered competitions in the past for their stock, and won a handful of awards over the years. Bushdocter was also one of the first coffeeshops to bring high quality cannabis concentrates (mainly wax) to Amsterdam, which they claim is produced through a solvent-free method. You are likely to find some on the menu, perhaps alongside some moonrocks and nederhasj. They also have a fairly robust selection on the weed-side of the menu. Genetics are largely old-school favorites here, with a few contemporary items thrown in the mix. There is also a decent list of pre-rolled joints, and space cakes if you are looking for an edible.

COFFEESHOPS

SHOP FEATURES

SHOP HOURS:

Daily:
9:00am-1:00am

CARMONA

ADDRESS: Tweede Jan van der Heijdenstraat 43, Amsterdam (Zuid)

MAP IT

Carmona Coffeeshop is located on Tweede Jan van der Heijdenstraat, in the Oude Pijp (Old Pipe) section of Amsterdam South. It is just two blocks to the east of Sarphatipark, the largest park in De Pijp. This park can be a serene escape from the city. It is large, lush, and quiet, with a beautiful lake in the middle. Beyond the park, this part of the city is mainly residential, and also quite beautiful. Even so, the Pipe neighborhoods are quite trendy. Around here you will find your fair share of small restaurants, shops, bars, and cafés.

The Shop

Carmona coffeeshop is a contemporary, yet unpretentious, establishment. Admittedly, the bright neon signage out front is not subtle. Anyone walking through the neighboring Van Woustraat shopping district probably cannot miss. Inside though, you find a shop that is moderate in size, and discriminating in its décor.

Carmona exists on one level, though is divided into two rooms. In the front, you will find the shop counter. Here you can buy cannabis products and basic refreshments. Once you make your purchase, you can move into the back. Here, you will find the shop's smoking lounge. This area is closed off from the staff and rest of the shop, which means that tobacco consumption is permitted on premises (this is a requirement of EU smoking laws).

In the smoking lounge, one will probably find ample seating in the form of padded leather chairs and benches. Tables are made of contemporary engineered wood. Though the room is tight, the furniture arrangement feels private. Glass panels let in some natural light from the front, which is augmented with well-placed accent lighting. The room has a look that reminds us of a small city café or coffee house. It is all quite cozy, with a vibe that is chill and quite conducive to a relaxing time.

The Menu

The cannabis menu at Carmona is fairly large for a local shop, with ample selection on both the weed and hashish side. For weed, they tend to stock mainly established favorites, although you might find a few strains based on contemporary USA genetics. The hashish selection usually consists of traditional pressed imports. In addition, they have an array of soda, juices, hot drinks, and snacks available for purchase. They are particularly serious about their coffee here. Expect to find a suitable cup if you are in the mood.

COFFEESHOPS

CONNOISSEUR GUIDE: AMSTERDAM

COFFEESHOPS

SHOP FEATURES

SHOP HOURS:

Daily:
9:00am-1:00am

CATCH 33

ADDRESS: Nassaukade 33-HS, Amsterdam (Oost)

MAP IT

Catch 33 is located on Nassaukade, near the southwest corner of Westerpark. This shop is just outside the s100 ring, which separates Amsterdam Centrum from surrounding neighborhoods. Though not a far walk from the city center, this shop is removed enough to be frequented primarily by locals. This section of the city is mainly residential as well, though Westerpark is an expansive and lush park that hosts many popular events. As such, this part of the city certainly still does welcome its share of visitors.

The Shop

The theme inside Catch 33 coffeeshop is distinctly Moroccan, with a vibe that is chill and artsy. Hand painted clouds on the ceiling creates a dreaminess to the atmosphere. This is complimented by hand textured walls, which blend in with the large polished wooden counter and accompanying trim. The Moroccan feel is well complimented by related works of art and sculpture, which are on display throughout. This all gives Catch 33 a much more polished appearance than most.

This shop is divided into two rooms. The front hosts the counter for purchasing cannabis, as well as drinks and snacks. The cannabis menu is moderate in size, with decent balance between weed and hash options. Expect under a dozen of each, but with enough variety to keep most customers happy. You can take your purchases into the back, where you find the shop's closed smoking room. Though not expansive, there are several tables and benches back here, and the artsy Moroccan theme makes it feel very comfortable. On sunny days, you can also find a couple of chairs and a bench out front, if you prefer an al fresco experience.

The Menu

The cannabis menu at Catch 33 is moderate in size. You can expect to find a half dozen items on each side of the menu. For weed, they generally stock a lot of old-school local genetics, though you are likely to find a contemporary strain or two as well. They seem more focused on hashish at Catch 33, where they feature mainly imports from Morocco. Some of their cannabis products are also available in pre-rolled joints, if you prefer not to have to roll our own.

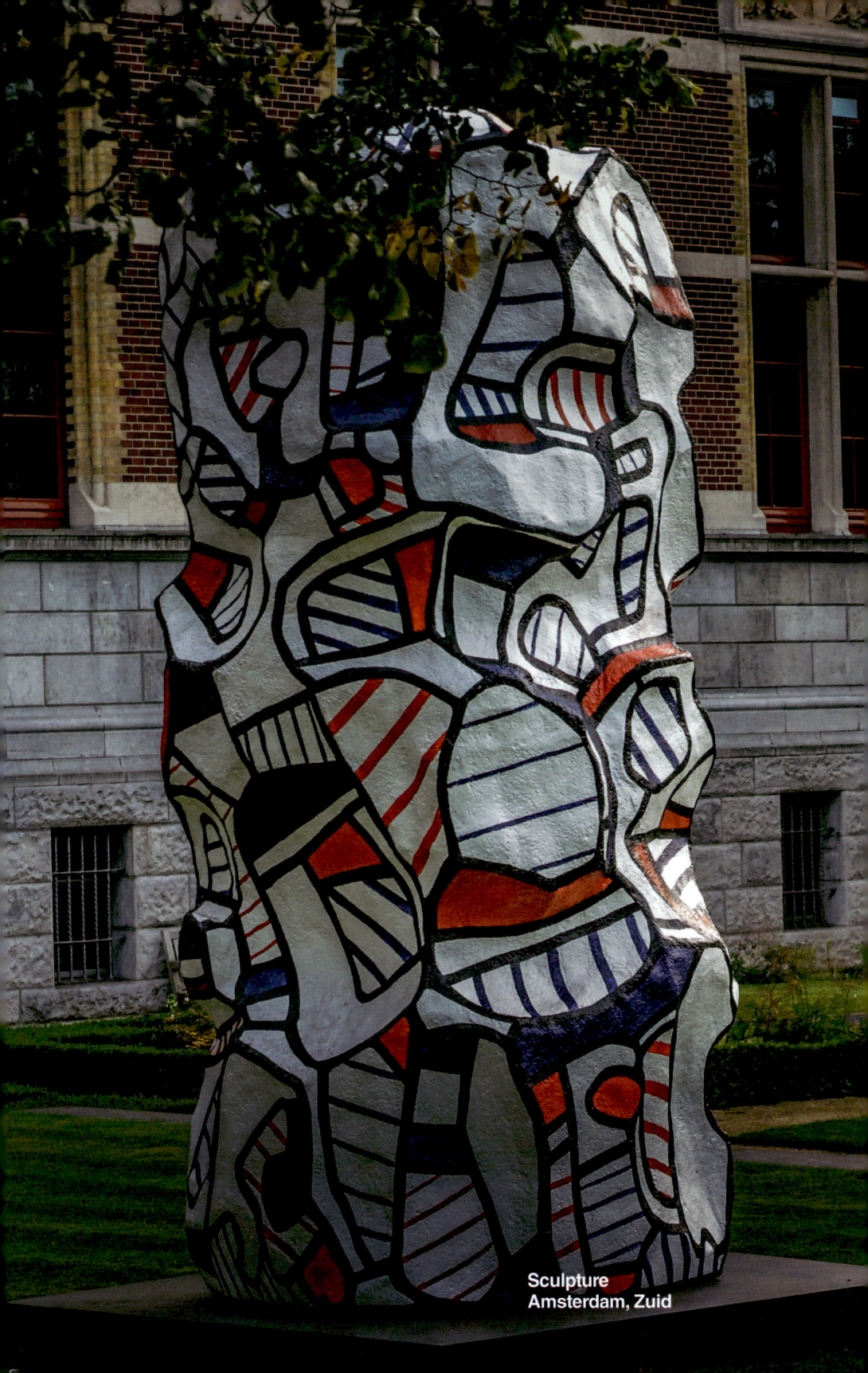

Sculpture
Amsterdam, Zuid

COFFEESHOPS

SHOP FEATURES

SHOP HOURS:

Daily:
7:00am-11:00pm

CENTRAL

ADDRESS: Prins Hendrikkade 89, Amsterdam (Centrum)

MAP IT

Central Coffeeshop is located on Prins Hendrikkade, across the street from Centraal Station. It is technically the closest coffeeshop to the train station, sitting just to the southeast of the main entrance. If you have just entered Amsterdam here and are heading south towards the Nieuwmarkt (New Market) area, it will likely be the first shop you come across.

The Shop

This is a small coffeeshop. Even so, they make good use of the space. Inside, one will find an artistic décor that seems to belie its simple "corner convenience store" façade. Central has gray tile floors, wainscot walls, and large hand-drawn murals. There are a handful of leather stools and some small tables as well, and a long wooden counter that runs along the front window. This place feels quite cozy for being on such a busy corner.

Though an interesting atmosphere, few people actually hang out here. Central is mainly a take-and-go establishment. Over the years this coffeeshop has gained a reputation for quality cannabis, and reasonable prices. The shop does not operate with a lot of frills. Their business has been distilled down to the essence of what is needed... good weed and hash, some coffee, drinks, and quick snacks for those on the go, and of course, fast service. Further, they open early, and close late. It is indeed a place of convenience, especially for cannabis-smoking travelers heading in and out of the city.

The Menu

The cannabis menu at Central Coffeeshop is visual. The flower (weed) and hashish comes pre-weighed in small plastic bags. A sample of each variety is clipped inside a glass display case, which is built into the main counter. The bags have prices affixed so you can see everything and know exactly what it costs without asking. This facilitates a fast transaction, especially on the part of the staff. The strains are largely of old-school genetics, and the hashish imported pressed varieties. The also have a decent selection of edibles here.

COFFEESHOPS

CONNOISSEUR GUIDE: AMSTERDAM

COFFEESHOPS

SHOP FEATURES

SHOP HOURS:

Daily:
9:00am-12:00am

CHAPITEAU

ADDRESS: Van Boetzelaerstraat 31, Amsterdam (Oost)

MAP IT

Chapiteau coffeeshop is located on Van Boetzelaerstraat, in a largely residential area of Amsterdam West called the Staatsliedenbuurt, or in English "the Statesmen neighborhood." It is just a bit to the south of Westerpark, one of the city's more notable green areas.

The Shop

The name Chapiteau is actually French for "Marquee". While the name might conjure up visions of a mega nightclub along the lines of Marquee in Las Vegas, Chapiteau is not actually a hangout spot... at all. While they do display a large sign here for Illimani Bolivian Coffee out front, this shop is exclusively a take-away location these days. As such, it is not really the place to look to sit down for a cup of coffee and some conversation.

The inside of Chapiteau features a small front ordering room, which has a clean and clinical appearance. The budtender stands behind the counter, where they are protected by a glass partition, similar to a bank. Transactions are handled via a small window in the center. Though a simple take-and-go, the management does try to bring a chill vibe to this shop. In addition to some basic trim artwork, the bank window is flanked on both sides by large fish tanks, which are built into the walls. Though you are only here for a quick pickup, the do make the room interesting.

The Menu

The cannabis menu at Chapiteau Coffeeshop is fairly large. There are usually more than a dozen strains on the weed side, typically a mix of old-school favorites for Amsterdam, as well as some more contemporary strains, for example West Coast USA Kush hybrids. They also have a nice selection on the hashish side. This is usually heavy on Moroccan hashish, though they usually carry a few imported black hashes as well, along with a domestic high potency isolator variety or two. A few pre-rolled joints round out their product list, and they also have basic accessories like papers, grinders, etc. if needed.

CONNOISSEUR GUIDE: AMSTERDAM

Tram 1 heading to the Leidseplein

COFFEESHOPS

SHOP FEATURES

SHOP HOURS:

Daily:
9:30am-1:00am

CHEECH AND CHONG'S

ADDRESS: De Clercqstraat 30, Amsterdam (Oost)

MAP IT

Cheech and Chong's coffeeshop is located in the Da Costabuurt neighborhood, a more residential part of the city in Amsterdam West. It is found just to the west of the Jordaan, so a bit out of the normal hustle and bustle. However, the immediate area surrounding Cheech and Chong's does have many small shops and cafés, and as a result, its share of foot traffic. Obviously, the name of this coffeeshop pays tribute to the world famous cannabis comedy duo from the USA. We have never seen either of them here personally, but hey, you never know. This is Amsterdam. Every famous stoner seems to make it here at some point, and where else would Cheech and Chong go?

The Shop

Inside, Cheech and Chong's coffeeshop feels very much like a small local bar. You know, the type of place that does not have too many frills, but is comfortable, serves your favorite beer, and feels like home when you get to know all the regulars. In short, the typical local hangout joint. We would say it looks like one too. Dark wood dominates the interior, and the furniture is primarily in the form of basic tables, benches, and stools. Nice. Unpretentious. You half expect them to draw you a pint when you enter. Unfortunately, Dutch law forbids it. It is cannabis only here.

Cheech and Chong's is split into two distinct rooms. The front is the ordering area, which features a large polished dark wood counter. There is matching shelving in the back, which probably accounts for much of this shop's "brown bar" vibe. In the back is the shop's closed off smoking room. Here, the consumption of tobacco is permitted. There is also a full-sized billiards table, and plenty of seating around the room. Mirrors make the area feel a bit more open than it is, but to be fair, this coffeeshop is large enough all things considered. Being in a less hectic neighborhood, it tends to have plenty of room to breathe most evenings.

The Menu

The cannabis menu at Cheech and Chong's is modest in size; usually a half dozen items or so on each side (flower, hashish). Though Chong may be big on California weed these days, this coffeeshop is focused primarily on local favorite (old-school) strains. Think of things like Amnesia, White Widow, Bubblegum etc. The hashish is imported, and often outranks weed with the number of options. Hash may be more in demand by their clientele, which is not uncommon with the more local shops.

COFFEESHOPS

CONNOISSEUR GUIDE: AMSTERDAM

COFFEESHOPS

SHOP FEATURES

SHOP HOURS:

Daily:
9:00am-1:00am

CITY HALL

ADDRESS: Oudezijds Voorburgwal 189, Amsterdam (Centrum)

MAP IT

City Hall Coffeeshop is located on Oudezijds Voorburgwal, off Damstraat. It sits just outside the Red Light District, at its western edge, a couple of blocks from Dam Square. This is in the heart of Amsterdam Centrum. The neighborhood around here can get very busy. If you like being in the thick of it, you will undoubtedly find yourself walking by this coffeeshop at some point.

The Shop

City Hall is found in the basement level of its building. As you step down to enter, you will notice what looks to be a traditional brown bar. There is a great deal of dark wood in here. The seating is mainly bench-style, barring a few loose tables in the back. A long bar, the dominant feature of the room, is set to one side. This is where you order cannabis and drinks. You half expect to find a running beer tap here too, but no such luck.

Although City Hall is a basement shop, it is not exactly dark. The pair of front windows seems to let in a fair amount of light. It is also well lit otherwise. This shop is canal-side too, and has an additional small area of outdoor seating street-side if you prefer some fresh air. This typically consists of a table or two, along with some chairs. As busy as this area is, the outdoor seating can be a great hangout spot for people watching.

The Menu

The cannabis menu at City Hall Coffeeshop tends to be extensive by most standards. Expect to find half a dozen or so types of hashish, and an even wider selection on the flower (weed) side. The genetics and stock are pretty traditional here. That means famous old-school strains of flower, and pressed imported hash. They also serve a decent selection of coffees, teas, juices, soft drinks, and basic snacks.

CONNOISSEUR GUIDE: **AMSTERDAM**

Oriental City for authentic dim sum, steps from City Hall

COFFEESHOPS

SHOP FEATURES

SHOP HOURS:
Mon-Thurs:
8:30am-12:00am
Fri:
8:30am-1:00am
Sat:
9:00am-1:00am
Sun:
9:00am-12:00am

CLUB MEDIA

ADDRESS: Gerard Doustraat 83-85, Amsterdam (Zuid)

MAP IT

Club Media coffeeshop is located in Oude Pijp (the Old Pipe), a trendy neighborhood in Amsterdam Zuid (South). There is an amazing diversity of independent restaurants, cafés, bars, and boutiques here. This coffeeshop also sits right adjacent to the Albert Cuypmarkt, the largest outdoor market in the Netherlands. This is undoubtedly a lively section of the city, attracting many locals and tourists alike. Club Media is a trendy independent shop itself, and seems to fit in quite well with the area.

The Shop

As you first enter, you will find the cannabis ordering counter. This is efficient. Club Media is a popular pickup spot for the locals. Hopefully you are here to stay a bit, though. The lounge area in the back is well worth some time. Inside, one will find a room that is open, welcoming, and bright. Club Media has a unique feel to it. It is a bit funky, a bit traditional, a bit urban. We would compare it to a modern restaurant that purposefully mixes contemporary and classical elements to create its own artistic expression. It is all quite cool.

Prime seating is found in the form of purple and black leather benches, which are pushed against many of the walls. They are soft but supportive, and very comfortable. In front of them are small café tables and pull up leather chairs. There are also in sets around the shop. In addition, you'll find some bar seating. They use thick chrome stools with round black and purple leather seats. It feels like they were ripped from a 1950s' diner. A nice touch. Off to one side is the tobacco lounge, which is closed-off behind a glass to comply with EU tobacco regulations.

The Menu

The cannabis menu is robust at Club Media. The weed-side typically carries more than a dozen strains. The genetics are a clear mix of old and new. You can expect some old-school Amsterdam strains here. Remember, this city cultivated so much of the genetics used in hybrids today. Some of these contemporary strains are probably sitting beside the classics here. The hashish side of the menu is smaller, but possibly even more noteworthy. We find this place to be a "Best of" location for hash, with an excellent variety of quality imports and more potent Nederhasj (Isolator). Another nice feature is the Volcano vaporizer. They also make great coffee, and have plenty of basic drinks and snacks.

COFFEESHOPS

COFFEESHOPS

SHOP FEATURES

SHOP HOURS:

Daily
8:00am-1:00am

COFFEESHOPAMSTERDAM

ADDRESS: Haarlemmerstraat 44, Amsterdam (Centrum)

MAP IT

CoffeeshopAmsterdam is on Haarlemmetstraat, a popular area of the city just southwest of Centraal Station. The immediate neighborhood hosts many small shops, cafés, and independent restaurants. This establishment has gone by a couple of other names in the past. Once it was named Pink Floyd, a vibrant smoke-filled tribute to the famous rock band, of course. In 2007, it was taken over by the owners of the famous "De Dampkring". Upon doing so, the décor was modernized, the menu expanded, and the shop's image revamped. More recently, however, it changed hands again. CoffeeshopAmsterdam is currently one of the most popular shops in this very competitive section of Amsterdam.

The Shop

CoffeeshopAmsterdam is aesthetically impressive, with a combination of exposed brick, modern furnishings, and cool lighting that makes this shop contemporary and inviting. At night, purple lighting even floods out onto the street from the upper floors. The whole corner seems to radiate the vibe of this shop, making it an extremely attention getting for those walking by. This is kind of a narrow shop, but long. It is also spread across three floors, which gives it a fair amount of seating room.

On the first floor, immediately as you walk in, you will find their large "Hash & Weed bar". Beyond this, you can step down to the back of the shop, where there are a few small tables and a juice bar. This area gets a lot of traffic from the staff and is not the most comfortable. Consequently, it is better to rest in one of two additional seating rooms upstairs. They are equally narrow, but have a great deal more tables and stools. There is room enough for about 75 people in this coffeeshop, which actually makes Coffeeshop Amsterdam the largest on Haarlemmerstraat. This is a section of the city generally known for small independent businesses, not large chains.

The Menu

The cannabis menu is extensive at CoffeeshopAmsterdam. Also, it hosts many strains from Amsterdam Genetics. Likewise, this location is regarded as being a connoisseur establishment. On the weed-side you will find many contemporary strains, along with a few old-school items. For hashish, they have a decent variety of imported types, along with a higher-potency domestic or two. They also have pre-rolled joints and space cakes here. Like most coffeeshops, this place does serve hot and cold drinks, along with basic snacks. There is enough to keep you comfortable here. The service is prompt also, so you won't expect to wait long for your order. The coffee is good here as well.

COFFEESHOPS

CONNOISSEUR GUIDE: AMSTERDAM

107

COFFEESHOPS

SHOP FEATURES

SHOP HOURS:

Daily:
9:00am-1:00am

CRASH LIGHT

ADDRESS: Pretoriusstraat 67, Amsterdam (Oost)

MAP IT

Crash Light coffeeshop is located in the Transvaalbuurt neighborhood of Amsterdam East (oost). It sits about equal distance between Oosterpark (Eastern Park) and Frankendael Park, noteworthy green areas in this part of the city. This section of Amsterdam is heavily residential. The surrounding blocks hold mainly multi-unit apartment buildings, with a dotting of small businesses on the ground floor. It is also not heavily trafficked by tourists. As such, Crash Light is mainly frequented by locals.

The Shop

Crash Light is a small Moroccan-themed coffeeshop. The décor is basic and unpretentious. This is all probably not that important though, as Crash Light serves as a take-and-go establishment only. They seem to do their business discreetly here, perhaps something that keeps them in good favor with the neighbors. They do not allow for outdoor seating, and we never see people loitering outside smoking joints. Barring the signs, you would probably miss the fact that this was a coffeeshop at all.

The Menu

The cannabis menu at Crash Light coffeeshop is modest in size. Expect to find just several options on each side of the menu. Not an abundance by any stretch, but seemingly enough to give you a decent variety. On the weed-side, they do seem to favor old-school genetics. Expect strains like White Widow and Amnesia. You might find a contemporary strain or two as well. The hashish-side of the menu has fewer options, but do not let this throw you. Crash Light is really a hash shop. They usually stock good quality flavorful Moroccan imports here. They also sell pre-rolled joints. Pricing tends to reflect the local clientele. In our experience, it is quite reasonable to shop here. If you are on a budget, you might want to check out a true locals' place like this.

Classic Architecture
Amsterdam Zuid

COFFEESHOPS

SHOP FEATURES

SHOP HOURS:
Daily:
10:00am-1:00am

CRUSH

ADDRESS: Marnixstraat 383, Amsterdam (Centrum)

MAP IT

Crush Coffeeshop is located on Marnixstraat, at the southwestern edge of Amsterdam Centrum. It is just north of the Leidseplein, one of the more popular destinations in the city center when it comes to nightlife. Crush is actually on a more residential street, however. As such, the area around here is a bit removed from the action, and does not get quite as crowded.

The Shop

Crush is located on the basement level of its building. Inside, one finds a fairly contemporary and artsy establishment. The seating area is small but open. There are low padded benches against the walls, and small footstools and tables in the center. A large flat screen television is hung against the back windows. There is also beautiful mural art on the wall, tile flooring, and plenty of modern wood trim. The place feels quite comfortable and cozy. Additionally, a closed room is found to the side. This is a tobacco lounge; allowing the shop to comply with EU smoking laws, and permit its consumption on premises. Also of note, we found Crush Coffeeshop to have one of the more well maintained restrooms in the city.

The Menu

The cannabis menu at Crush Coffeeshop is moderate in size. Expect maybe a dozen options on the flower (weed) side, and maybe half that for hashish. For weed, they focus mainly on traditional old-school Amsterdam strains, which you may find alongside a bit of contemporary genetics here and there. The hashish is mainly imported from Afghanistan and Morocco. You might find a little isolator (nederhasj) if you look, though. Additionally, they have pre-rolled joints and space cakes. Aside from cannabis, you can also order coffees, teas, and basic snacks here.

COFFEESHOPS

CONNOISSEUR GUIDE: AMSTERDAM

COFFEESHOPS

SHOP FEATURES

SHOP HOURS:
Daily:
8:00am-1:00am

D&L

ADDRESS: Govert Flinckstraat 323, Amsterdam (Zuid)

MAP IT

D&L Coffeeshop is located on Govert Flinckstraat, to the east end of De Pijp neighborhood. De Pijp translates into "The Pipe" in English. At present, this is amongst the more trendy neighborhoods in Amsterdam. Here, one will find the outdoor marketplace Albert Cuyptmarkt, and Sarphatipark, among other popular destinations. The street D&L rests on is largely residential, with one way traffic and few businesses on the street level. As such, it is a bit more quiet around here than you generally expect in this busy neighborhood.

The Shop

This is a small and fairly practical Dutch shop. The owner has not gone over-the-top with décor and amenities. However, that is not to say the shop is not worth hanging around at. This is not simply a take-and-go. There is a fair amount of seating in a Moroccan-themed lounge in the back. Here you will find a large table, surrounded by long benches. There are a couple of TV's as well. Once making a purchase at the front counter, the budtender will buzz you back into this closed area.

The Menu

The cannabis menu at D&L Coffeeshop is moderate in size, with roughly twenty items at any given time in our experience. This shop is somewhat more known for its hash offerings, having competed in cannabis competitions (and won some awards) in the past. This reputation persists, and the shop seems to stock a nice variety of imported hard-press items of quality to maintain it. This shop also has a decent selection of coffees, basic drinks, and snacks if you are thirsty or hungry. They also have WiFi for their customers, if you need to stay connected.

Rembrandt Square

COFFEESHOPS

SHOP FEATURES

SHOP HOURS:
Daily:
10:00am-1:00am

DAMPKRING

ADDRESS: Handboogstraat 29, Amsterdam (Centrum)

MAP IT

Dampkring Coffeeshop (formally De Dampkring) is located on Handboogstraat (Longbow Street), in the famous upscale shopping area surrounding Kalverstraat. The name De Dampkring means "The Atmosphere" in Dutch. It may be an ideal choice. Dampkring has grown to be one of the most famous coffeeshops in the city. Much of this has to do with its décor and atmosphere.

The Shop

Dampkring is simply stunning, inside and out. When one first approaches this place, the first thing they notice is the ornate façade. With hand-carved panels and pillars alongside stained glass, it is arguably the most intricate in the coffeeshop business. We would put it amongst the most notable in the city. It is that beautiful.

Inside, the shop is no less interesting. As you walk in, you immediately notice that the entire room is encased in art and color. It is difficult to put it into words. Trying our best to explain it, we sum it up like this. The walls are all painted in a textured 60s psychedelic-style. There are columns holding up the custom ceiling, which is also painted and abstract in its form. The tables, bar, and counters are similarly all custom made of beautiful polished wood, and with trippy abstract textures. Lights can be found throughout, some taking on the shape of distorted bubbles or ball clusters. The management describes the décor as having a combination of Arabic, Bohemian, and Buddha influences. All we know is, it looks amazing.

Dampkring coffeeshop is perhaps most noted for being featured in the major motion picture Oceans 12. The famous scene featured George Clooney, Matt Damon, and Brad Pitt. The appearance catapulted the profile of this shop to that of a major Amsterdam attraction. Damprking is now on many visitors "must see" list, some of whom are not even cannabis smokers... they just want to see the coffeeshop featured in Oceans 12. Management has even name a strain after the movie. Ocean's 12 Haze has been a long-standing basic (and popular) item on the menu ever since.

The Menu

Dampkring has long had a reputation for quality cannabis. This is identified as a connoisseur establishment. Further, they have one of the most extensive cannabis menus in the city. On any given day they may list roughly two dozen flower (weed) strains, and a dozen or so types of hashish. The menu details each strain type (indica or sativa dominant) or hashish origin, along with a description of its smell, taste, and effect. The marijuana products are purchased in the back of the shop, where they have a special counter and extensive display of the offerings. This shop also has plenty of options for coffees, teas, juices, soft drinks, and snacks if you plan on staying.

COFFEESHOPS

CONNOISSEUR GUIDE: AMSTERDAM

COFFEESHOPS

SHOP FEATURES

SHOP HOURS:

Mon-Thurs:
2:00pm-11:00pm
Fri-Sat:
2:00pm-12:00am
Sun:
1:00pm-9:00pm

DE BOMMEL

ADDRESS: Balboastraat 19, Amsterdam (Oost)

MAP IT

De Bommel Coffeeshop is located on Balboastraat, in the De Baarsjes ("The Perch") neighborhood of Oud-West Amsterdam. This is one of the city's most diverse areas; quite youthful and professional in its demographics. De Bommel is just a stone's throw away from Rembrandt park. This is one of the city's most beautiful green areas, and a literal hotspot in the summer. The immediate neighborhood is also quite popular among tourists and residents alike, and hosts many trendy bars, restaurants, and cafés. De Bommel was the first coffeeshop in this neighborhood, and has been in business for more than 30 years.

The Shop

The english translation for "De Bommel" is "The Bumblebee." However, the shop mascot here is a smoking bear. We are not sure where the bumblebee comes in, but that is not really important. The shop itself is unpretentious, but comfortable. We would say traditionally Dutch in its practicality. They are not big on flash here, but the shop does have some extra amenities such as WiFi and a tobacco smoking room. There is also a retro arcade machine, projector, and dart board. The clientele is mainly local during the winter, and a mix during the summer season.

The Menu

This shop tends to have a robust cannabis menu. On the weed-side, it tends to feature old-school favorites, as well as some newer contemporary (West Coast USA) strains. For hashish, they tend to have a similar size selection, mainly imports from the traditional hashish regions. They have pre-rolled joints if that is your preference. Their menu changes here every couple of months or so, which seems to keep the offerings fresh. According to the budtender Willem, their catchphrase here is "De Bommel, we don't sell shit!" Simple, and to the point.

COFFEESHOPS

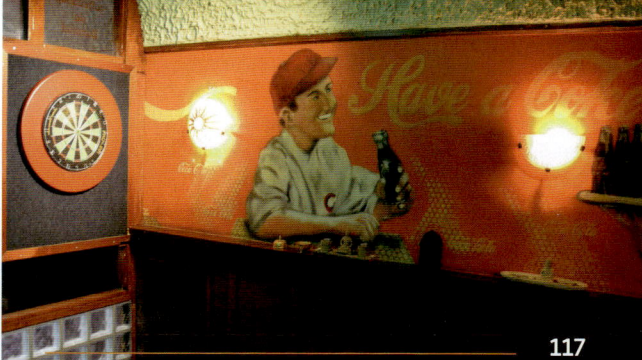

CONNOISSEUR GUIDE: AMSTERDAM

COFFEESHOPS

SHOP FEATURES

SHOP HOURS:

Daily:
10:00am-11:00pm

DE KADE

ADDRESS: Stadionkade 107, Amsterdam (Zuid)

MAP IT

De Kade Coffeeshop is located on Stadionkade, in the south (Zuid) part of the city. The name of this shop translates into "The Quay". This likely refers to the location of this shop, which sits on "Stadium Quay" road, directly across from the Amstel Canal. This is a very picturesque and predominantly residential part of the city. This section of the Amstel canal is not a tight busy passageway either. It is much more open and tranquil than the Amstel typically is further north. On a nice sunny day, we suggest taking a stop waterside before you wander off. Relax and enjoy the shade and views. De Kade is in such a beautiful spot here. It should not be missed.

The Shop

The atmosphere of De Kade is best described as chill and unpretentious. The décor is artsy, but basic. The wooden tables are pretty standard, and the leather seats a bit more cushy than normal, but not extravagant. This is very much a sit, smoke, and just relax type of place. That is not to say they are sparse on amenities. To the contrary, they offer quite a bit in addition to cannabis here. For starters, they are big retro gaming fans. They have legitimate old school pinball machine(s) here, a multi-arcade, a table football game (foosball), and a television. How about a game of chess? Just ask at the counter. This shop is basically a hybrid combination: small arcade, local pub, and your living room.

The Menu

The cannabis menu at De Kade is large, and has a diverse selection on offer. They usually have numerous exceptional options on the weed side in particular, which has garnered this shop recognition as a connoisseur establishment. They appear to be working hard with their growers to produce high quality USA genetics. So, you definitely can expect to find some of the more modern and noteworthy strains here. On the hash side, you can first find some quality imported pressed hashish. Beyond that though, they usually do have some higher potency domestic isolates as well. They also offer the requisite pre-rolls, and quite an expanded collection of edibles as of late.

After the cannabis products and amenities, it should be noted that this is also a pretty good shop for drinks. They serve a nice selection of juices here, and make damn good coffee as well. If tea is your preference, you will find no shortage of options here too. They also have enough by way of basic snacks and munchies, so worry not. If we had to sum up this shop in one word it would be "comfort". Not the chairs or couches mind you, but the vibe of this place. They do an excellent job of making you feel at home here. That applies to both locals and tourists. Everyone should feel equally welcome in here.

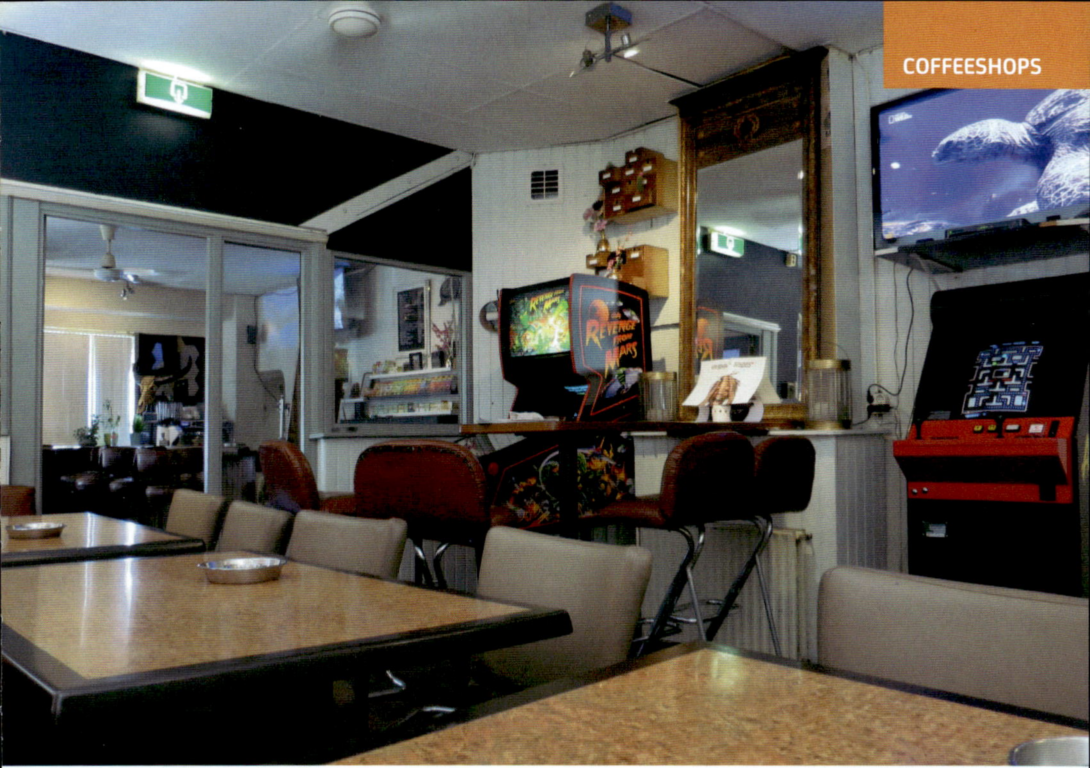
REVENGE FROM MARS

A SMILE IS THE PRETTIEST THING YOU CAN WEAR
BRAINS
Kush
Candy-Kush
Power-Plant
White-Widow
Amnesia-Kush
Pineapple
Pipe-Screens
Island
White-Widow
Amnesia
Secret Box
tip-Box

De Kade
Keep away from Children & Pets!
Original Vanilla Muffin
Use Responsibly
Less is more & Be patient
18+
Dosage: +/- 0,5 Per Serving
Best Before: 17-10-'17

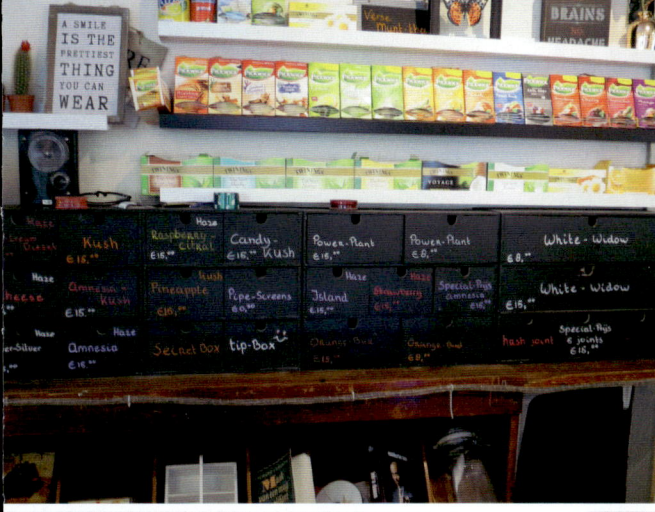

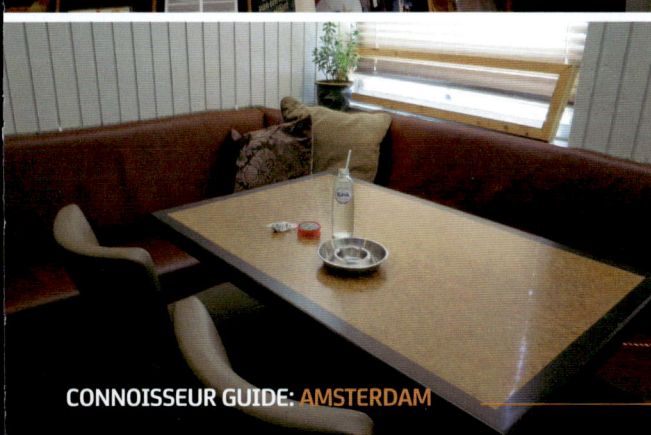

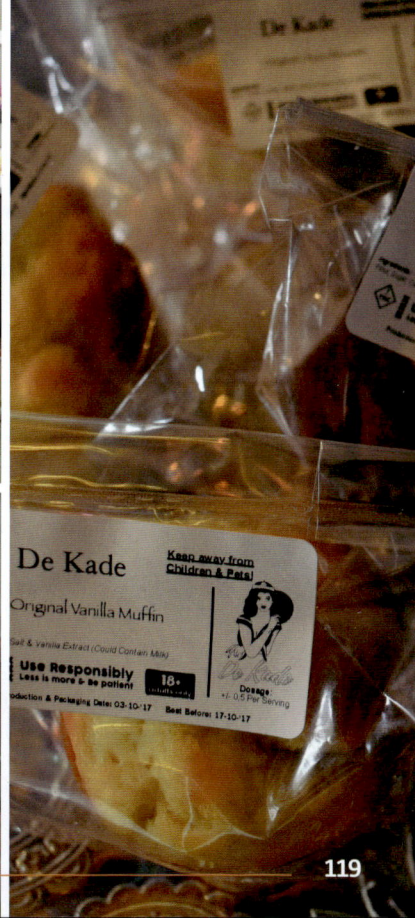

COFFEESHOPS

SHOP FEATURES

SHOP HOURS:

Daily:
9:00am-1:00am

DE KEEPER

ADDRESS: Van Woustraat 193, Amsterdam (Zuid)

MAP IT

De Keeper Coffeeshop is located on Van Woustraat, in the Diamantbuurt section of Amsterdam-Zuid (south). Diamantbuurt translates into "Diamond Neighborhood" in English. This was once Amsterdam's diamond district, built up during the early 1900s next to the famous diamond cutter Asscher. While this part of the city is no longer identified as a jewelry center, it is a well developed residential area, with a good share of restaurants, cafés, and other businesses. If looking for a change of pace, you might find it in a neighborhood like this.

The Shop

"De Keeper" translates into "The Keeper" in English. This refers to a goalkeeper or goalie, a pivotal position in the game of football; soccer to Americans. For those wondering if the sport was the intended imagery, and not another for De Keeper, look no further than the shop logo. It is a stick-figure of a goalkeeper guarding a net holding weed.

Inside De Keeper one will find a coffeeshop with basic décor. Comfortable and real, just not flashy. The front room hosts a quick pickup window, for those just looking for a quick weed purchase. If you are for more than a buy and fly though, the back of the shop hosts its smoking lounge. This includes a glassed-off partition, to legally allow for tobacco smoking. In the lounge you will find some leather couches and a large flat screen TV. It is a nicely furnished room and comfortable. If you are looking for somewhere to watch the game, De Keeper coffeeshop might serve you well.

The Menu

The cannabis menu at this coffeeshop likely reflects its predominantly local clientele. It is moderate in size, and tends to list more traditional items. This means Amsterdam favorite strains of weed. Think of items like Amnesia, White Widow, and Silver Haze; strains that made Amsterdam genetics so famous. On the hashish side, this means mainly traditional imported pressed varieties of hashish, though they have been known to stock stronger domestic isolator too. In addition, you can find the basic pre-rolled joint (weed and hash), and the standard option space cake.

COFFEESHOPS

CONNOISSEUR GUIDE: AMSTERDAM

COFFEESHOPS

SHOP FEATURES

SHOP HOURS:

Daily:
8:00am-1:00am

DE KROON

ADDRESS: Oudebrugsteeg 26, Amsterdam (Centrum)

MAP IT

De Kroon coffeeshop is located on Oudebrugsteeg, or "Old Bridge Alley." The term "alley" is appropriate here, as this shop is indeed found on a very narrow and short connecting street. Normally, it is the type of street you would probably not walk down. But this is the heart of Amsterdam, right in a very busy shopping district. There is extremely heavy foot traffic around this shop. They say in business location can be everything. While we would not say it defines De Kroon, it certainly ensures this shop is rarely empty.

The Shop

In English, De Kroon means "The Crown." We assume this is meant to convey a sense a quality to potential customers. With a name like this, you risk not being taken seriously if you fail to deliver a memorable experience. Fortunately for De Kroon, they have built quite a nice shop here. De Kroon stands out for its lounge. We would argue, it is one of the more comfortable chill spots in this bustling part of the city center.

Immediately as you enter, you will notice they have converted the area at the front window into a seating area with large benches. This type of seating is mirrored in the back, where you will find two larger plush leather-topped benches, complete with throw pillows and small movable tree-stump tables. In-between, a series of small contemporary tables are fitted to the wall. The décor in here is a mix of natural wood and jungle theme; a green on brown combination that is very appealing. Though this space is not big, it is definitely quite comfortable.

The Menu

The cannabis menu at De Kroon is moderate in size. They seem to like old-school favorites on the weed side. You will probably come across some Haze strains, or things like White Widow or AK-47. However, do not be surprised if you find a contemporary (USA) strain or two as well. The hashish options also tend to be traditional. This is mainly in the form of imports, from places like Morocco and Afghanistan. They also have a variety of pre-rolled (weed/hash) joints, or space cake, if preferred.

COFFEESHOPS

CONNOISSEUR GUIDE: AMSTERDAM   123

COFFEESHOPS

SHOP FEATURES

SHOP HOURS:
Daily:
10:00am-12:00am

DE OVERKANT

ADDRESS: Nieuwe Herengracht 71, Amsterdam (Oost)

MAP IT

De Overkant coffeeshop is located on Nieuwe Herengracht (New Herengracht). It sits just outside of the city centre, in Amsterdam Oost (East). The name of this shop translates into "The Other Side". This coffeeshop is actually situated directly across the canal from Amsterdam's famous Hortus Botanicus, or botanical gardens. It is also formally known as De Overkant Hortus; perhaps the name refers to its location on the other side of the gardens. Incidentally, these botanical gardens are amongst the oldest in the world. They were first built in 1638 for the cultivation of medicinal herbs (quite appropriate, don't you think?). They are most certainly worth a visit if you are in the area.

The Shop

This coffeeshop is fairly low-key in its décor. It is a modest establishment, what you expect with most local Dutch coffeeshops. There are not a lot of needless frills in here. While it may not be expansive in size, they do provide seating. In the front of this shop are two large windows, with long wall mounted tables. Pull-up stools provide a great place to sit, have a smoke, and watch the crowds outside pass by. Splashes of color and eclectic prints on the walls also give this place feel a bit of an artsy feel. De Overkant is a down-to-earth and chill coffeeshop.

The Menu

The cannabis menu at De Overkant is moderate in size. It is quite strong on the hashish-side, where they feature a wide number of imported hard-pressed items. They also have a fairly strong mix of flower as well, with well known old-school favorites sure to be on the menu, typically alongside a few more contemporary items. They are very big on pre-rolled joints here. You can find both pure weed and tobacco-mixed varieties, as well as hash joints. Additionally, this shop has a wide variety of drinks/sodas/juices, and a decent selection of quick snacks if needed.

SHOP FEATURES

COFFEESHOPS

SHOP HOURS:
Daily:
8:00am-11:30pm

MAP IT

DE PRIJS

Surinamestraat 7I, Amsterdam (West) **:ADDRESS**

De Prijs coffeeshop is found on Surinamestraat, at the north end of the Hoofddorppleinbuurt (Hoofddorp Square neighborhood). This is a largely residential area of Amsterdam South. De Prijs actually sits right between Vondelpark and Rembrandtpark, two of Amsterdam's most popular green areas. This is one of the most beautiful sections of the city, especially during the warmer months, when you can really appreciate the surroundings. If you find yourself walking between these two parks, De Prijs will be hard to miss, as it is right beside the main canal crossing on s106.

The Shop

The décor in De Prijs coffeeshop is decidedly Indian-themed. The shop itself is quite big. Upon entering, you will notice plenty of seating around the front. In the back it also hosts a large open room, with both a pool table and a table football game (foosball). The vibe of De Prijs is somewhat of a mix between a local bar and a billiards hall. If you prefer mixed joints, you will also find a small closed-off tobacco room in the back. A cigarette machine is by the front door if you are short on mix.

The Menu

The cannabis menu at De Prijs is modest in size, which is common in areas like this, which tend to draw a smaller tourist crowd. They seem to focus more on the weed-side, which usually outnumbers the hashish options by a fair margin. Strains are largely established old-school favorites. They do still have several options on the hashish-side. These are usually Moroccan imports, something they seem to specifically specialize in. Likewise, the small selection may just reflect particularity in supply. Like most shops, they have a variety of pre-rolled options if desired.

In English, one way to translate De Prijs is into "The Price." With shops that cater mainly to locals, the management usually has to keep things reasonable when it comes to the menu prices. In that regard, this translation may be apt. However, it is not so "on point" that we would say the defining characteristic of this place is low prices. The best way for us to sum up De Prijs, is to say that this establishment is a comfortable local hangout, especially if you enjoy getting stoned and playing billiards.

COFFEESHOPS

SHOP FEATURES

SHOP HOURS:

Mon-Thurs:
9:00am-11:00pm
Fri-Sat:
9:00am-12:00am
Sun:
10:00am-11:00pm

DE REPUBLIEK

ADDRESS: Tweede Nassaustraat 1B, Amsterdam (Oost)

MAP IT

De Republiek coffeeshop is located on Tweede Nassaustraat, in the Staatsliedenbuurt section of Amsterdam West. This translates in English as the "Statesman Neighborhood." De Republiek is very close to the busy s100 ring, just off on a side street. While Amsterdam West is generally more quiet and residential than the city center, the immediate neighborhood around De Republiek is actually quite busy given its crossing such a main motorway.

The Shop

This coffeeshop is relatively small in size. It is split over two levels, however. The front room has a counter for ordering cannabis, basic drinks, and snacks. Stools pull up to a long bar along the front window, providing a bit of space to hang out and roll up your purchase. There is also a small loft upstairs. It overlooks the main shop area, and provides an area of seating, if you prefer a longer stay. The shop is basic in its amenities, but also quite relaxed and chill in its atmosphere. It is not a bad place to sit for a while.

The Menu

This coffeeshop is actually owned by the proprietors of Siberië, The Loft, and De Supermarkt. The management is pretty serious about their cannabis. On the weed-side of things, they often focus on more contemporary high-potency strains, such as those coming out of West Coast USA in recent years. For hashish, they like imported pressed varieties from Morocco and other parts. The quality is usually very high. To that, they provide lab tests on a majority of their stock. The reports should include a full cannabinoid profile; giving you some solid information about the products you are considering.

COFFEESHOPS

COFFEESHOPS

SHOP FEATURES

SHOP HOURS:
Daily:
11:00am-11:00pm

DE SUPERMARKT

ADDRESS: Frederik Hendrikstraat 69-HS, Amsterdam (Oost)

MAP IT

De Supermarkt coffeeshop, which as you may have guessed, translates into "The Supermarket", is located on Frederik Hendrikstraat, in the West section of Amsterdam. You will find it a bit more residential in this part of the city as compared to the Centre. Historic tall apartment buildings and small street-level cafés, boutiques, and a variety of shops dominate the immediate neighborhood. The pace may be slightly slower here, but not by much. Being just outside the canal ring, there is still a lot of activity in this part of the city.

The Shop

This particular coffeeshop is on one level, and is split into two rooms. In the front you will find a narrow long room, which serves as the smoking lounge. Stools, wooden benches, tables, and chairs provide basic comforts for visitors. This establishment is relaxed and unpretentious in its appearance. It is chill and practical, without unnecessary frills. Green accent lighting provides a bit of a contemporary touch. Otherwise, this is a fairly traditional Dutch coffeeshop.

Behind the smoking lounge is a glass door, which leads to the shop's counter. Here you can buy cannabis, or choose from a selection of coffees, drinks and basic snacks.

The Menu

De Supermarkt is actually owned by the same group as Siberië, The Loft, and De Republiek. As such, expect to find a high quality cannabis menu here. The weed list should include a decent mix of contemporary high-potency strains, along with some more established genetics. On the hashish-side, expect a nice selection of quality imported pressed varieties. It is also of note that this is one of the few shops that invests in lab testing its inventory. We are not sure how up-to-date they are, but you should be able to find reports at the counter. If they are not on display, just ask. Each should include a fairly thorough cannabinoid profile.

Beyond cannabis, they serve some good coffee here. Like any good supermarket, they also have a thorough selection of sodas, juices, energy drinks, and your basic collection of candy and packaged snacks.

COFFEESHOPS

CONNOISSEUR GUIDE: **AMSTERDAM**

DE WATERSNIP

ADDRESS: Lodewijk van Deysselstraat 37, Amsterdam (West)

MAP IT

De Watersnip is a juice-bar and coffeeshop located in the Slotermeer-Zuidwest neighborhood of Amsterdam West, not far from Sloterplas. This is a predominantly residential part of the city, mainly hosting large block apartment buildings, along with the occasional ground-level business. This part of Amsterdam is not widely visited by tourists. Consequently, the clientele at De Watersnip consists mainly of locals, and the odd city visitor that just so happens to be staying in this area.

The Shop

This shop is named after the Watersnip, also known as the Common Snipe. It is a short but husky long-billed bird that can be found in various wetlands throughout much of Northern Europe, including Holland. Older locals will also remember it from the Dutch 100 Guilder bill, which of course has long since replaced by the Euro.

De Watersnip is a take-away establishment. Upon walking in, you will see their ordering counter, along with a small selection of drinks, snacks, and rolling papers available in a vending machine. There is also a cigarette machine, for those looking for some tobacco to mix with. Though there is no smoking lounge here, the lobby has just enough space to roll a quick joint before heading back into the neighborhood.

The Menu

The menu at De Watersnip is modest in size. This is common with the more local places, which usually do not see as much traffic, or particularity among visiting cannabis connoisseurs. They just need to keep the regulars happy. As such, expect just 3-6 options of weed or hash on most days. The weed strains will likely be old-school, the type of long-standing genetics that made Amsterdam famous. The hashish is imported; from the traditional places like Morocco and Afghanistan. Otherwise, you can also pick up the pre-rolled joint, if preferred.

Nearby Sloterplas park

COFFEESHOPS

SHOP FEATURES

SHOP HOURS:
Daily:
9:00am-1:00am

DNA

ADDRESS: Achillesstraat 104, Amsterdam (Zuid)

MAP IT

DNA Coffeeshop is located on Achillesstraat, in Amsterdam-Zuid (South). It is specifically in the Stadionbuurt section of the Oud Zuid (Old South). This translates into Stadium Neighborhood, which refers to the Olympic stadium that was built here for the 1928 Olympics. It still stands, and remains a popular sports venue for Amsterdam. The immediate neighborhood around this shop is almost exclusively residential. These streets host large block-style apartment buildings, and have a fairly low density of shops, at least until you walk a few streets over. The surrounding architecture is often historic, and quite beautiful.

The Shop

This coffeeshop was formerly named Jabba The Hut. That establishment was not very high on the radar. Things seem to be changing, however. This shop has since seen a complete overhaul. First, the new DNA Coffeeshop location has been updated quite a bit. The interior is quite modern now in appearance. The room here is clean, open, and clinical. Menus are hosted on a computer screen, and the choices presented are in detail as to their effects and composition. We would say it is all quite reminiscent of an American dispensary.

There is a small smoking room to the side. There is not much room in here, and it is not the type of place you would hang out with a group for any extended amount of time. It is really just a place to prep your smoke, have a quick puff, and be on your way. DNA is really a take-and-go location. Again, another trait very reminiscent of a USA dispensary.

The Menu

DNA would still be low on the radar if it were not for another big change. This shop now appears to be working very closely with Amsterdam Genetics. This is a local seed breeder that is linked with the Boerejongens (Farmer Boys) chain of connoisseur shops. Amsterdam Genetics also supplies several other connoisseur shops in the city. As such, expect to find connoisseur-grade cannabis on the menu here. The selection is generally contemporary, and high quality. This means some West Coast USA genetics, in high demand these days.

The hash menu is equally impressive here. You can usually find some soft, rich, and flavorful imported varieties. The edibles have been exceptional here too. They go well beyond the basic space cake, and never seem to cheap out on the ingredients (cannabis) like some other shops do.

COFFEESHOPS

SHOP FEATURES

SHOP HOURS:

Daily:
10:00am-1:00am

DOLPHINS

ADDRESS: Kerkstraat 39, Amsterdam (Centrum)

MAP IT

Dolphins Coffeeshop is located on Kerkstraat (Church Street), towards the southwest edge of the city center. It is close to the Leidseplein, which is among the most popular destinations in Amsterdam for food, shopping, and nightlife. The front door of Dolphins is just a few steps off Leidsestraat, the main road leading to the Leidseplein. Likewise, the area around here is heavily trafficked with city visitors.

The Shop

Upon walking into this shop you will almost certainly first notice the décor. It is elaborately handcrafted from top to bottom, and takes on a deep sea theme. Dolphins, coral, sea urchin surround you in unbelievably detailed 3D sculptures and plaster decorations. Much of the remaining exposed parts of the walls are painted in sea blue color. You feel like you are on a Disney ride, "Under The Sea" most appropriately.

Upstairs you will find the counter for ordering cannabis products, as well as a variety of coffees, teas, drinks, and snacks. You will also find a station with two large glass vaporizers. These are Verdamper style; a hybrid between a traditional bong and a whip vaporizer. There are also a handful of tables up here with high top seating.

Downstairs "Under the Sea" takes on a whole new meaning. When you enter this room you will feel like you climbed into a 20th century submarine. Once again, the presentation is incredibly intricate and beautiful. This room is the coffeeshop lounge. It is much more open than the upstairs, and hosts a section of huge padded booths. Tobacco smoking is permitted here, as the basement is closed off from the rest of the shop. The area is well ventilated. It is also at street level, so the front windows can be opened when the weather is nice. There are flat screen TV's down here, and a vending machine for snacks if you are just a bit too relaxed to trek back upstairs.

The Menu

The cannabis menu at Dolphins Coffeeshop is not extensive. It includes maybe a half dozen flower (weed) strains, and several varieties of hashish. Most are named after the shop; items such as "Dolphin Kush and White Dolphin." They also sell pre-rolled joints, and make a mean Space Muffin edible. It is of note that this shop has a history of entering cannabis competitions. At times, their entries have definitely stood out for their quality. You can usually find some solid product here, even if the selection is not vast.

COFFEESHOPS

CONNOISSEUR GUIDE: AMSTERDAM

COFFEESHOPS

SHOP FEATURES

SHOP HOURS:

Daily:
7:00am-1:00am

EASTWOOD

ADDRESS: Pieter Vlamingstraat 286, Amsterdam (Oost)

MAP IT

Eastwood Coffeeshop is located on Pieter Vlamingstraat, in Amsterdam Oost (East). It is not far from Oosterpark, in a heavily residential section of the city. The area is quite nice. The tree-lined streets are a nice change of pace from the Centrum.

In 2015, this shop was actually forced to close, as the building hosting it was torn down for reconstruction. Eastwood was out of business for a while, but has since reopened. It is still in roughly the same spot, but now on the ground level of a beautiful modern new building. Given this relocation, Eastwood is technically one of the newest coffeeshops in the city of Amsterdam, at least from a building perspective.

The Shop

Inside Eastwood, one will find contemporary décor that matches well with the new building. The color scheme is mostly shades of grey and black; the furniture mica-topped (modern). Ceiling-to-floor windows in the front let in a lot of natural light during the day. At night, ample track lighting keeps the place well lit. The place feels very much like a small café. Simple, clean, comfortable. The smoking lounge in Eastwood Coffeeshop is not large, but being this far out of the city center, it usually does not draw in massive crowds. You will presumably find a place to chill… perhaps on the plush leather benches in the back.

The Menu

The cannabis menu at Eastwood Coffeeshop is fairly large. This shop seems to strongly favor weed with its number of options. Expect to find well over a dozen strains. These will likely be a mix of traditional Amsterdam favorites, as well as more contemporary strains from USA (think Kush, Gorilla Glue, etc.).

The selection is much shorter on the hashish-side; usually less than six items. However, this could mean the shop is very selective; only stocking a few items they think are worthwhile. Beyond that, Eastwood has plenty of pre-rolled joint options, as well as some basic drinks and snacks. They also have a formidable coffee machine, so expect to find a decent cup if you are looking.

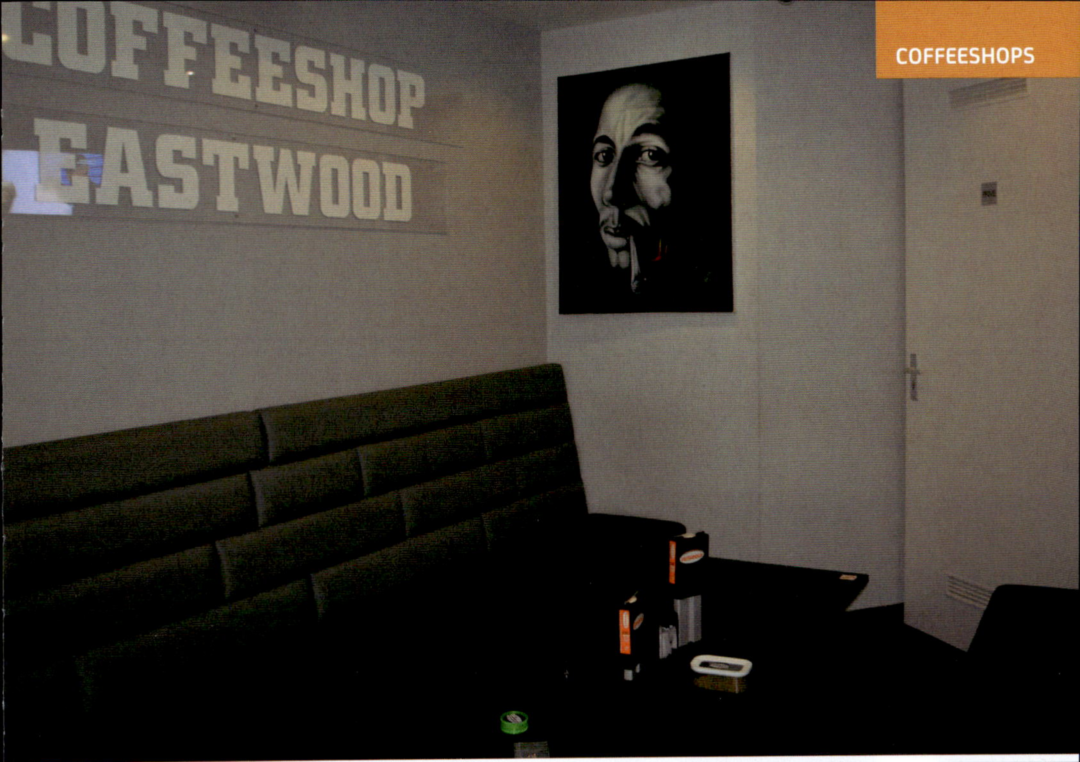

COFFEESHOPS

CONNOISSEUR GUIDE: **AMSTERDAM**

COFFEESHOPS

SHOP FEATURES

SHOP HOURS:

Daily:
9:00am-1:00am

EASY TIMES

ADDRESS: Prinsengracht 476, Amsterdam (Centrum)

MAP IT

Easy Times Coffeeshop is located on the Prinsengracht (Prince's Canal), close to the Leidseplein. The immediate neighborhood surrounding this establishment is highly commercial. Walking the narrow streets here, you will find seemingly no end to the number of small restaurants, bars, munchies sellers, and souvenir shops. As you would expect, this area is also densely packed with tourists. This is one of the more popular destinations in Amsterdam, especially in the evenings. If you are looking for a lively night out, the neighborhood around here may be a good option.

The Shop

This coffeeshop is quite modern in its appearance. Easy Times is best described as a mix between an upscale café and urban nightclub. One of the first things you notice as you walk up is the outdoor seating. The sidewalk extends out quite far, and the building Easy Times sits in is relatively wide. This provides ample room for five or so tables and accompanying chairs. The tables are polished wood, a nice touch. There are also a couple of potted trees outside, which really adds to the "al fresco" patio feeling. Remember, this is a prime canal-side location. Their outdoor seating is hard to beat on a warm day or evening.

Velvet ropes mark off the entrance to the shop itself. They lead you inside, where you will notice a coffeeshop with a bit of a nightclub vibe. Leather stools and seats, curved modern tables, glass partitions, and purple accent lighting all add to the effect. The shop is divided into two rooms. In the front is the main counter. Here you can order cannabis, along with an assortment of coffees, teas, juices, and drinks. Of note, they make fresh mint tea and milkshakes, so it is a bit more than a "just the basics" kind of place. In the back, you will find the shop's smoking lounge. It is behind an entire wall/door of glass, and has a very open feeling.

The Menu

The cannabis menu in Easy Times Coffeeshop is quite extensive. They tend to list well over a dozen strains on the flower (weed) side. Here you will typically find a good mix of contemporary and old school strains. If you are looking for a popular new West Coast USA strain, it might be here. While not as extensive, their hashish menu tends to be quite formidable as well. Further, the quality of many of their pressed imports is often great. You are sure to find something soft, strong, and flavorful here. They also sell pre-rolled joints and edibles. The latter selection is quite good, and includes a variety of muffins, brownies, and cakes. Vaporists will likely appreciate the two Volcano vaporizers, which are setup on their own table in the front room.

COFFEESHOPS

CONNOISSEUR GUIDE: AMSTERDAM

COFFEESHOPS

SHOP FEATURES

SHOP HOURS:

Daily:
7:00am-1:00am

EL GUAPO

ADDRESS: Nieuwe Nieuwstraat 32, Amsterdam (Centrum)

MAP IT

El Guapo Coffeeshop is found on Nieuwe Nieuwstraat, a short walk to the south of Centraal Station. The name of this street translates into "New Newstreet", oddly enough. In spite of its name, New Newstreet is a modest side street. It is not very new in appearance. There are a few businesses here, some residences, and a bunch of back walls to other places (read: it is more of an alley). Most people come across El Guapo when cutting across this street traveling to/from the main shopping area around Nieuwendijk. This is a surprisingly quiet spot though, as compared to much of the immediate area. It makes El Guapo a bit of an oasis, if you will.

The Shop

El Guapo is a chill and artsy shop. One of the most notable features of the interior is an airbrushed scene, which covers one full wall, front to back, top to bottom. It is a beautiful and colorful work, presented in a sort of urban spray paint style... the kind of thing you expect to see on an old New York Subway car. They are also fond of another Amsterdam tradition here, stickers! You will find a few large patches of them around the shop, a little bit left behind from different visitors. They also feature a nice plaque of international currencies. This is truly an international city, and Guapo illustrates that well.

Seating is mainly provided in the form of long leather benches, which run the length of one wall. In front of these are several large wooden tables, which provide plenty of room to spread out and handle your smoke. This is a one-room shop, not especially large. In the front is seating, and in the back a large counter for making purchases. The doors open wide in the summer though, and there is a large window above that lets in quite a bit of light.

The Menu

The cannabis menu here tends to be quite robust on the weed-side. It is not unusual to find them stocking more than 30 different strains. They keep them handy in bins right behind the counter, so you have plenty of options to look at when buying. The hashish selection is much smaller, but still ample by most standards. Otherwise, this shop has few amenities. It is fairly basic. Some drinks, coffee, a few snacks dispensed from a coin-operated machine. Overall, El Guapo is best described as an intimate coffeeshop. Not a lot of frills, but a fun and friendly atmosphere.

COFFEESHOPS

CONNOISSEUR GUIDE: **AMSTERDAM**

COFFEESHOPS

SHOP FEATURES

SHOP HOURS:
Daily:
9:00am-1:00am

EL MARSSA

ADDRESS: Witte de Withstraat 106, Amsterdam (West)

MAP IT

El Marssa Coffeeshop is located on Witte de Withstraat, in the De Krommerdt neighborhood of Amsterdam-West. Like many areas of Amsterdam, this neighborhood is growing. It is youthful, diverse, and upwardly mobile. The immediate area around El Marssa has many families of Turkish, Moroccan, and Surinamese descent, and is home to one of the city's strong Muslim communities. It is largely residential here. Expect quieter walks, and fewer bars and nightclubs than you find in many other areas close to the centre. El Marssa is also between two picturesque tree-lined canals. We highly recommend taking a stroll beside one when you are in the area.

The Shop

While we would not regard this coffeeshop as large, El Marssa is still fairly roomy. In the front, one will find a counter for ordering cannabis products. They also serve juices, soft drinks, and basic snacks here, and make a variety of hot coffees and teas. Once you make your purchase, you can get buzzed into the closed room in the back. Here you will find the shop's smoking lounge area.

The lounge at El Marssa is not especially elaborate or luxurious. However, we would describe it as both comfortable and "real". This is largely a locals' place... people know each other here, and they are not coming for the fancy décor. Do not let this deter you if you are visiting the city. In our experience, they welcome anyone in the door. There is also a closed tobacco smoking room in the back, so that this shop can stay in compliance with EU smoking regulations. If you prefer mixed joints, be sure to take advantage of it.

The Menu

The cannabis menu at El Marssa is moderate in size. This is not a big shop with strain hunters. On the weed-side, expect to find several old school favorites, alongside a couple of more contemporary items. While interesting, this shop is much more known for its hash. On menu here are usually pressed imports from Morocco. Though the selection is not vast, the quality can be exceptional. This shop seems to be quite popular with local hash smokers. With consistent product at a fair price, we can understand why.

Wide Canals (Amsterdam, West)

COFFEESHOPS

SHOP FEATURES

SHOP HOURS:

Daily:
9:00am-1:00am

FAMILY FIRST

ADDRESS: Amstel 36, Amsterdam (Centrum)

MAP IT

Family First Coffeeshop sits canalfront on the Amstel, in the middle of Amsterdam Centrum. It is just to the north of the Rembrandtplein (Rembrandt Square), which is a popular destination among visitors to the city. This area is packed with shops, restaurants, and cafés, and sees a great deal of street and foot traffic. It is especially popular at night, where its high density of bars and nightclubs makes it a major draw. Family First is among the newest coffeeshops in Amsterdam, at least from an ownership perspective. This shop was a Bushdocter location for a long time, but changed hands in early 2018.

The Shop

This coffeeshop is not expansive. Family First exists on one level. The décor is largely a holdover from the previous owners. We would describe it as interesting and artsy. Green dominates the inside of this shop. The tables are painted with colorful abstract images, which are infused with the occasional marijuana leaf. The walls are not bare, but full murals floor-to-ceiling. Actually, the top of the walls curve in, with one side melding in with the ceiling. This is a unique effect that makes the space feel encased in the artwork it is decorated with.

Seating here is mainly in the form of stools, which pull up to the tables. They look like they came from a diner in the 1980s; maybe 50s. We are not exactly sure of the era. They are, however, quite comfortable, and compliment the lounge-vibe of this place well. So too does the sofa. You will find it pressed against the back wall. This is arguably the most desirable seating in the house; plush and comfortable.

The Menu

The cannabis menu at Family First is moderate in size. On the weed-side they typically have a bit shy of a dozen items. The strains carried are usually a mix of old school favorites and contemporary USA genetics. The hashish-side of the menu is roughly the same size. The selection here includes traditional pressed imports, as well as higher potency Nederhasj varieties. We have also found some exceptional wax and moonrocks at Family First. At present time, our early experience with the product here, particularly the hashish/concentrates, warrants its classification as a connoisseur establishment. We hope to see Family First continue with great quality offerings.

COFFEESHOPS

CONNOISSEUR GUIDE: AMSTERDAM

COFFEESHOPS

SHOP FEATURES

SHOP HOURS:

Daily:
10:00am-1:00am

FEELS GOOD

ADDRESS: Oudezijds Voorburgwal 36-HS, Amsterdam (Centrum)

MAP IT

Feels Good Coffeeshop is located on Oudezijds Voorburgwal, just a bit north of the De Oude Kerk (The Old Church). It is also within the Red Light District, towards the north end. This is one of the busiest sections of the city center, especially with visitors. Consequently, the narrow road that hosts this coffeeshop sees a great deal of foot traffic daily. Some nights, the area gets downright packed.

The Shop

The first thing you notice about this shop is the turnstile at the front doorway. Perhaps they want you to feel like you are entering an amusement park? Pushing through brings you to their front room. It is dimly lit, with strong accent lighting in green neon. You make your purchase at a counter here, which is fully behind a clear partition (bank teller style). The menu is written all over neon blackboards, adding to the accent lightning.

It has an interesting vibe; feels like you have walked into a small neighborhood nightclub. In the back of the shop is the smoking lounge, which is partitioned-off behind a glass door. The décor is basic. Wooden tables and benches. Old wooden floors. The odd bit of artwork or photographs hung on the walls. It is fairly spacious though, and has a bit of privacy with the shape of the room and its sunken/elevated areas.

The Menu

Feels Good Coffeeshop has a reputation for quality cannabis at not-so-extreme prices. As such, you tend to find many locals in this place. Though also welcoming of tourists, the dark no-frills nature of this shop tends to put it lower on the list of "go-to" establishments. This might be a benefit to the savvy traveler. At Feels Good one may trade a bit of the unnecessary extras like table service and a fancy décor, for a more "real" Dutch coffeeshop experience. When you distill it to its basics, this means quality weed, a chill environment without any pretense, and perhaps some good conversation with your neighbor.

SHOP FEATURES

SHOP HOURS:

Daily:
10:00am-12:00am

COFFEESHOPS

MAP IT

FLASHBACK

Hudsonstraat 138-HS, Amsterdam (West) **:ADDRESS**

Flashback Coffeeshop is located on Hudsonstraat, in the Hoofdweg en Omgeving section of Amsterdam West. The surrounding neighborhood here is a strong mix of commercial and residential. Hoofdweg means "main road" or "highway" in English, and the full translation of Hoofdweg en Omgeving is essentially "Main Road and Surroundings." Though it is a bit removed from Amsterdam Centrum, there is a lot of activity in this neighborhood; a bit busier than you commonly find out in the West. At the same time, however, the Hoofdweg is also quite lively with cafés, restaurants, coffeeshops, and other shopping/entertainment. This coffeeshop is also just a few blocks East of Rembrandtpark, one of the city's most popular green areas.

The Shop

Flashback is a local Moroccan-owned shop. The décor is basic, but comfortable. This shop does feature a large smoking room in the back, and it is not rare to find it packed with locals. However, with the place being so accustomed to serving locals, do not be surprised (or offended) if they ask you to smoke your goods elsewhere. It kind of depends on the mood of this place, in our experience. Sometimes they are quite welcoming and chill. At others, they probably feel new visitors will mess with the locals-only vibe, and politely suggest you move on.

The Menu

This place offers plenty of hot and cold drinks for their regulars, as well as a fairly standard cannabis menu. Here you will find mainly old-school strains of weed in stock, as well as imported pressed hashish products. If you are able to get the budtender to show you their menu, you will find their selections to be quite affordable. Perhaps the price is what brings the locals back time and time again.

COFFEESHOPS

SHOP FEATURES

SHOP HOURS:
Daily:
11:00am-1:00am

FLOWER POWER

ADDRESS: Rozengracht 139, Amsterdam (Centrum)

MAP IT

Flower Power Coffeeshop is located on Rozengracht, near the western edge of Amsterdam Centrum. This part of the city sees a bit less tourist traffic than the main areas of the center, though still provides an ample supply of restaurants, boutique shops, nightclubs, etc.

The Shop

While most shops in the center are small and somewhat "closed in" due to traditional architecture, Flower Power has a much more modern façade. The front and side of the building are mostly glass. This lets in a tremendous amount of light, and allows the occupants of the shop to relax and watch people walk by.

The décor in Flower Power coffeeshop is fairly basic, but quite nice at the same time. Inside one will find a wooden bar on one side, some wood tables and stools, long counters in front of the windows, and a lot of wood trim. It feels a lot like a neighborhood bar, though of course no alcohol is served here. It is of note that they do have an arcade and pinball machine. Score another one for neighborhood bar, though we are dating ourselves a bit. Today, of course, pinball and arcade games are rare in European cities like Amsterdam, given their size and the premium on space. So if you fancy these classic games, this shop might be a nice find.

The Menu

The cannabis menu at Flower Power coffeeshop is not extensive, but does provide a nice variety of options. On the weed-side of the menu, they tend to stock a mix of traditional and slightly more contemporary genetics. For hashish, they have a few imports from places like Morocco and Nepal. There is also a standard and "special" section for each, with the latter usually being their higher priced items. They also sell pre-rolled joints and space cakes. This shop reportedly sells cannabis bonbons from time to time as well, which is a nice change of pace. The drink menu lists various coffees, tea, juices, and soft drinks.

COFFEESHOPS

CONNOISSEUR GUIDE: AMSTERDAM

COFFEESHOPS

SHOP FEATURES

SHOP HOURS:

Mon-Sat:
10:00am-1:00am

Sun:
10:00am-12:00am

FREE I

ADDRESS: Reguliersdwarsstraat 70, Amsterdam (Centrum)

MAP IT

Free I Coffeeshop (Roman numeral, so "Free 1" or "Free One") is located on Reguliersdwarsstraat, a venue for some of the city's popular LGBT establishments. Here you will find no shortage of gay-friendly bars and nightclubs, and at least one other coffeeshop that identifies as such (The Other Side). Free I also identifies as an LGBT-friendly establishment and are welcoming to all visitors here.

The Shop

Free I Coffeeshop is an interesting place. The décor in here is part "tropical tiki bar" and part "underneath the freeway overpass". Let us explain.

The tiki bar theme is apparent as soon as you walk in. There is bamboo all around the main level of this place. It is very deliberate, such that you half expect your drinks to be served in a hollowed coconut shell. Unusual, but can be a fun break from the norm. The "freeway overpass" décor is found downstairs, in the shop's basement seating room. This is a part of the shop that some people LOVE while other people HATE. The cellar has low ceilings, exposed concrete, and just a few small areas of seating. There is nothing polished or frilly here. You feel like you are hiding out, having a smoke with your buddies where nobody will catch you. If this brings back fond memories of disobedience and camaraderie for you, then you are likely going to love it in here. Another notable feature of the Free I Coffeeshop is that the front wall of the basement has a wide window. On sunny days it can be opened, giving everyone in this room a nice on-level view of the sidewalk outside.

The Menu

The cannabis menu at Free I is fairly large. On the weed side, they tend to stock close to a dozen strains. Most are old-school Amsterdam genetics, usually with a few contemporary USA items. They seem to be fonder of hashish, though. This side of the menu is listed first, and usually has more options. The stock largely consists of imports from places like Morocco, Nepal, and Afghanistan. However, you may find some more potent isolator (nederhasj) as well. This shop also has a variety of coffees, teas, basic drinks, and snacks.

COFFEESHOPS

COFFEESHOPS

SHOP FEATURES

SHOP HOURS:
Daily:
10:00am-1:00am

FREEDOM

ADDRESS: Van Hogendorpstraat 201, Amsterdam (West)

MAP IT

Freedom Coffeeshop is located on Van Hogendorpstraatmin in Amsterdam West, just to the south of Westerpark. Though this area is a bit outside of the center, and thus more likely to be frequented by locals (and less tourists), we find the shop quite welcoming. Freedom has a Statue of Liberty on its sign. We will take this as confirmation that all city visitors are invited to visit.

The Shop

There is a Moroccan theme inside Freedom coffeeshop. It is a bit chill and funky, but very down to earth. The first thing you will notice when entering is likely the shop's hand carved wooden counter. This is where you can order cannabis, of course.

Once you make your purchase, head on back to the smoking lounge. The room is fairly big for this type of local shop, and not likely to be overcrowded. The furniture is basic, but comfortable. Because it is closed off from the main shop and is not serviced by the staff, it complies with European smoking regulations. Tobacco is allowed here; mixed joints always welcome.

The Menu

The cannabis selection here is small by most standards. There are usually just a few items on each side of the menu. For flower (weed), this shop seems to favor the old-school favorites. Think Amnesia…White Widow. These are the types of strains that made Amsterdam famous. For hashish, you will usually find a couple of imported pressed varieties. Pre-rolled joints are also on the menu. They do serve coffee here too, as well as a handful of basic drinks and snacks.

COFFEESHOPS

SHOP FEATURES

SHOP HOURS:
Daily:
7:00am-1:00am

FUNKY MUNKEY

ADDRESS: Marnixstraat 333, Amsterdam (Centrum)

MAP IT

Funky Munkey Coffeeshop is located on Marnixstraat, at the very western edge of Amsterdam Centrum. It is within the Jordaan neighborhood, which is one of the more picturesque parts of the city center. This area is home to many small trendy shops, cafés, and restaurants, as well as beautiful historic apartment buildings and canal homes. You may have to head east a couple of blocks to see the best of it, though.

The Shop

The décor inside this shop is well maintained, and arguably very comfortable. Leather couches and chairs line the walls, next to polished wooden tables. The floor is some type of hardwood, smooth and shiny. The walls and ceiling are all painted in a complex interconnected design as well, making this seem somewhat of a "theme" coffeeshop, if the theme were simply "cool".

The best way to describe Funky Munkey would be to say it is a cross between a city coffee house and "man cave". There is a pool table in the center of the room. A chess table rests in here as well. A giant representation of a dartboard is hung on one wall. There is a flatscreen TV, some neon, a vending machine when you need a quick snack fix... it is a really comfortable place to chill. On the same note, the management here is big into music. You will find live concerts here on occasion, and some really funky beats on the speakers otherwise. There are a lot of windows in here too, and bench seating out front if you prefer some fresh air.

The Menu

The cannabis menu here is moderate in size. Further, it is simply a mess of taped on amendments. It is impossible to see what the original menu looked like, as it has been updated so many times. This establishment tends to rotate its stock quite a bit, and seems little concerned about the look of the menu in the process. As for the stock, on the weed side we tend to find a bit under a dozen items, mostly old-school strains. The hashish selection is smaller, consisting mainly of Moroccan imports. Do not skip over it. The owner here is serious about the hash they sell. There is usually some high quality product on hand.

COFFEESHOPS

CONNOISSEUR GUIDE: AMSTERDAM

COFFEESHOPS

SHOP FEATURES

SHOP HOURS:

Daily:
10:00am-10:00pm

FUNNY PEOPLE

ADDRESS: Tt. Vasumweg 4C, Amsterdam (Noord)

MAP IT

Funny People Coffeeshop is located on Tt. Vasumweg, on the edge of the Tuindorp Oostzaan neighborhood of Amsterdam Noord (North). The immediate area here is largely industrial. You will find many businesses in the marine industry as it is waterside, but also plenty of other service and manufacturing-oriented companies. For a change of pace, the area to the north is decidedly more residential, and Buik Sloterbreek park is just a short walk to the east.

The Shop

The theme of Funny People coffeeshop is "classic comedians." The shop logo is a tribute to the Marx Brothers, though there are plenty of other famous faces plastered around this place…Laurel and Hardy, Charlie Chaplain, Abbott and Costello, Aykroyd and Belushi as the Blues Brothers, Fred Gwynn. The vibe is fun and very reminiscent of a local café or coffee shop (non-cannabis). The trim is largely light colored woods and grey paint. The color scheme is earthy, and makes the place feel green and hip.

This coffeeshop is divided into three rooms. In the front, an entrance that could serve as a waiting area, or a take-away-counter if they decide to close off the rest. In the middle room you will find the counter, along with several wooden tables and chairs for seating. The furnishings are basic, but comfortable. In the very back of the shop is a closed off smoking room. This is probably the best place to chill. Bench seating lines the walls; and there are cushions and throw pillows to make it a bit more cozy. Tobacco (mixed joints) smoking is, of course, allowed in here.

The Menu

Being quite removed from the city center, Funny People coffeeshop is not heavily visited by tourists, barring those that find themselves staying in a nearby hotel. As such, the cannabis menu may not be quite as extensive as one of the major shops. On the weed-side you can expect to find several strains, mainly old-school city favorites. There should also be several imported pressed concentrates on the hashish-side. They do serve pre-rolled joints if you prefer, as well as decent coffee and some basic snacks. Local clientele also means the pricing tends to be more reasonable. If you are in the area, it might be worth a stop to check out the inventory.

COFFEESHOPS

CONNOISSEUR GUIDE: AMSTERDAM

COFFEESHOPS

SHOP FEATURES

SHOP HOURS:

Daily:
9:30am-1:00am

GET DOWN TO IT

ADDRESS: Korte Leidsedwarsstraat 77-79, Amsterdam (Centrum)

MAP IT

Get Down To It Coffeeshop is located on Korte Leidsedwarsstraat, or the "short cross street of Leidsestraat". In case you were wondering, there is also a long or "lange" cross street. This street leads right into the Leidseplein, one of the city's most popular destinations for nightlife. Get Down To It is right outside, though close enough that we would consider this one of the shops in the Leidseplein. This coffeeshop is found in the basement of the building. As such, there is not much natural light that enters. Still, the shop is well lit.

The Shop

The layout is such that you are presented with a glass counter upon entering. This is for ordering your cannabis products. Once you make a purchase, you can walk around into the shop's smoking lounge. It is quite large. Three interconnected rooms full of tables, chairs, and booths. There are even two pool tables in here, and enough room to actually play.

The décor throughout this coffeeshop would be best described as abstract. There is some classic tiling on the floors, unique brass lighting fixtures, and mural artwork all around. It all does a good job of making the place feel more open (and above ground) than it actually is.

The Menu

The cannabis menu at Get Down To It Coffeeshop is fairly large. There are usually well in excess of a dozen strains on the weed (flower) side. For hashish (concentrate), not quite as many, but still a diverse product selection. Having a closed smoking area, this coffeeshop also allows for tobacco consumption. Additionally, Get Down To It promotes itself as an "Internet Café Coffeeshop". This is perhaps not quite the draw it once was, but you can for sure stay connected while visiting the basement. They also serve coffees, teas, juices, soft drinks, and some basic snacks.

COFFEESHOPS

SHOP FEATURES

SHOP HOURS:

Daily
10:00am-1:00am

GOA

ADDRESS: Kloveniersburgwal 42, Amsterdam (Centrum)

MAP IT

Goa Coffeeshop is located on the Kloveniersburgwal canal, just south of Nieuwmarkt Square. It is close to the Zuiderkerk, or "Southern Church". This beautiful church was built back in 1611, and was once painted by Monet. It now serves as a concert and event hall. This is the very center of Amsterdam. There is incredible history all around. Consequently, it is also one of the busiest parts of the city with visitors. As such, it can get pretty crowded around here. If you like to be in the middle of the action though, this is a great neighborhood for it.

The Shop

The décor of this shop would be best compared to a nicer sit-down Asian restaurant. A lot of the furniture here is dark wood, and Asian in style. There are also red couches, black leather stools, hanging birdcage lights, and Asian inspired artwork throughout. It is all very black and red, and quite traditional. The shop itself is one large open room. The seating is pushed to the sides, and a counter is in the center- back for ordering drinks and cannabis. They usually have chill tunes on the radio, perhaps some reggae or modern ambient music.

The Menu

The cannabis menu at Goa Coffeeshop is moderately large. You will find about a dozen items on the weed side, mainly older and well-established strains, with a contemporary item or two thrown in. There are roughly as many options for hashish. These are usually imports, though they may have a higher potency local isolator variety or two. They also sell pre-rolled joints here.

The electronic menu system here has the pricing for all items in the shop, and breaks the cannabis products down to common quantities; usually 1 gram, 2 grams, and 5 grams. We haven't caught any price breaks for larger purchases, but these things always change. They also serve a selection of hot drinks (various coffees and teas) here, as well as juices, soft drinks, and basic snacks.

Canal heading to the Zuiderkerk.

COFFEESHOPS

SHOP FEATURES

SHOP HOURS:

Daily:
9:00am-1:00am

GREEN HOUSE CENTRUM

ADDRESS: Oudezijds Voorburgwal 191, Amsterdam (Centrum)

MAP IT

Green House Centrum Coffeeshop is part of the famous Green House Amsterdam brand. It is located on Oudezijds Voorburgwal, a small side-street off Damstraat, just outside the Red Light district. This shop sits canal-side, in one of the busiest parts of the city center. Though it isn't the largest or most beautiful of the Green House shops, it is likely the most popular.

The Shop

Green House Centrum has an artsy modern décor inside. The bar counter and tables are custom made - all carved wood with a high gloss finish. In front of them are fixed cloth-topped stools, which are anchored into the hardwood floor with metal bases. Many of these bases are large metallic cannabis leafs, which adds a really cool effect. The walls are also decorated with tiny rocks and shells; and behind the bar is a giant wall of pebbles. Additionally, there are accents like dark wooden shelving, custom glass/lighting, and chrome fixtures. It all ties together to make this one of Amsterdam's more upscale establishments. Unfortunately, this place can get so packed at times that it can make it difficult to take in its beautiful décor. Too many people to see it all together!

The Menu

The Green House brand is associated with not only coffeeshops but cannabis breeding. They have entered many competitions over the years. Many of the decorations in their shops are a testament to the quality of their work. In the back of this location in particular, one will find numerous display cases showing off various trophies and other awards that Green House has won. They also have a "wall of celebrities" in the far corner. As you will see, this shop has had no shortage of famous customers over the years.

The cannabis menu in all Green House shops is similar, and extensive. The offerings tend to be heavier on the weed-side (flower), with typically more than a dozen varieties grouped into several different categories such as "Haze, Organic, Special". The hashish side of the menu is not short of offerings either, typically both domestic and imported varieties.

A volcano vaporizer is also available for use here. They also offer pre-rolled joints, and an ample menu of coffees, teas, drinks, and snacks. Perhaps it is the award winning cannabis, the celebrity clientele, or both, but Green House Centrum is inarguably one of the most famous of Amsterdam's coffeeshops.

COFFEESHOPS

CONNOISSEUR GUIDE: AMSTERDAM

COFFEESHOPS

SHOP FEATURES

SHOP HOURS:

Sun-Thurs:
7:00am-12:00am

Fri-Sat:
10:00am-1:00am

GREEN HOUSE NAMASTE

ADDRESS: Waterlooplein 345, Amsterdam (Centrum)

MAP IT

Green House Namaste Coffeeshop is located on Waterlooplein (Waterloo Square). This square is the site of a famous daily flea market, dubbed the Waterlooplein Markt. It is also a section of the city with a great deal of art and culture. Nearby one can find the National Opera and Ballet House, Rembrandt House Museum, and the Jewish Historical Museum.

A "namaste" is a greeting in Hindu culture. It is usually spoken with a slight bow, and conveys a sense of respect and welcome to the recipient. It is likely this sense of welcome was the intended atmosphere for Green House Namaste. The décor is arguably soothing. It is an intermingling of polished wood with abstract art and fixtures all around. Light boxes are even set into the side wall, displaying a collection of Hindu statues and other bits of art. It is the type of highly detailed surrounding you would expect at a high end spa or hotel.

The Shop

The shop itself is small, but luxurious. Seating is provided in the form of plush leather and suede covered couches. Throw pillows provide additional comfort and class, not that they are needed. Custom carved tables sit in front, and provide just enough room to rest your things, along with a few drinks or snacks. There is also a nook in the back, which is bounded by exposed brick and a "rock slide" display. A stained glass skylight is featured above. It is all very beautiful, and makes this among the nicest shops, aesthetically speaking, in the city.

The Menu

The cannabis menu is connoisseur grade at this coffeeshop, as all Green House Amsterdam locations. If you have any doubts just check the glass display case in the front. It holds just a small sampling of the great many competition victories held by this shop. Though some may argue of the politics of cannabis competitions, there is not much arguing about the stock quality here once you have sampled it enough. It is very consistent. Expect to see a large selection on both the flower (weed) and concentrate (hashish) side.

COFFEESHOPS

CONNOISSEUR GUIDE: AMSTERDAM

COFFEESHOPS

SHOP FEATURES

SHOP HOURS:

Sun-Thurs:
10:00am-12:00am

Fri-Sat:
10:00am-1:00am

GREEN HOUSE DE PIJP

ADDRESS: Tolstraat 91, Amsterdam (Zuid)

MAP IT

Green House Pijp coffeeshop (also known as Green House Tolstraat) is the original of four Green House Amsterdam locations. It is also, perhaps, the most famous, at least among those "in the know". Just take a look around the shop… the many pictures lining the walls. The place is packed with photos of red-eyed celebrities. But wait. If you are a fan of the Green House chain, you will notice that many of the same celebrity photos are hung in the other locations as well. Fact is, many of these photos were taken right here at Green House Pijp.

The Shop

This shop might just be THE place for the celebrity stoner visiting Amsterdam. Why? For one, the atmosphere is upscale. The menu is also excellent, and boasts many internationally famous strains. Perhaps most importantly though, the shop is far enough from the city center that it is rarely loaded with throngs of tourists.

Let's get to some more specific details. First, the interior. Green House Pijp is on one level, though they used to have an upstairs smoking room (currently closed). The shop has a highly handcrafted appearance. There are elevated and sunken wooden floors, and a great deal of sculpted trim all around. The architecture is forward thinking, and the décor quite luxurious. Seating is ample. Comfortable leather booths and couches line the shop. They are arranged in separate sections, however, which makes each area feel more private. The shop is large enough for a decent sized group, but not expansive. It would be aptly described as an intimate place. The large mirror on the back wall does give the illusion of more space, though. The music on the radio is likely to be some form of modern jazz, R&B, or hip hop.

The Menu

The Green House cannabis menu (similar at all shops) is one of the most famous in Amsterdam. The selection is large, with the weed and hash offerings subdivided into categories such as Bio Organic, Haze, G-House Specials, and G-House Exclusives. To attest to the quality of their options, this coffeeshop has no shortage of trophies and awards. You will notice them scattered throughout the Tolstraat location, just as the other three (they have won enough to spread them out!).

This shop also has a Volcano vaporizer at the bar, an increasingly popular choice among the "cannabis connoisseur" crowd looking for maximum flavor. Overall, everything at Green House Pijp seems to tie together very well, creating an upscale but comfortable and private coffeeshop experience. It is no wonder so many famous people visit.

COFFEESHOPS

CONNOISSEUR GUIDE: AMSTERDAM

COFFEESHOPS

SHOP FEATURES

SHOP HOURS:
Daily:
9:00am-1:00am

GREEN HOUSE UNITED

ADDRESS: Haarlemmerstraat 64, Amsterdam (Centrum)

MAP IT

Green House United Coffeeshop (also sometimes called Green House Lounge) is one of the most famous shops lining Haarlemmerstraat. This street is found to the north end of the Jordaan. This surrounding neighborhood is regarded as one of the more "hip locales" in the city, and is known for an abundance of small craft shops, trendy restaurants, and independent boutiques. It is also home to a few of Amsterdam's more upscale coffeeshops. Green House United is unquestionably counted among them.

The Shop

One of the first things you notice as you walk up to Green House United is that the entire front of the shop is made up of side-by-side glass panels that open up wide. It makes the place feel spacious and airy. You will find one of the most beautiful counters in Amsterdam to the left. Beyond it, leather booths and tables on both sides of the main floor. The seating is posh, and the décor is very detailed. The shop is also lit as if it were a nightclub. Combine this with modern but relaxed music, and you have a really cool and chill atmosphere.

The split-level setup in the back is another nice surprise, and provides extra room both upstairs and downstairs. Something that also stands out in here, very noticeably, is the wall of celebrity pictures. There are framed photos hanging all over one of the walls in the shop. Many of them are signed. The subjects are a literal "who's who" of canna-supportive celebrities and bands. Big name visitors to the Green House Amsterdam shops have included 50 Cent, Ludacris, Bill Maher, Snoop, Cypress Hill, The Roots, Miley Cyrus, and Mike Tyson, to name just a few.

The Menu

With the slogan "Creators of Champions", the Green House Amsterdam brand clearly recognizes that without top quality cannabis, even terrific ambiance would not give them world recognition and reputation. They have such a reputation as a result of years of hard work. This shop has more contest victories than we could count, and likely more than any other shop. Take a look at some of the trophies that are prominently displayed throughout.

The cannabis menu at Green House is not to disappoint. You have a large selection of weed strains broken down by category such as outdoor grown, organic, and exclusive. Their hash selection is also plentiful, and includes both imported and higher potency local (nederhash) varieties. Many of the options are likely to be competition winning varieties. For those that prefer vaporizing over smoking, you will notice a Volcano for use on their main counter. Just ask for the necessary ballon (valoon) and filling chamber.

The regular menu is also exceptional. This is one of the few shops in Amsterdam that serves hot food. They offer a full menu, with options including hot breakfast items (eggs, pancakes), burgers, steak, steak sandwiches, salads, and milkshakes.

COFFEESHOPS

SHOP FEATURES

SHOP HOURS:
Daily:
8:00am-1:00am

GREEN PLACE

ADDRESS: Kloveniersburgwal 4, Amsterdam (Centrum)

MAP IT

Green Place Coffeeshop is located on Kloveniersburgwal, just to the south of the Nieuwmarkt (New Market). This is an extremely busy part of Amsterdam. The street is lined with many businesses of all types including small cafés, restaurants, and shops. It also sits directly on the Kloveniersburgwal canal, giving Green Place some pricey real estate. The area is beautiful and historic, and brings in a lot of visitors. Further, it also serves as a central hub for many of the attractions/other areas that Amsterdam has to offer.

The Shop

This coffeeshop is modest in size. It resides in an area where space is at a premium. What it lacks in size, however, it does seem to make up for in other areas, namely a really "cool vibe". Starting at the front of the shop, the interior is nice, but not plush. Wall mounted tables, funky lighting, and a long bar make this place feel a bit like a local pub or café. Seating in this room is mainly in the form of leather-topped stools. These are lined along the shop's wrap-around bar, and in front of the tables. Exposed air conditioning ducts give it a bit of an industrial feel. It is functional and artsy.

In the back of Green Place, there is a closed smoking lounge that is a bit more opulent in design. Here you will find leather topped couches that wrap around the room, along with a couple of small tables. The room is not large, but open enough to be a busy corner of this shop. The trim throughout Green Place is a bit Arabian, with a touch of modern. You cannot put our fingers on it exactly, but Green Place tends to be a really fun, comfortable, happy place to visit. Perhaps it is the cool lighting, the abstract symbols on the walls, the chill music, or simply the staff and people we find here.

The Menu

With regard to their cannabis, Green Place is presently considered a connoisseur establishment. They have entered numerous competitions in the past, and have some wins to their credit. You can find a couple of their medals displayed on the walls. Likewise, the cannabis menu here is fairly robust. You are likely to find some highly contemporary weed (flower) strains in this shop, as well as some more potency concentrate (hashish) varieties. Their edibles are excellent as well. They also sell pre-rolled joints, if you prefer. Lastly, no shop will keep you comfortable for long without some decent coffee, tea, juices, drinks, and snacks. On that front, Green Place also seems to deliver.

COFFEESHOPS

CONNOISSEUR GUIDE: AMSTERDAM

COFFEESHOPS

SHOP FEATURES

SHOP HOURS:
Daily:
9:00am-1:00am

GREEN PLANET

ADDRESS: Spuistraat 122, Amsterdam (Centrum)

MAP IT

Green Planet Coffeeshop is located on Spuistraat (translates as Lock Street), not far from the famous Amsterdam city landmarks of the Royal Palace and De Nieuwe Kerk (The New Church).

The Shop

This is a fairly unassuming shop from the outside. It is located in the basement of a building with only a couple of small windows in front. The immediate area also tends to see traffic passing through than hanging around. Though its building's brick façade is quite beautiful, it can still be easy to miss Green Planet.

This is far from the largest coffeeshop in Amsterdam. The room inside Green Planet is small. Further, its two small windows do not let in a whole lot of natural light. That would not be to say this is an unappealing coffeeshop, however. To the contrary, the interior is quite updated and contemporary. Seating is provided in the form of small table/stool sets and full-sized benches. It is quite an interesting mix, actually. There is a modern grey mica counter where you order your cannabis products and extras, with a lot of cool neon accent lighting around. It feels like a nightclub; the kind of place that features black (UV) lights or a bubble machine. Only, there is not much room to pack the people in here. This shop is much more personal and private.

The most notable feature of Green Planet is probably the outdoor seating. On warm sunny days, they setup tables and chairs outside. Spuistraat has a wide sidewalk, so there is plenty of room to stretch out and enjoy some time at a coffeeshop "al fresco."

The Menu

Green Planet has a cannabis menu that is moderate in size. On the weed-side, you should find a lot of tradition favorites; though they are likely to also stock a few contemporary strains. Hashish is mainly in the form of imports from Morocco. Though this shop is in the city center, pricing tends to be a touch more reasonable here than in some of the more high-profile shops. They also serve some basic drinks and snacks here.

The Royal Palace, Dam Square

COFFEESHOPS

SHOP FEATURES

SHOP HOURS:
Daily:
9:00am-1:00am

GREENHOUSE EFFECT

ADDRESS: Nieuwmarkt 14, Amsterdam (Centrum)

MAP IT

Greenhouse Effect Coffeeshop is located directly on Nieuwmarkt Square. This is among the top tourist spots in the city, dense with both historic buildings and modern businesses. Greenhouse Effect is actually one of several coffeeshops directly on the square, which is arguably prime real estate for such businesses. This shop was formerly located on Warmoesstraat, and was attached to a small hotel. It was a popular place. With the changing of regulations in the red light district, however, the coffeeshop was forced to move. In the Nieuwmarkt, it is now taking up the old space of Hill Street Blues coffeeshop. The old hotel in the RLD, unfortunately, is now closed. Incidentally, Greenhouse Effect is not affiliated with the Green House chain of coffeeshops in Amsterdam.

The Shop

The best way to describe Greenhouse Effect would be to say that it seems like a mix of a juice bar and a coffeeshop. The first thing you notice when you walk in, is that the front is bright and open. The shop has a long café counter here in its front room. You can view their cannabis offerings which are on display behind its front glass panel, in see-through plastic containers. Like many coffeeshops, the setup is such that you place your order in the front room, before venturing further on into the shop.

It is worth noting that the food and drinks are a big feature of this place. In the front room, you will notice a large selection of cakes, marijuana edibles, and even fresh fruit on display. Greenhouse Effect seems to be pretty serious about their coffee, juices, and desserts, and proud to show it off. We would say this establishment is more "gourmet snack bar coffeeshop," than simply a place to buy weed, sit, and get stoned. Amsterdam coffeeshops are often a bit lacking in the food department. Greenhouse Effect seems focused on making sure you want to stay when you get the munchies.

As you go on further, into the back of Greenhouse Effect coffeeshop, one will find a smoking room. This lounge area features numerous tables, along with wooden bench and chair seating. There is a small elevated balcony in here as well, which gives this room a split-level feeling. The furniture is comfortable enough, and the room has a pretty "chill" vibe to it. The décor is not opulent. The shop feels down to earth. Perhaps of greater interest, however, this coffeeshop makes good use of the wide sidewalk in front of the shop. Like many businesses in the Nieuwmarkt, they feature a nice stretch of outdoor seating. With the density of foot traffic here, we would argue there are few places better to sit and relax on a warm sunny day. That is, if the bustling crowds of the Nieuwmarkt do not bother you.

COFFEESHOPS

CONNOISSEUR GUIDE: AMSTERDAM

COFFEESHOPS

SHOP FEATURES

SHOP HOURS:

Daily:
12:00pm-8:00pm

GREY AREA

ADDRESS: Oude Leliestraat 2, Amsterdam (Centrum)

MAP IT

Grey Area Coffeeshop is found on Oude Leliestraat (Old Lily Street). It resides in the Grachtengordel-West neighborhood, which translates into Canal Ring West. This is one of the more picturesque parts of the city, with a great many old residences, small restaurants, trendy boutiques, and three of the city's most beautiful canals. Likewise, this is one of the more popular areas among tourists, and where you will likely find the greatest concentration of al fresco dining options (we have not actually done the calculations).

The Shop

Grey Area Coffeeshop is small. In fact, it is one of the smallest in the city when it comes to square footage. Inside there is just enough room for a few tables, a shelf with a few pull-up stools, and a counter for serving cannabis products. Do not expect over-the-top décor either. The decorating in here is cheap yet ingenious at the same time. The walls, tables, pretty much every flat surface in here is covered in stickers and rolling papers that have been applied by visitors. If you take some time to look at them, you will find many small notes of greeting. Grey Area is, indeed, a global phenomenon. There are messages from every corner of the globe here.

This shop is short on amenities. Do not expect a TV, hot food, or much by way of snacks or coffee. While management will provide its visitors with some basic needs, that is not really what this place is about. Grey Area is about one thing and one thing only: cannabis. This shop has long established itself as among the most recognized connoisseur coffeeshops shops in Amsterdam. They have entered (and won awards) in countless competitions over the years, and their menu items include weed stock from some of the most awarded breeders.

The Menu

Its focus on quality has made Grey Area one of the city's most famous coffeeshops. Likewise, it has been host to no shortage of celebrity clients. If there is a big concert in town and the band members enjoy weed, there are very high odds they (or someone from their crew) will make a trip here. Lines are usually long at Grey Area Coffeeshop, in spite of the fact that customers are often here just to make a quick purchase. This is a likely a testament to their focus on quality. While we would not argue this shop has "THE" best weed in the Dam (we have not found any one shop to stand above all others in this regard), it is indeed one of the most consistent for high quality connoisseur bud.

COFFEESHOPS

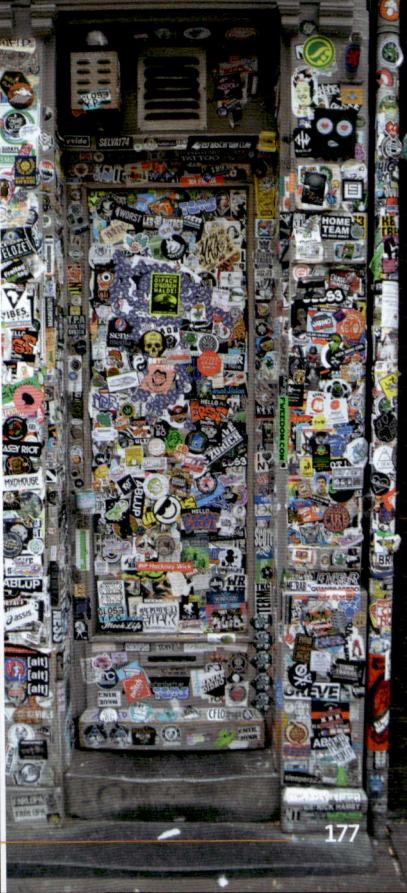

CONNOISSEUR GUIDE: AMSTERDAM

COFFEESHOPS

SHOP FEATURES

SHOP HOURS:

Mon-Fri:
9:30am-12:30am

Sat-Sun:
10:00am-12:30am

HAPPY DAYS

ADDRESS: Amsteldijk 139, Amsterdam (Zuid)

MAP IT

Happy Days Coffeeshop is located on Amsteldijk, in the Rijnbuurt (Rhine neighborhood) of Amsterdam South. This coffeeshop sits right on the main s110 motorway, which runs along the Amstel river here. This is a beautiful and highly residential part of the city. The streets are mainly lined with large apartment buildings, though there are enough bushes and trees around to give it a more tranquil feel. Mind you, you still know you are in the large city of Amsterdam. But the pace is more relaxed here.

The Shop

We would start off by stating that Happy Days is not quite a traditional Dutch coffeeshop. It is largely frequently by residents from the area. It is a true locals' establishment. But it is somewhat more polished than what one usually expects with these types of places. Often, they have a more traditional "old wood" feel, and eschew fancy décor. Instead, Happy Days coffeeshop has a decidedly contemporary appearance. Leather benches, dark wooden tables, and purple backlighting all give this place somewhat of an urban nightclub feel. It is not over the top, but definitely designed.

Taking away from the nightclub vibe a little, however, is the fact that this shop is not especially large. However, they do make very good use of the space, and provide a fairly comfortable if not intimate environment to hang out in. There is a billiards table and a table football game (foosball), and enough additional space to fit several bench seats, which are deep and restaurant-style. Even with this, the place seems open. The large front window probably helps.

The Menu

The cannabis menu at Happy Days Coffeeshop is not expansive, but sufficient for most. Expect to find half a dozen varieties or so on the weed-side. They usually favor traditional Amsterdam strains here, but often have a contemporary strain or two on offer as well. They offer fewer (but still several) types on the hash-side of the menu. Again, think traditional choices… imported pressed hashish from Morocco. They also have pre-rolled joints, and "space muffins" for edibles. These muffins can be a nice change of pace from the chocolate cake (space cake) that most shops sell. Lastly, they make a good cup of coffee here, and have enough basic snacks to hold anyone over for a while.

CONNOISSEUR GUIDE: AMSTERDAM

HENNEP KAAS
HOLLANDSE KAAS & HENNEP ZADEN
Hemp Cheese

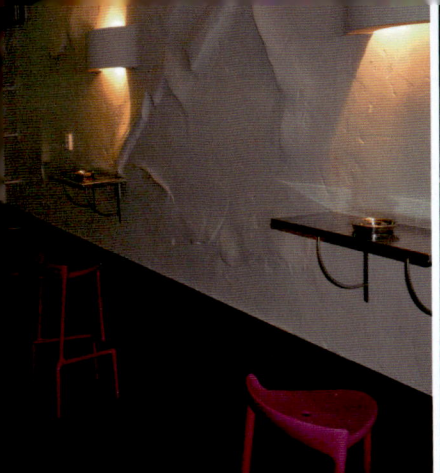

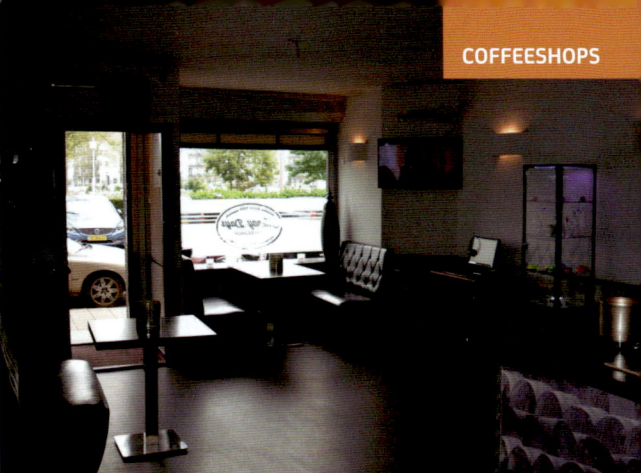

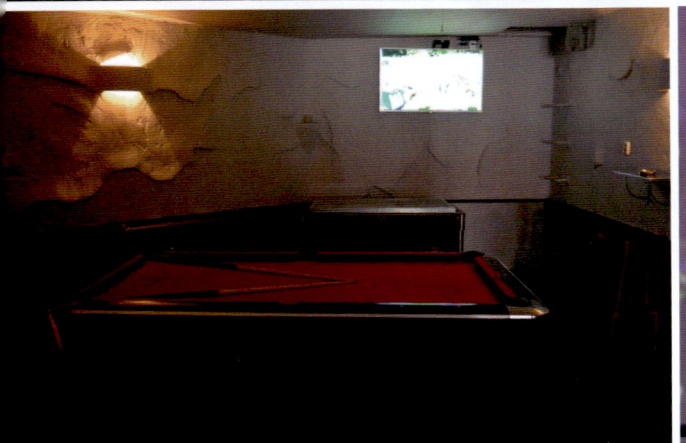

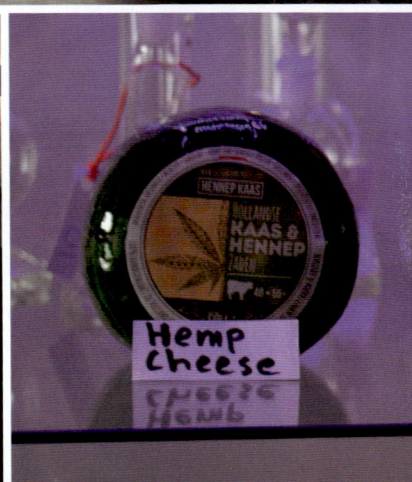

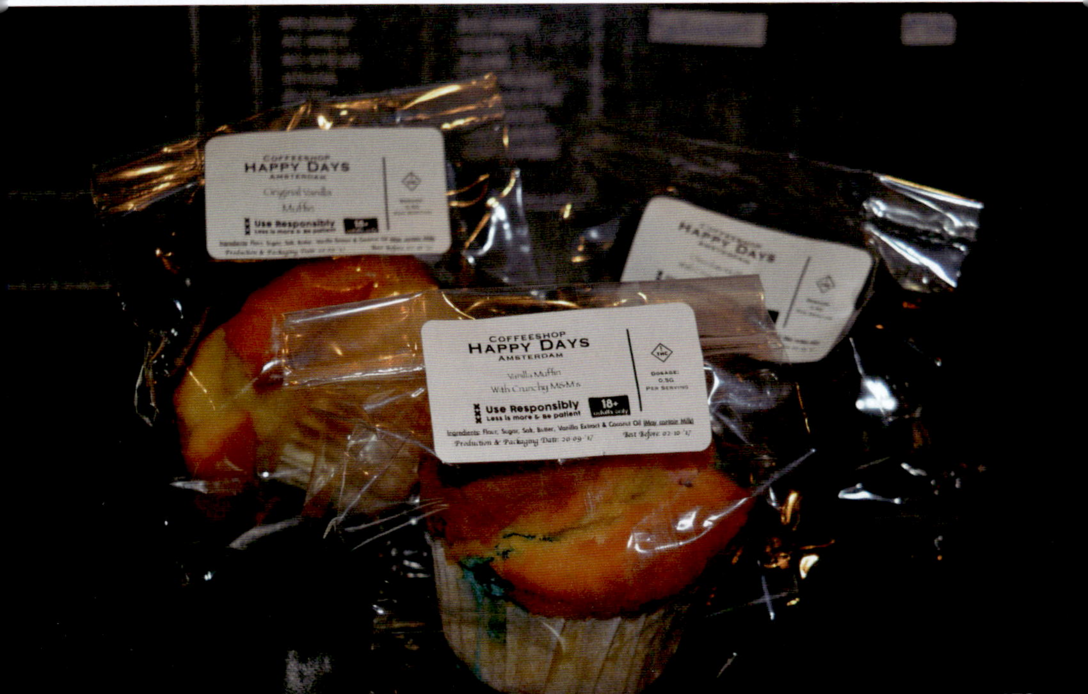
COFFEESHOP
HAPPY DAYS
AMSTERDAM
Original Vanilla Muffin
Use Responsibly
COFFEESHOP
HAPPY DAYS
AMSTERDAM
Vanilla Muffin
With Crunchy M&M's
Use Responsibly
Less is more & be patient
18+ adults only
THC
Dosage: 0.5G Per Serving
Ingredients: Flour, Sugar, Salt, Butter, Vanilla Extract & Coconut Oil (May contain Milk)
Production & Packaging Date: 20-09-'17
Best Before 02-10-'17

COFFEESHOPS

SHOP FEATURES

SHOP HOURS:
Daily
9:00am-1:00am

HAPPY FEELINGS

ADDRESS: Kerkstraat 51, Amsterdam (Centrum)

MAP IT

Happy Feelings Coffeeshop is located on Kerkstraat (Church Street). It is just a bit outside of the Leidseplein, known for its abundance of nightlife venues like bars, nightclubs, coffeeshops, and restaurants. It is a busy area, but also one with a great deal to see and do.

The Shop

This coffeeshop refers to itself as the "happiest coffeeshop in town." While we have no way of objectively evaluating this, we can say the vibe in here is usually pretty upbeat and fun. Being just outside one of the city's hotspots probably helps. It keeps this shop quite busy with, well, happy guests, which undoubtedly keeps the shop happy as well.

You walk through a turnstile upon entering Happy Feelings coffeeshop. Upon doing so, you are presented with a shop that is distinctly contemporary (dare we say trendy) in appearance. There are several standout features of the décor. For starters, the walls of the shop feature large sections of exposed brick. Both track and recessed lighting are overhead. Together, these give the room a city industrial feel. The front counter, which seems to be built out of a glowing cube, provides strong accent lighting for the room. Polished dark black tables and leather/chrome stools accommodate guests, and finish off the modern interior of this shop quite well.

The Menu

The cannabis menu is considerable in size at Happy Feelings. The menu is found on a digital screen built into the front counter. It separates the weed (flower) strains by indica or sativa dominance. Hashish (concentrate) products are also available, as are pre-rolled joints. For those who prefer vapor to smoke, they also have several De Verdamper vaporizers. These are a cross between a traditional bong (water pipe) and a whip-style (tube draw) vaporizer. A little more tricky to use than a Volcano, but does the trick.

Lastly, you will find a stereo microscope on the counter. This is for examining your purchase up close; a good sign this shop is confident about its stock. Happy Feelings has the basic amenities to make your stay comfortable. It is of note, however, that they really seem to like employing vending machines here. They have separate machines for selling soda, chips and candy, and rolling papers. So these other bits are "self serve," so to speak.

COFFEESHOPS

CONNOISSEUR GUIDE: AMSTERDAM

COFFEESHOPS

SHOP FEATURES

SHOP HOURS:
Daily:
7:00am-1:00am

HAPPY PEOPLE

ADDRESS: Dapperstraat 2, Amsterdam (Oost)

MAP IT

Happy People is located on Dapperstraat, near the Eastern Docklands in Amsterdam Oost (east). This shop sits canal side, in a predominantly residential part of the city. This is a very pleasant area to walk around and enjoy the scenery, especially during the warmer months. The greenery is calming and lush, and the architecture impressive. Happy People is also a short walk from the Artis, Amsterdam's famous Royal Zoo. The Artis is brimming with both history and exotic animals, and is highly recommended if you are looking for something interesting to do on a free afternoon.

The Shop

Clean and unassuming on the outside, Happy People is the corner business at a large historic building. Inside, the feel is quite different. We would say the theme is Garden of Eden, with a modern mythical twist. There is a beautifully painted meadow on the bathroom door, which is surrounded by intense vines, gargoyle and dragon candle holders high on the walls... Celtic mirrors. All of these accents must have taken a great deal of time to acquire, and they laid them out perfectly, to create a splendid smoking sanctuary.

They have one large smoking lounge in Happy People coffeeshop. The furnishings are basic but ample. There is plenty of high-top and bar seating to make use of in here.

They also have a big screen TV, and a full size pinball machine (rare for Amsterdam shops), in this case Tron Legacy. They also have seating outside - two wooden picnic tables. On a warm day, this is quite a nice place to rest and people watch.

The Menu

The cannabis menu at Happy People coffeeshop is moderate in size. On the weed-side, expect to find short of a dozen options. These are typically old school Amsterdam strains in our experience. Think of items like White Widow and Amnesia; flavorful potent strains that have drawn in visitors to this city for decades. The hash side is typically much smaller, but will still have several options for you to choose from. These are usually imported pressed hashes from places like Morocco and Afghanistan. Of course, pre-rolled joints are ample here as well. Pricing should be reasonable, as they cater more to regulars than city visitors here, so cost is a big consideration.

Sunset on the Canal

COFFEESHOPS

SHOP FEATURES

SHOP HOURS:

Daily:
9:00am-12:00am

HET BALLONNETJE

ADDRESS: Roetersstraat 12, Amsterdam (Centrum)

MAP IT

Het Ballonnetje Coffeeshop is located on Roetersstraat, just behind the University of Amsterdam. It is on the east side of the city, in a neighborhood known as the Plantage. This is one of Amsterdam's "green neighborhoods". It is noted for its lush parks, including the beautiful botanical gardens (Hortus Botanicus). The Artis Royal Zoo (Natura Artis Magistra) which is also found here, is one of the oldest zoos in mainland Europe. This section of the city is slightly outside of the city center, and the pace seems just a bit more relaxed. Given its proximity to the University, The Plantage is also a noticeably youthful neighborhood, with a high density of students.

The Shop

The name of this shop translates into "The Balloon" in English. Het Ballonnetje is one of the oldest coffeeshops in the city, opening its doors in 1978. So, this is a historic place. It is also one of the more quintessential Dutch-local establishments. There are not a lot of frills here. The inside is basic, but clean and well maintained. Wooden chairs and tables provide seating.

The décor in Het Ballonnetje is on the artistic-side. Featured is a beautiful large hand-painted mural of a person hovering over the city in a red balloon; pretty cool. The lighting is funky, and the other art and pictures add to the artsy vibe. So let us be clear. While we consider the furnishings basic, this shop is also "real"... artistic without being an over-polished tourist trap. Do not worry if you are a tourist. Being a historic shop, plenty of people make a special trip here, and the staff is known to be especially welcoming of visitors.

The Menu

For a coffeeshop that is frequented by locals, the menu selection at Het Ballonnetje tends to be more contemporary than you would probably expect. The management here seems to be into their cannabis more so than many others, particularly the flowers (weed). While you can expect to find some old-school strains here, you should also see many modern favorites, including some popular West Coast USA strains. The quality tends to be very high. The hashish-side is quite robust, as well. In addition, they have a large list of pre-rolled joints, along with some basic Space Cakes for edibles.

COFFEESHOPS

COFFEESHOPS

SHOP FEATURES

SHOP HOURS:

Daily
10:00am-1:00am

HET GELDERSE

ADDRESS: Geldersekade 54-HS, Amsterdam (Centrum)

MAP IT

Het Gelderse Coffeeshop is located just to the south of Centraal Station. Though it resides in a very busy section of the city, its immediate block is actually one somewhat less traveled. As such, this can be, at times, a bit more relaxed of a place to visit, though we would dare not say serene. The hustle and bustle of the city centre surrounds this location. The respite you may find here is likely to be short, but noteworthy.

The Shop

The Dutch phrase Het Gelderse translates into "The Gelderland" in English. It may be referring to the Dutch province of the same name, or perhaps the canal outside, which is named the Geldersekade. Either way, it is an external reference. We do not see it represented in any special theme inside the coffeeshop.

If there was a theme, it would be that of a tribute to the Argentinean revolutionary Che Guevara. His likeness is used in the shop's logo and menu, and is seen in a few spots inside. Otherwise, Het Gelderse is a fairly nondescript location. The interior is small, and wood dominates the décor. They do have a large front window, which lets in a lot of light. It makes the room feel a bit larger than it actually is. The view is quite nice here as well, being that the Geldersekade is one of the city's more picturesque canals. Otherwise, do not expect a lot of frills here.

The Menu

The cannabis menu is considerable in size at Het Gelderse. They tend to list a dozen or more strains on the weed (flower) side, though perhaps half as many types of hashish (concentrate). They do not work with any particular cannabis breeders of note, at least none that are featuring on the menu. They also sell pre-rolled joints, if you prefer. Otherwise, not a lot of extras are to be found. This seems to be a down to basics coffeeshop. Some weed, some drinks, a nice view.

COFFEESHOPS

SHOP FEATURES

SHOP HOURS:
Daily:
7:00am-12:45am

HUGO

ADDRESS: Frederik Hendrikstraat 123-hs, Amsterdam (West)

MAP IT

Hugo Coffeeshop is located in the Frederik Hendrikbuurt section of Amsterdam West. This is just to the west of the Jordaan district, and has some similarities to that famous neighborhood. Frederik Hendrikbuurt is also a largely residential, historic, and slightly more relaxed part of Amsterdam compared to what you generally find in the center of the city. That stated, we would not describe the area as quiet. Rather, it can be quite lively with people, and has easy access to plenty of restaurants, cafés, bars, and other small businesses.

The Shop

The name of this establishment is formally "Hugo de Groot" or "Hugo The Great" in English. It is named after a famous Dutch jurist, who is credited with helping to shape international law. We do not see much by way of tribute to Hugo the Great inside, however. Instead, the theme of this establishment seems to be birds. At least, the shop logo appears to be a Green Macaw parrot, and you are likely to find the real shop mascot, presumably that same bird, sitting on a perch inside the shop to greet visitors. An unusual find in an Amsterdam coffeeshop, no doubt... and quite a beautiful creature. Hugo is also female owned. Not the only such shop of course, but worth noting as most shops in the city are owned by men.

Coffeeshop Hugo is a pickup location only. However, that has not stopped the shop from creating a beautiful interior. Hugo is nicely decorated; dare we say decidedly upscale. The hardwood accents and stone-lined walls are extravagant, and seems to stretch right out into the street. Stone tiles on the floor and soft accent lighting make this shop feel like the lobby of a fancy spa or hotel. Were there an actual lounge to hang out and smoke in, we would consider Coffeeshop Hugo among the more nicely appointed operations in the city. Unfortunately, you will only be here for a quick purchase.

The Menu

The cannabis menu at Coffeeshop Hugo is moderate in size. On the weed side of the menu they tend to have just shy of a dozen strains. These are likely to be mixed genetics. That is, you will see a lot of old-school favorite strains that local smokers are most familiar with on the one hand. On the other, they also stock some contemporary strains, typically West Coast USA hybrids. The hashish-side of the menu is much more trim; usually just several options to choose from. These are imported pressed varieties from places like Morocco and Afghanistan. If preferred, they also have a small selection of pre-rolled joints, and a space cake if you are looking for an edible.

COFFEESHOPS

CONNOISSEUR GUIDE: AMSTERDAM

COFFEESHOPS

SHOP FEATURES

SHOP HOURS:

Daily:
7:00am-1:00am

HUNTER'S

ADDRESS: Utrechtsestraat 14, Amsterdam (Centrum)

MAP IT

Hunter's Coffeeshop is located on Utrechtsestraat, near Rembrandtplein. Hunter's is one of just a handful of multi-shop brands in Amsterdam. They established their first location in the Red Light District back in 1985. Since that time, they have opened several other shops in the city (and closed a few as well). Currently they have several other shops operating in Amsterdam Noord and West. At one time this particular coffeeshop went under the name Sevilla. However, it was taken over by Hunter's some years back. It now appears to be the brand's flagship location following the closing (de-licensing) of the original Hunter's in the RLD.

The Shop

This shop is perhaps most known for its unique seating. In front of polished wooden tables one will find legitimate movie theater seats, complete with drink holders in the armrests. They are quite comfortable, as one might expect of chairs that you are expected to sit in for two hours at a time. No, they are not complimented by an actual indoor movie theater (the shop is not quite big enough for that). However, Hunter's Coffeeshop is an otherwise contemporary and warm place. You probably will not be in a rush out. Alternative seating options include a windowsill couch, and outdoor tables and chairs (al fresco style).

The Menu

As a brand, Hunter's Coffeeshop tries to bring consistency in its cannabis offerings, offering similar menus across all shops. These list a fairly large selection of both weed (flower) and hashish (concentrate) options. They also sell a variety of pre-rolled joints, and space cakes for "edibles". This shop also has a fairly comprehensive coffee, tea, drink, and snack menu; enough options to keep you deep in movie seats for a good stretch.

SHOP FEATURES

COFFEESHOPS

SHOP HOURS:
Daily:
9:00am-11:00pm

MAP IT

HUNTER'S BROS

Waterlandplein 7, Amsterdam (Noord) **:ADDRESS**

Hunter's Bros Coffeeshop can be found in a shopping center in the Waterlandpleinbuurt section of Amsterdam-Noord (North). This roughly translates into "the Waterland Square" neighborhood in English. This is a largely residential area, far away from the hustle and bustle of the centrum. Though not popular with tourists, those who make it out here will find a beautiful, green, and peaceful neighborhood. Bros is very close to the Schellingwouderpark. This park sits on the river Ij, and is also connected to a tranquil lake to the north. It is a hidden gem that few tourists see.

The Shop

A neon sign above the door is probably the only thing you notice about this coffeeshop from the street. Well, perhaps that or the suit-wearing bouncer often positioned at the door. We are not sure how much trouble the management runs in to out here. But it does provide a sense of security for a cash-only business. This coffeeshop is now part of the Hunter's brand. This should provide some consistency for those that like the other Hunters-linked establishments.

Bros used to be a takeaway-only place. Since being taken over by Hunter's, however, they have upgraded the shop and opened a smoking lounge, which you will find to the right of the main counter as you enter. The décor inside is contemporary. Modern fixtures and light-colored wood floors and trim provide an urban café feel. A giant window in the front of the lounge lets in a lot of natural light, making the room feel very open. The main counter also wraps around into the lounge, so you can order cannabis products or refreshments during your visit. Seating is in the form of small tables/chairs, and pull-up bar stools.

The Menu

The menu in here is fairly robust for a neighborhood shop. There are most options on the flower (weed) side, where they typically carry well over a dozen strains. The genetics are a mix of old-school favorites and more contemporary hybrids, such as those coming from the West Coast USA. For hashish, they like both domestics and imports. For the latter, they carry a lot of Moroccan hash. The former, usually several options of isolator, also known as high potency nederhasj. They carry un-pressed kief from time to time. Being all the way up here in Amsterdam Noord, this is almost exclusively a place for locals. As such, expect prices to be more reasonable than they are down in the city center.

COFFEESHOPS

SHOP FEATURES

SHOP HOURS:

Daily:
9:00am-11:00pm

HUNTER'S FILIAAL

ADDRESS: Papaverweg 2, Amsterdam (Noord)

MAP IT

Hunter's Filiaal coffeeshop is located on Papaverweg, in the Volewijck section of Amsterdam Noord (North). The Volewijck actually has a dark history. Once, very long ago, it was the site of the city gallows. The story about this is quite interesting if you want to look it up. We will spare you the gruesome details. Today, the Volewijck is a beautiful and strongly residential part of the city. If you make it out here, enjoy exploring. The Noord definitely runs at a different pace than the centrum. You might even want to visit Noorderpark, an exceptional (though perhaps lesser known) green area quite close to this shop.

The Shop

Het Filiaal was the name of this shop before it was sold to Hunter's. In English, Het Filiaal means "The Branch." We are not certain of the exact meaning in the context of this business. Perhaps they mean an olive branch; peace. Perhaps it is just another way for saying "the location", as we might see in English. Either way, it does sounds cool. And now that it is a location for the famous Hunter's chain, I guess we can say it fits.

Inside Hunter's Filiaal you will find a down-to-earth establishment reminiscent of a local sports bar. This furnishings are wood and basic, but comfortable. Seating is in the form of high top tables and bar stools. The room has dartboards and a big screen tv, as you would expect in a sports bar. This is a lively shop, popular among residents in the area. As one would expect in an atmosphere with such amenities and seating, they have a plentiful hot and cold drink selection.

Perhaps the most notable feature about Hunter's Filiaal is found behind the shop. There is a door in the back door that leads to a large patio area. It feels very much like the backyard of a family home. There is ample outdoor furniture to relax in: wicker chairs and comfortable cushion-topped benches. There is plenty of room to throw a nice party back here, if you so wished. Of course, this is a popular hangout on warmer days.

CONNOISSEUR GUIDE: AMSTERDAM

SHOP FEATURES

SHOP HOURS:

Daily:
9:00am-12:00am

COFFEESHOPS

MAP IT

HUNTER'S MERCATOR

Orteliusstraat 193, Amsterdam (West) **:ADDRESS**

Hunter's Coffeeshop is located on Orteliusstraat, in the Van Galenbuurt section of Amsterdam West. It is very close to Mercatorplein (Mercator Square), a popular shopping area in this part of the city. The surrounding neighborhood here is quite beautiful. It is largely residential, full of tree-lined streets and contemporary block-style apartment buildings. Hunter's is also just to the north end of Rembrandtpark, one of the most popular (and lush) green areas in Amsterdam. In warmer months, this is a great place to enjoy the outdoors.

The Shop

Before joining the Hunter's chain, this place was known as Coffeeshop Happiness. It largely served as a take-and-go establishment in recent years, catering mainly to local clientele who just stop in for a quick purchase. The smoking lounge in the back of the shop is once again open. As such, feel free to relax a while here. The lounge is not especially large or luxurious, but has enough of the basics to keep you comfortable. Several tables and chairs provide seating, and there is a flat screen TV if you want to catch a game.

The Menu

Being part of the Hunter's chain now, you can expect some consistency with other locations as far as the cannabis menu goes. The Hunter's menus tends to be moderate in size, with ample options to choose from. On the weed-side, expect to find both contemporary (USA) hybrid genetics, as well as some more traditional Amsterdam local strains. The hashish is largely in the form of imported pressed varieties, from the usual regions. Like most shops, they also have sufficient stock of pre-rolled joints on the ready. The do make a space cake here too. While simple in concept vs. the more gourmet edibles starting to make the rounds in Amsterdam, Hunter's usually puts some effort into their products; edibles included.

COFFEESHOPS

SHOP FEATURES

SHOP HOURS:

Daily:
10:00am-1:00am

IBIZA

ADDRESS: Hemonystraat 16, Amsterdam (Zuid)

MAP IT

Coffeeshop Ibiza is located in Amsterdam Zuid (South), near the eastern edge of the Oude Pijp (Old Pipe) neighborhood. The Old Pipe area is a popular and lively section of the city; one of Amsterdam's hotspots. It is densely populated, and has no shortage of bars, restaurants, cafés, and boutique shops to keep you occupied. Generally speaking, however, the streets around Ibiza are a little quieter than that of the Oude Pijp.

The Shop

Ibiza is the largest coffeeshop in the immediate neighborhood. The place is ornate, starting with the shop's bright blue painted façade. The interior décor is similarly intricate. The shop has a bright blue and white color scheme as you enter, funky accent lighting, beautiful handcrafted light fixtures, and plenty of artwork - presenting a fun, upbeat vibe. Presumably named after the Mediterranean island, the theme here would best be described as "island smokers' paradise". The coffeeshop mascot/logo is a joint… which is depicted alone on an island… relaxing with a bottle of beer and a joint of its own.

The building that Coffeeshop Ibiza is in has an expansive split level layout. There are actually four distinct lounge areas in here. The first is on the main level, and hosts the shop's bar. Here you can purchase your cannabis, as well as from a large selection of drinks and snacks. Bar stools, tables, and chairs provide ample seating. Behind the bar is lounge number two, a glass-enclosed smoking room. This is to comply with European tobacco smoking laws. Mixed joints (tobacco/cannabis) are allowed in here, normally banned in coffeeshops without such facilities.

At the back of the shop are stairs leading up and down to the remaining two lounges. Downstairs you will find the third, a wide room with various chairs, tables, and bench seating. It feels more private here, probably because visually you are separated from the rest of the shop. Upstairs is the fourth lounge. This open room has a balcony overlooking the main floor. The décor is largely traditional wood-trim. There are plenty of chairs, tables, and more importantly, several deep plush leather couches here. These are comfy to say the least. We would argue it is the "prime" seating here.

The Menu

The cannabis menu is fairly large. On the weed side, expect to find a dozen strains or so. They offer both old-school strains and contemporary items. The hashish-side of the menu is roughly half the size of the weed. Still, there are several selections to choose from. These are traditional imports mainly from Morocco, Nepal, and India. They also have a fairly extensive selection of pre-rolled joints.

COFFEESHOPS

CONNOISSEUR GUIDE: **AMSTERDAM**

COFFEESHOPS

SHOP FEATURES

SHOP HOURS:
Daily:
9:30am-12:00am

JOHNNY

ADDRESS: Elandsgracht 3, Amsterdam (Centrum)

MAP IT

Coffeeshop Johnny is found on Elandsgracht (Elks Canal), in the more residential and upscale Jordaan district. This is a beautiful section of the city center, packed with historic buildings and tranquil canals to enjoy.

The Shop

This coffeeshop is easily spotted when walking on the street by its bright white and red wooden façade out front. Inside, Johnny is a modern shop. Its décor includes cleanly painted walls, contemporary light-colored wainscoting on the walls, plenty of additional wood trim, and thick, white mica counters. Glass-shelved display cases also show off the shop's cannabis stock, various smoking accessories, and shop memorabilia. The best way to put the interior of Johnny into words would probably be "high-end clinical".

Seating at this shop is limited. It is largely a take-away establishment, though there are a couple of stools if you want to sit at the counter, and a few more by the front window. Otherwise, patrons will find a small smoking area to the side of this shop. This is partitioned off from the main counter area with a wall/door of glass. This allows tobacco smoking in the establishment, of course. Most, however, use the area to roll a quick joint before hitting the road.

The Menu

The cannabis menu at Coffeeshop Johnny reflects the modern feel of this shop. It has been computerized; found on screens that have been built into the main counter. This shop has recently started working with Amsterdam Genetics, an established, reputable breeder. As such, the quality of their menu should be very high. On the weed-side, expect to see many modern hybrids. For hashish, a mix of domestic (isolator) and imported sieved and pressed varieties, including the highly flavorful block hashes from Morocco.

In addition to cannabis, Johnny serves a variety of coffees, tea, and soft drinks.

COFFEESHOPS

CONNOISSEUR GUIDE: AMSTERDAM

COOFFEESHOPS

SHOP FEATURES

SHOP HOURS:
Daily:
10:00am-1:00am

JOLLY JOKER

ADDRESS: Nieuwmarkt 4a, Amsterdam (Centrum)

MAP IT

Jolly Joker Coffeeshop is one of the many businesses directly bordering the Nieuwmarkt (New Market), a bustling square in the city center. This corner of the city is highly trafficked by tourists. Consequently, most of the businesses in this area cater to that clientele. The Nieuwmarkt is most noted for the Waag, a beautiful and massive old building that served as a gate in the city's outer wall back in the 15th century. Now there is a restaurant here. The building that holds Jolly Joker is actually quite old itself, though not nearly as much. So, there is a lot to admire here, even if simply the building architecture in the surrounding area.

basic down-to-earth Dutch coffeeshop. You can step in here and find some weed or hash; just do not expect the menu to be dominated by award-winning strains or high potency extracts.

Aside from cannabis, they serve basic comforts such as coffees, teas, juices, and sodas, as well as a list of simple snacks.

The Shop

The Jolly Joker coffeeshop is very traditional in its décor. There is a lot of wood inside; bar, tables, benches, trim. It all has a very "corner pub" feeling to it. Not a lot of frills. It does have the benefit of very large front windows on both sides of the shop, being this is a corner building. As such, the place gets in a lot of light, making for a very open feel. The Nieuwmarkt is also a great place to sit and people watch, as the crowds in this area can literally be massive on a warm sunny afternoon.

The Menu

The cannabis menu is moderate in size, and in our experience does not feature any special breeders. They are a

The Waag, Nieuwmarkt Square

COFFEESHOPS

SHOP FEATURES

SHOP HOURS:

Daily:
10:00am-1:00am

KADINSKY 1

ADDRESS: Rosmarijnsteeg 9, Amsterdam (Centrum)

MAP IT

Kadinsky Coffeeshop on Rosmarijnsteeg is one of three Kadinsky locations in Amsterdam. The name of this street translates into "Rosemary Alley." It is very close to the Begijnhof, which was a court of houses built as a beguinage in the 17th century. A beguinage is a complex to house religious laywomen seeking to join like-minded communities. Perhaps it had to do with one of the old churches in the area. Either way, this neighborhood is no longer dominated by religion. Today, it is in the heart of Amsterdam city center, with a great amount of activity both day and night.

The Shop

From the outside, Kadinsky looks like your average neighborhood pub. Once you step in, however, you find a much more interesting place. The shop has a split-level floor plan, which provides a couple separate seating areas. Here, patrons are not presented with basic wooden tables and chairs, but comfortable leather benches and decorative stools. The rooms are filled with modern furniture, exposed lighting, and other contemporary décor that give it a decidedly urban feel. The whole place looks like a small, artsy nightclub... far from your average bar.

This shop also has a notable feature. Its large front window consists of two separate panels. The bottom panel opens up. In front of it, a long table. This is great in the summertime, as it opens up the room. It gives the shop a bit of an indoor/outdoor feel, without actually having the space for outdoor seating.

The Menu

If you are familiar with the Kadinsky coffeeshops, you know they boast a sizable cannabis menu. There are typically over a dozen types of flower (weed), and though not as many, still a formidable selection of concentrates (hashish) as well. Kadinsky is actually known for its hash. If you are debating between the two types of product, lean towards this. They also have pre-rolled joints, if you prefer not to roll you own. As for the non-medicated menu, this coffeeshop also serves good coffees, along with a selection of teas, soft drinks, juices, and simple snacks.

COFFEESHOPS

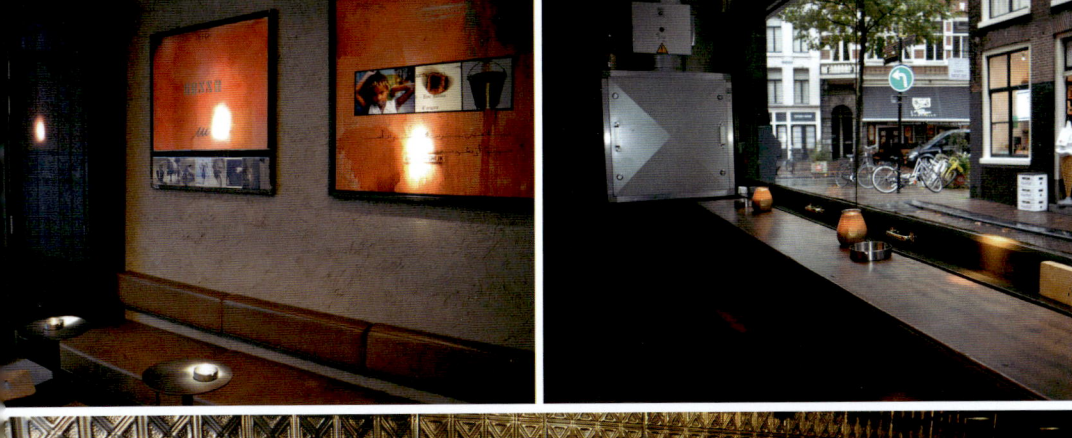

CONNOISSEUR GUIDE: AMSTERDAM

COFFEESHOPS

SHOP FEATURES

SHOP HOURS:

Daily:
9:30am-1:00am

KADINSKY 2

ADDRESS: Zoutsteeg 14, Amsterdam (Centrum)

MAP IT

Kadinsky Coffeeshop (on Zoutsteeg) is one of three Kadinsky coffeeshops. For Amsterdam, this is one of the more notable chains. In English, the name of this street translates into "Salt Lane." It is a side street off the Damrak, a main thoroughfare in and out of Amsterdam Centraal. On the other side is Nieuwendijk, one of the city's most popular shopping streets. Zoutsteeg is quite small, more of an alley. What is more, this little alley sees a great deal of foot traffic. It can get quite crowded, as can the area in general.

The Shop

From the outside, this Kadinsky location is rather nondescript. You see a lot of glass, a lot of wood. It feels like it could be anything, but easily a neighborhood pub. This is something we would say about all the Kadinsky shops. On the inside, however, the shop has a much different vibe. The interior of this place is modern, artsy, and urban. The brick walls, exposed lighting, and overhead wood beams really make you feel like you are in an intimate city café or coffee house somewhere.

Seating in this coffeeshop is mainly in the form of long benches covered in plush leather pillows. Small tables are positioned in front, and provide enough room for some smoking gear and coffee. Thought this shop is fairly small, it is quite comfortable, worth the time to chill at. With Kadinsky being such a known brand, and the very busy surrounding area, it can be tough to find a seat here sometimes. If you can, however, you have yourself a nice respite from the hustle and bustle outside.

The Menu

The cannabis menu at Kadinsky is considerable in size. They are likely to have a dozen or more strains on the weed (flower) side, and nearly as many options for hashish (concentrate). Genetics are definitely a mix of old and new. Expect things like White Widow and Amnesia to be side by side with Pineapple Kush and Gorilla Glue. While the weed is more prominent on the menu, we would say the shop is better known for its hashish. They seem to specialize in Moroccan imports, specifically, but do often carry some domestic isolator too. They also sell pre-rolled weed and hash joints, as well as space cakes.

Aside from cannabis, they serve gourmet coffees and tea here, along with the regular selection soft drinks, juices, and snacks.

COFFEESHOPS

COFFEESHOPS

SHOP FEATURES

SHOP HOURS:

Daily:
10:00am-1:00am

KADINSKY 3

ADDRESS: Langebrugsteeg 7-A, Amsterdam (Centrum)

MAP IT

Kadinsky Coffeeshop on Langebrugsteeg is one of three shops operating under the Kadinsky brand. The street name translates into "Long Bridge Alley", which references one of the city's historic (in this case 16th century) wooden bridges. Deconstructed in the 1930s, it is long gone. A lot has changed. This is the Jewelry Quarter now, home to many of the city's jewelers, jewelry galleries, and gold/silver smiths. There is also many high-end clothing, accessory, and other shops in this area, making this a fairly popular neighborhood for tourist traffic.

The Shop

The outside of this Kadinsky coffeeshop location is quite aesthetically pleasing, and fits well with the higher priced businesses of the area. The front has a beautiful large window, and the outer façade is of handcrafted polished wood. It gives the shop an upscale city pub feel.

Inside, this shop is also quite nice. The interior is small, but well cared for. There is a lot of wood in here, some handcrafted. Red color dominates, and recessed lighting overhead provides a nice contemporary feel. It is not really needed during the day, however, as the front window lets in a lot of natural light. There is limited seating downstairs. An additional seating room can be found on the floor above, at the top of a creaky narrow staircase. Wooden chairs and tables accommodate the customers in both. The interior still has a city feel to it, but it is a bit more urban café than brown bar.

The Menu

The cannabis menu at the Kadinsky coffeeshop locations is formidable. There are typically over a dozen strains of weed (flower) available, and a sizable selection of hashish (concentrate) products. While the weed menu is quite diverse and comprehensive, Kadinsky is really known for its hash. They have a reputation for importing some very clean and potent product, particularly from Morocco. They do often stock some more potent domestic nederhasj (Ice-O-Lator) as well.

This brand is known for keeping its customers comfortable, at least with the basics on offer, such as good coffee and teas, and a decent enough selection of soft drinks, juices, and simple snacks.

COFFEESHOPS

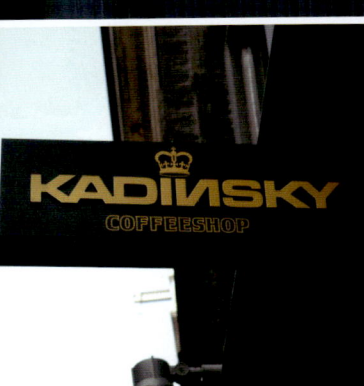

COFFEESHOPS

SHOP FEATURES

SHOP HOURS:
Daily:
10:00am-1:00am

KASHMIR

ADDRESS: Jan Pieter Heijestraat 82, Amsterdam (Zuid)

MAP IT

Kashmir Coffeeshop is found on Jan Pieter Heijestraat, in Amsterdam's Oud-West (Old West) neighborhood. This is a diverse part of the city that boasts high real estate prices, and is home to the established and upwardly mobile. There has been seen strong economic development here in recent years. The area around Kashmir now features a mix of modern architecture with beautifully maintained historic buildings. Combined with it being situated close to, and roughly equidistant from, both Rembrandt Park and Vondelpark, it is clear why this neighborhood is so desirable. Do not just come here. Take a long stroll around...

The Shop

The coffeeshop part of Kashmir is modest in size. It features a small lounge area in one long room on the ground floor, and a bar on one side for ordering cannabis products. The inside is appointed with eclectic colorful artwork throughout, and lined with low, cushy couches and small tables. It is very Asian and Middle Eastern in influence, and quite comfortable.

The individuals behind this establishment also run the Kashmir Lounge across the street, as a compliment to their coffeeshop. This smoke-friendly bar was formed when the alcohol ban on coffeeshops was instituted. The Lounge is a bit larger, with a similar eclectic appearance.

They have a full bar with mixed drinks and a formidable beer collection. There is a separate smoking room for tobacco consumption, to comply with EU smoking laws. Otherwise, they are fine with weed being smoked throughout (until such time as a law prohibits it).

The Menu

The cannabis menu at Kashmir is considered moderate to large in size. Most days, there are many weed options, typically a mix of both old-school strains and new imported genetics. If this shop was known for one thing over the other, it would be hashish (concentrate). They typically have a diverse selection of imports from different regions, and the quality is generally above-average in our experience. You can also find a large list of available pre-rolled joints, if you would rather not do the work.

CONNOISSEUR GUIDE: AMSTERDAM

COFFEESHOPS

COFFEESHOPS

SHOP FEATURES

SHOP HOURS:

Sun-Thurs:
10:00am-12:00am

Fri-Sat:
10:00am-1:00am

KATSU

ADDRESS: Eerste v/d Helststraat 70, Amsterdam (Zuid)

MAP IT

Katsu Coffeeshop is located on Eerste van der Helststraat, just adjacent to the famous outdoor market Albert Cuypmarkt. This shop rests in the De Pijp (The Pipe) neighborhood, a trendy part of the city with a great density of popular bars, nightclubs, restaurants, and an endless selection of enticing shops and cafés. In such a hip section of Amsterdam, it is hard to stand out but Katsu most certainly does. Arguably, it is a bright beacon in this busy neighborhood. In the city-wide coffeeshop scene, this shop is equally noteworthy, and carries a solid reputation for quality and comfort.

The Shop

One of the first things that stands out about Katsu is that this is an extremely artsy place. You can see this even from the outside, where the façade is painted from the street to the top of the building's first level. The look is very unusual; an intense blue and green background with splashes of color. With the 3D KATSU logo prominently displayed, it almost feels like the splash screen to a video game; but this is a building!

The artistic vibe continues on the inside, where you will find beautiful paintings, photographs, handbills, and other bits pasted throughout this split level shop. It is vibrant and colorful in here. Simply appointed with wooden benches and tablets, but quite comfortable. The outside seating area is perhaps the real star of the shop. On warm sunny days you will find a sectioned-off area of tables and chairs.

This beautiful shop attracts a lot of tourists. It may be a bit outside of the city center, but people often make a special trip here. The menu is presented in both English and Dutch to accommodate the international crowd it attracts. The shop is known for quality cannabis and fair prices, all things considered. You will find a lot of locals here too. So grab some cannabis, order up a coffee, and find a bench. You should find your time at Katsu quite enjoyable.

The Menu

This is typically regarded as a connoisseur shop with regard to its cannabis menu. They have entered and won cannabis competitions in the past. Look around. You will see some awards on display. The menu is robust, with many options on both the weed (flower) and hashish (concentrate) side. The weed tends to be a solid mix of old-school favorites, and contemporary strains. They seem to be constantly updating things here too, which keeps things fresh. The hash-side is equally impressive; many options of pressed import to choose from. This shop also offers pre-rolled joints (mixed and pure weed), and space cakes.

COFFEESHOPS

CONNOISSEUR GUIDE: AMSTERDAM

COFFEESHOPS

SHOP FEATURES

SHOP HOURS:

Daily:
10:00am-1:00am

KOOI

ADDRESS: Amstelstraat 35, Amsterdam (Centrum)

MAP IT

Kooi Coffeeshop is located on Amstelstraat, just to the east of the Rembrandtplein. The street outside is a busy thoroughfare in and out of the city centre. With all of the beautiful canal-side restaurants, cafés, and coffeeshops in the immediate area, it can be easy to pass on by with the traffic, and overlook this small shop. Many visitors may also remember it as Old Amsterdam, a long established (but quite basic) locals' shop. It actually changed hands in early 2018. The new owners have revamped this place so much, that it is unrecognizable once you step inside.

The Shop

The word "kooi" is Dutch, and translates into "birdcage" in English. It is an element present both in the logo and in the shop itself. Inside, one will find a stunningly beautiful décor. One of the most notable features is the overhead lighting. These custom fixtures contain bare light bulbs, encased in old-fashioned gold birdcages. They shine through the front window as you walk by. It draws the eye, and gives the place a highly contemporary feel. Much about this place is equally impressive, especially the three-dimensional walls. We will let the pictures explain.

Kooi coffeeshop is not especially large, though we would say that there is still sufficient room in the lounge most days. Especially cozy are the long leather benches in the back. There is also an area by the front window, with both wide bench and stool seating. The windows up front run nearly floor to ceiling, and let in a lot of light on sunny days. This area can be quite comfortable. It is hard to put this shop in words, but abstract, artistic, and modern keep coming to mind. Though one of the newest shops in the city, we would definitely say Kooi coffeeshop is an Amsterdam original.

The Menu

The cannabis menu at Kooi coffeeshop is moderate in size. The weed-side of the menu is generally more robust in its number of selections, which include a lot of traditional Amsterdam strains. However, these do sit alongside some contemporary USA genetics… think Gorilla Glue… Kush hybrids. The hashish-side of the menu is smaller, but includes both imported varieties, and more potent Dutch isolator (Nederhasj). They also have pre-rolls, and quite a nice selection of edibles. If you are looking for something better than the basic "space cake", you might want to give this shop a try.

COFFEESHOPS

CONNOISSEUR GUIDE: AMSTERDAM

COFFEESHOPS

SHOP FEATURES

SHOP HOURS:
Tues-Sat: (only)
11:00am-1:00am

LA TERTULIA

ADDRESS: Prinsengracht 312, Amsterdam (Centrum)

MAP IT

La Tertulia Coffeeshop is located canal-side on Prinsengracht, the outermost waterway in Amsterdam's central canal ring. It resides on the western edge of the "De 9 Straats" neighborhood, or "The Nine Streets". This is a famous shopping area in the Jordaan district, which features a multitude of small boutiques, restaurants, and indoor/outdoor cafés. La Tertulia coffeeshop blends in well with the neighborhood. It is an artsy place, with a large outdoor seating area. This coffeeshop opened back in 1983, so it is a well-established member of the city's coffeeshop culture.

The Shop

The name La Tertulia translates into "The Salon" in Spanish. This appears consistent with the vibe they cultivate. When you walk in, you will find a very open split-level coffeeshop. There are a lot of plants, some large crystals including actual meteorites. It all makes for a spa-ish feel. You almost feel ready to check-in and grab a robe. The other décor is primarily in the form of colorful paintings. The selection of colors is vibrant, which makes the room feel bright and lively.

This shop is essentially divided into three sections. Upstairs is a balcony area, which overlooks the rest of the shop. You will find some basic tables and fold-out chairs here. Downstairs, you will find additional seating, as well as the shop's counter. However, it is outside where you find the most notable feature of the shop. Their summertime outdoor seating consists of four tables and sixteen chairs. The furniture may be more practical than comfortable but the canal-side location is hard to beat. The section is also beside a giant mural depicting one of Van Gogh's outdoor scenes - creating a perfect "al fresco" coffeeshop experience.

The Menu

The cannabis menu is moderate in selection, listing perhaps a dozen strains on the flower (weed) side. They tend to have a much smaller selection of hashish (concentrate), though some of the varieties are usually of high quality and potency. If you want to examine your purchases up close, they do sell budscopes here. This generally signals the shop's confidence in their product. They also offer pre-rolled joints, and are also known for their weed brownies (edibles). Additionally, it is of note that they have a "de Verdamper" vaporizer.

Cannabis aside, La Tertulia appears to be quite serious about their non-medicated menu too. It features gourmet coffees, teas, juices, and a variety of snacks. You will also find a selection of hot "toasties" and other sandwiches if you are seeking more of a light meal. Al fresco dining, indeed.

COFFEESHOPS

CONNOISSEUR GUIDE: AMSTERDAM

COFFEESHOPS

SHOP FEATURES

SHOP HOURS:

Mon-Thur
9:00am-11:00pm
Fri-Sat:
9:00am-12:00am
Sun:
10:00am-11:00pm

LOFT

ADDRESS: Jan van Galenstraat 285, Amsterdam (Oost)

MAP IT

The LoFt coffeeshop is located on Jan van Galenstraat, near the southwest corner of Erasmuspark. This is De Baarsjes, a trendy section of Amsterdam West. The surrounding area is strongly residential, but also hosts an ample collection of small cafés, restaurants, and independent shops. This is a hip neighborhood, as noted by its increasing popularity with the artsy and young professional crowds alike. It is well worth a stroll around.

The Shop

The look and feel of this particular coffeeshop is best described as an "urban café". One of the first things you will notice as you approach the shop is the small outdoor seating area. A few planters provide some privacy, so you feel like you are dining street-side or "al fresco". Inside, the café vibe continues. There is a small smoking lounge in front. The floor walls and trim are mostly wood. The main glass window runs nearly floor-to-ceiling, and lets in a ton of natural light. It all makes this place quite comfortable and open.

The Menu

The same group that owns Siberië, De Republiek, and De Supermarkt Coffeeshops also owns the LoFt. The management is generally quite serious about their cannabis menu. On the weed side, expect a mix of high quality strains. They generally include a selection of contemporary items, some of the same genetics that you would encounter in Colorado or California, USA. The hashish-side of the menu is also formidable. Expect to see some flavorful, soft, and potent imports, and possibly domestic isolators as well. It is also worth noting that this shop is one of very few in Amsterdam that publishes potency and cannabinoid profile testing on their items. This should provide a lot more insight into what you are consuming. If you do not see the reports, ask at the counter.

COFFEESHOPS

COFFEESHOPS

SHOP FEATURES

SHOP HOURS:

Daily:
12:00pm-12:00am

LOS ANGELES

ADDRESS: Derde Oosterparkstraat 142 /BG, Amsterdam (Oost)

MAP IT

Coffeeshop Los Angeles is located in the Oosterpark-buurt section of Amsterdam East. This translates into the neighborhood around Amsterdam's "Eastern Park", one of city's lush and expansive green areas. The streets surrounding Los Angeles Coffeeshop are largely residential, mainly hosting apartment buildings, with the occasional business on the ground level. As expected in an area like this, the clientele is largely local. However, we have always found this shop to be welcoming to city visitors.

The Shop

While this Moroccan-owned coffeeshop may be far from California, it carries a slight West Coast vibe. Well, perhaps not contemporary Los Angeles. The theme here is best described as American Wild West - the days of cowboys and gunslingers. The furnishings in here are basic, but suitable. Wooden tables and chairs, as you would expect of any decent Old-West saloon. The vibe is down to earth, no pretenses here. They do have a billiards table though, and a TV if you want to catch a game.

The Menu

The cannabis menu at Coffeeshop Los Angeles is fairly small, which is common with the more local shops. However, the selection is diverse, at least on the weed-side. They tend to stock not only Amsterdam mainstay (old school) strains, but also some contemporary West Coast USA genetics, such as they Kush hybrids so popular in the California marijuana scene. The hash side of the menu is even smaller, but has the standard imported varieties from Morocco and other parts.

Aside from cannabis, this shop also makes some good coffee and tea, and has a decent selection of basic snacks in case you need something to hold you over.

Amsterdam's Eastern (Ooster) Park

COFFEESHOPS

SHOP FEATURES

SHOP HOURS:

Daily:
10:00am-1:00am

MASSAWA

ADDRESS: Chasséstraat 4, Amsterdam (West)

MAP IT

Coffeeshop Massawa is located in the Chassébuurt neighborhood in Amsterdam West. This is a largely residential area, which was recently redeveloped to bring in residents with greater income diversity, and to be a more family and community-oriented place. Though there are a fair amount of businesses here on the ground level of many of the apartments, it is still a fairly quiet area, and can be a nice place to take a stroll. Massawa is in a beautiful corner location in this neighborhood, right on the wide Kostverlorenvaart Canal.

The Shop

This coffeeshop takes its name from Massawa, a coastal African city that was once a key location in the Ottoman Empire. Today it is part of the independent country of Eritrea, though its rich history is still celebrated. The owners here are Moroccan, though we would be hard pressed to say there is a strong Moroccan theme in this establishment. The shop logo is a camel smoking a large hookah. That aside, the hardwood floors, polished wood trim, and circular "grand bar" make this place feel much more like an upscale neighborhood pub or hotel bar than a coffeeshop with any particular theme. It is a simple but nice place; very well maintained.

The building here is fairly big. As such, they host a large smoking lounge at Coffeeshop Massawa. Seating is mainly in the form of comfortable leather-cushioned benches, as well as high top tables and bar stools. There are also some extras in here including a jukebox and flat screen tv's, if you want to pick the music or catch a game. There is an additional glass-enclosed smoking room. This is so tobacco smoking (mixed joints) can be permitted on premises separate from other customers as well as staff. The tobacco smoking room at Coffeeshop Massawa is large, comfortable, and just as nice as the rest of the shop.

The Menu

The cannabis menu is fairly small here. This is likely owing to the largely local clientele. With such shops we usually see a tight selection that the regulars are accustomed to, versus having an extensive menu that caters more to strain-hunting tourists. On the weed-side, you are likely to find mainly Amsterdam old-school items here. For hashish, traditional imported pressed varieties, mainly from Morocco. If we were to choose, we would say the shop probably favors hashish. If indecisive, go with that. Lastly, Coffeeshop Massawa has an extensive drink menu, if you are looking for some refreshments.

COFFEESHOPS

CONNOISSEUR GUIDE: AMSTERDAM

COFFEESHOPS

SHOP FEATURES

SHOP HOURS:
Daily:
9:00am-1:00am

MEDITERRANÉ

ADDRESS: Spuistraat 80, Amsterdam (Centrum)

MAP IT

Coffeeshop Mediterrané is located on Spuistraat, which runs north-to-south inside the canal ring of Amsterdam Centrum. This is an extremely busy road that receives an enormous amount of foot traffic. Off Spuistraat, one can find easy access to popular points of interest in Amsterdam such as Centraal Station, Dam Square, the Royal Palace, De Nieuwe Kerk (The New Church), and Spui Square, to name just a few. If you are visiting the city center, there is a good chance you will find yourself walking past Coffeeshop Mediterrané at some point.

The Shop

Living up to its name, there is a Mediterranean theme in this establishment. First, on the outside of Coffeeshop Mediterrané you will notice its two large overhead signs, which display a small tropical island. The shop is wrapped in painted murals displaying theme-related scenery on the inside… a little bit desert, a little bit tropical. Small tables and wicker seats add a "poolside" feel to round out the theme. The room here is narrow and long, with ample seating. There is also a separate glass-enclosed smoking room to one side. Tobacco consumption (mixed joints) is allowed in there.

The Menu

The cannabis menu at Coffeeshop Mediterrané is usually moderate in size. You will probably find a half dozen items or so on each side of the menu. For weed, they have a lot of the old-school genetics that made Amsterdam famous. They are probably more focused on hashish though. On this side of the menu, they seem to be big on Moroccan imports. If you are in the market, it is probably worth taking a look at the offerings. They also have pre-rolls and space cake.

There is also an ample menu of teas, coffees, juices, soda, and basic snacks here.

SHOP FEATURES

SHOP HOURS:
Daily:
10:00am-12:00am

MAP IT

MILLENNIUM

Jan Hanzenstraat 109, Amsterdam (West) **:ADDRESS**

Coffeeshop Millennium is found in the Kinkerbuurt section of Amsterdam Oud-West (Old West). This triangular neighborhood is essentially bordered on all sides by canals, though technically the area's main shopping street of Kinkerstraat marks its southern edge (a few blocks short of the canal). This part of the city runs at a slower pace than the centrum, is a bit more green, and largely residential.

The Shop

Being in a residential area, Coffeeshop Millennium largely caters to a local crowd. Most use it as a quick and affordable buy-and-fly location. However, if you are looking to stay a while they do have a nice seating area in the back. Their Moroccan roots shine through here, with beautiful paintings of camels on the walls, and themed couches and décor lining the smoking room. The place is chill, comfortable and unpretentious.

They also have a billiards table at this coffeeshop, undeniably the main attraction of the smoking area. With space being such a premium in a city like Amsterdam, it is fairly uncommon to find one inside a coffeeshop. If we had to sum up the vibe in here, we would say it reminds us of a down-to-earth local pool bar. A cool hangout spot, for sure.

The Menu

For a locals' place, the cannabis menu at Coffeeshop Millennium is fairly robust. They are likely to have roughly a dozen items on the weed-side. While these are mainly old-school (long established) Amsterdam favorites, you will probably see some modern genetics creeping in here as well. The menu is not quite as large on the hashish-side, maybe a half dozen options. These are mainly traditional imported pressed varieties, from Morocco and other regions. They also have space cake here, and several pre-rolled options.

COFFEESHOPS

SHOP FEATURES

SHOP HOURS:

Daily:
10:00am-1:00am

MR. K & CO.

ADDRESS: Tweede Laurierdwarsstraat 44C, Amsterdam (Centrum)

MAP IT

Mr. K Coffeeshop is found on Tweede Laurierdwarsstraat, which is the second cross street of Laurierstraat (translates into Laurel street). It is located in the Jordaan district, which is a famous neighborhood full of high-end boutiques and even higher-end real estate prices. Mr. K rests on a relatively quiet residential block here. It blends in well with the surrounding upscale neighborhood, perhaps even standing out a bit with its intricate and polished wood façade and beautiful stained glass windows.

The Shop

The interior of Mr. K is more basic than its outer appearance lets on. Inside, it is a fairly traditional Dutch coffeeshop. There are not a lot of frills. Instead, the décor is mainly in the form of posters and a multitude of small statues, bits of pottery, tribal masks, and other trinkets on display. Though a small shop, they have several distinct forms of seating including wooden chairs, benches, and a couple of rocking chairs.

There is also a very comfortable pillow-filled nook and elevated couch in the upstairs glass-enclosed smoking room, arguably the shop's prime seating. Additionally, you will find outdoor seating in the form of a single bench. We would not say this is the best location for people watching, nor does Mr. K have a stunning view. Still, this is a peaceful neighborhood, and a rest here might be called for.

The Menu

The cannabis menu at Mr. K is moderate is size. They tend to list under ten strains of flower (weed), and perhaps a half dozen types of hashish (concentrate). Do not be mistaken, however, into thinking the lack of an extensive selection equates to a lack of interest in their products. To the contrary, they seem to be about quality here, and even feature name brand genetics on their menu. The pricing tends to be reasonable as well, as this is not a shop that is inundated with tourists. Mr. K also needs to cater to a local clientele, which to their credit do seem to keep coming back.

COFFEESHOPS

CONNOISSEUR GUIDE: AMSTERDAM

COFFEESHOPS

SHOP FEATURES

SHOP HOURS:
Daily:
10:00am-1:00am

NACHTEGAAL

ADDRESS: Krugerplein 22, Amsterdam (Oost)

MAP IT

Coffeeshop Nachtegaal is a small take-away only establishment, which is found in the Transvaalbuurt section of Amsterdam Oost (East). The surrounding area is largely residential. The streets are tree-lined and host large apartment buildings, small parks, and playgrounds, and are surprisingly quiet for being in such a large city. They even have some stretches of brick road here. It is quite a beautiful part of Amsterdam.

The Shop

In English, Nachtegaal translates into "nightingale". You will notice the nightingale, a small bird found in Europe and parts of Asia and Africa, featured on the shop logo. It is known particularly for the beautiful song of the male bird, typically heard at night. While we are not entirely certain why this name was chosen for the coffeeshop, we suspect it has something to do with celebrating your night on the town. For many, of course, that means having some bud or hash to top it off.

The Menu

Being a small buy-and-fly shop that caters almost exclusively to local residents, they do not host a very large cannabis menu here. Expect to find three to four items on each side (weed, hashish). The weed stock is very traditional here; famous old-school Amsterdam strains along the lines of White Widow and Amnesia. The hashish is, as well. You will find a few pressed imported varieties from the regular source countries. They also have pre-rolls and "space bonbons" at Coffeeshop Nachtegaal, the latter being a nice change of pace from the usual offerings.

You can grab a coffee or soda on your way out as well, but they do not really specialize in the extras here. This place is really about one thing: keeping the locals happy with quality cannabis at low prices.

SHOP FEATURES

COFFEESHOPS

SHOP HOURS:

Daily:
9:00am-1:00am

MAP IT

NEW TIMES

Spuistraat 260, Amsterdam (Centrum) **:ADDRESS**

New Times Coffeeshop is found on Spuistraat, not far from the Amsterdam Historical Museum. It is a few blocks north of Spui Square, which is regarded as a main cultural center for the city. The surrounding neighborhood is dotted with a dense collection of small bookstores, cafés, and boutiques. Like many businesses in the area, New Times has an independent, small shop feel to it. It fits right in around here. It exists on one level, so it is not quite considered expansive. What this coffeeshop lacks in size, however, it seems to make up for in other areas, like with its décor.

The Shop

New Times would be best described as a modern coffeeshop. The interior is polished. Clean hardwood floors line the room, and the shop is accented with purple lighting and trim. They use recessed lighting, and a variety of other contemporary fixtures in here. Seating is provided in the form of leather-topped chairs. These are quite plush and comfortable to sit in. The wood is dark. The walls are papered with Arabian-themed images. These little touches are lovely; though perhaps tie in together even more nicely. Few shops display such attention to detail.

If you prefer some fresh air, New Times also has the benefit of a large sidewalk out front. When the weather is nice, the shop is sure to take advantage of it. Typically, they will put several wooden table and chair sets outside. Spuistraat is a very busy thoroughfare for foot traffic, making the New Times "al fresco" seating section a perfect place to relax and people watch.

The Menu

The cannabis menu is fairly comprehensive at this coffeeshop. They tend to stock roughly a dozen strains of weed (flower), and nearly as many varieties of hashish (concentrate). On occasion you may see a competition winning strain here, or at the very least some contemporary imported genetics from the USA. They also sell pre-rolled joints as well as some space cakes.

For the non-cannabis related offerings, they appear to be pretty big into coffee here. If that is not to your taste, they also sell a variety of teas, juices, and soft drinks. New Times also makes great milkshakes, and has enough by way of basic snacks to keep guests sated. Nobody likes to leave a good time just to satisfy the munchies, after all.

COFFEESHOPS

SHOP FEATURES

SHOP HOURS:

Daily:
10:00am-1:00am

NICE PLACE

ADDRESS: Van Ostadestraat 290, Amsterdam (Zuid)

MAP IT

Coffeeshop Nice Place is located in the Nieuwe Pijp (New Pipe) section of Amsterdam Zuid (South). Generally speaking, the Pijp area is quite lively; a city hotspot. However, this particular coffeeshop is found on a quiet, brick tree-lined road near Sarphatipark (City Park), in an almost exclusively residential neighborhood. As such, Coffeeshop Nice Place is largely for locals. That stated, we have always found the business to be very welcoming of city visitors.

The Shop

The name of this shop is to the point: Nice Place. This begs the obvious question, is it actually a nice place to visit? We would have to say "Yes." The interior of this shop is fairly large, contemporary, and well-appointed. Comfortable leather benches and chairs make up the seating. The wood trim - clean and polished. White tile floors and a large front window make the place feel open and bright. It all comes together nicely and gives you the feeling of being at a local café or small restaurant.

The Menu

The cannabis menu is modest in size at Coffeeshop Nice Place. This is expected of shops that cater mainly to local residents. For them, it is usually more important to have a consistent product at a good price, than to try and stock a large menu for strain-hunting tourists. There is usually about half a dozen items on the weed-side… mainly old school items. For hashish, a bit less. These again are usually traditional imports. Uniquely, they also have both banana and chocolate space cakes. Most small shops in this part of town will only stock a chocolate cake option. Note: this shop also has an enclosed area for smoking, which means that tobacco consumption is permitted on premises.

Coffeeshop Nice Place also has a robust drink and snack menu. Granted, it consists mainly of the basic coffees and packaged goods - soda, juice, energy drinks, teas, candy bars, a baked good or two… but all together you are looking at dozens of options.

Monument in Sarphatipark

COFFEESHOPS

SHOP FEATURES

SHOP HOURS:

Daily:
9:00am-12:00am

NIEUW AMSTERDAM

ADDRESS: Hoofdweg 226, Amsterdam (West)

MAP IT

Coffeeshop Nieuw Amsterdam is found in the De Baarsjes area of Amsterdam West. The neighborhood here is fairly residential, with a moderate mix of businesses on the ground level of many of the buildings. This shop was once known as Coffeeshop Sinbad but has since been renamed. As you may have guessed, the new name of this coffeeshop means "New Amsterdam" in English. Although there has been an "Old Amsterdam" coffeeshop for quite a long time now, to have another coffeeshop named after the city was perhaps overdue.

The Shop

When walking into Coffeeshop Nieuw Amsterdam, you will see an extravagantly decorated service counter on your left. In the first area of the shop you can grab coffee, some smoke, and roll joints while sitting on the bar stools on the side of the ordering counter. You can relax and grab a snack or drink from vending machines. If you keep walking just a few more feet, you will see a glass-enclosed tobacco-friendly room in the back.

The décor inside Coffeeshop Nieuw Amsterdam is a bit artsy, a bit funky. Let's pick out a few features that stand out in its smoking lounge... dark marble tile on the floors, purple accent lighting, comfortable plush couches with vibrant abstract printed fabric. This place feels very much like a small artsy nightclub, the likes of which you might find in Los Angeles or New York. It is intimate, colorful, and hip. This is a hang out place, for sure.

The Menu

The cannabis menu is sizable at Coffeeshop Nieuw Amsterdam. Expect to find a dozen or so choices on the weed (flower) side. They favor Amsterdam old-school favorites here, and seem to especially love their Haze strains. The hashish-side of the menu is not quite as robust, about half the size. It still has enough to choose from for most visitors. These are largely imported pressed hashish varieties, from places like Morocco and Afghanistan. There are plenty of pre-rolled joint options here too.

COFFEESHOPS

CONNOISSEUR GUIDE: AMSTERDAM

COFFEESHOPS

SHOP FEATURES

SHOP HOURS:
Daily:
9:00am-1:00am

NOGAL WIEDES

ADDRESS: Czaar Peterstraat 122, Amsterdam (Noord)

MAP IT

Nogal Wiedes Coffeeshop in located in a quiet residential neighborhood in Amsterdam Noord (North) called Czaar Peterbuurt. It is right near the Het Funen, which translates roughly into "The Fun". This part of the city is home to the famous Funenpark. It is not quite a park though, but a recently built architectural development project, in the middle of a lovely green area. The homes are stunningly abstract. If you are in the area and want to see something unique and creative, we highly recommend it. Better yet; take the walk to Funenpark after visiting a local coffeeshop and go in a creative state of mind. You might appreciate it even more.

The Shop

Nogal Wiedes is a small coffeeshop that primarily serves as a take-and-go location. A large counter with a glass partition greets you as you enter, where you make your purchase. If you are looking to chill a bit, fret not. There are two small smoking rooms behind the counter. While each area only has one table and can seat just a handful of people, each has a good amount of privacy to enjoy here. Each table also has its own flat screen television, so this is not a bare minimum experience. Note that you can enjoy mixed tobacco weed/hash joints in Nogal Wiedes. The smoking area is closed off from the rest of the shop including the staff, so to comply with EU smoking regulations.

The Menu

The cannabis menu is moderate in size at Nogal Wiedes. For flower (weed), they usually carry a bit shy of a dozen strains. These are mostly old-school favorites. The hash menu is much smaller, just several options to choose from. Again traditional items; imported pressed hashish from the usual countries. As one would expect from a shop that supplies mainly the neighborhoods residents, the pricing is much more reasonable here than most shops in the tourist-packed city centrum.

SHOP FEATURES

SHOP HOURS:

Daily:
10:00am-1:00am

COFFEESHOPS

MAP IT

PACIFIC

Balthasar Floriszstraat 10, Amsterdam (Zuid) **:ADDRESS**

Coffeeshop Pacific is located in Duivelseiland, one of the smallest neighborhoods in Amsterdam Zuid (South). It is situated between the Museum Quarter, and the lively De Pijp area. Duivelseiland is "Devil's Island" translated into English. This part of the city is named after the former and infamous French prison colony in Guiana. We are not exactly sure why. The picturesque brick, tree-lined streets that make up this beautiful residential neighborhood seem anything but sinister.

The Shop

This establishment is found at the corner of a large red brick building. On the outside, the look of the place is classic modern brick. The inside, however, is far more contemporary. The color scheme of Coffeeshop Pacific is a bit industrial: black, grey, and off white. The comfortable black leather-topped benches, light-colored wooden stools, and polished tables make you feel as if you are in a gourmet bakery or café. Add a large screen TV, some track lighting, and a few classic paintings, and you have got one impressive smoking lounge.

The Menu

The cannabis menu is fairly small here. Coffeeshop Pacific is mainly a locals' place. Shops like these tend to focus more on consistency than variety. The weed-side of the menu is going to feature mostly old-school strains; Amsterdam favorites. The hashish-side, traditional imported pressed varieties from Morocco and other parts. They have plenty of pre-rolled joint options too, and a fairly good selection of basic coffees, drinks, and snacks. Pricing tends to be reasonable, which you would expect from the less tourist-focused shops.

COFFEESHOPS

SHOP FEATURES

SHOP HOURS:
Mon-Fri:
8:00am-1:00am
Sat:
9:00am-1:00am
Sun:
10:00am-1:00am

PAPILLON

ADDRESS: Van der Helstplein 8, Amsterdam (Zuid)

MAP IT

Papillon Coffeeshop is located on Van der Helstplein, in Amsterdam-Zuid (south). This shop is found in a busy square, lined by many small cafés, bars, and restaurants. On most evenings the immediate area around this shop is crowded, and lively with activity. You will find many young people shuffling from place to place, enjoying the night out. If you are looking for someplace to go in the evening but are not exactly sure where, this neighborhood is worth considering.

The Shop

The inside of Papillon is modern in appearance. Though not especially large, the main lounge area is open and lined with comfortable leather couches. Small, square tables are in front of each. The room has a very cubic and contemporary feel to it. You could easily see this as the waiting area for an advertising agency, or luxury car dealership. On one side of Papillon, there is also a glass-enclosed smoking room, so this shop accommodates those with a preference for mixed (tobacco/cannabis) joints.

The Menu

The cannabis menu at Papillon is moderate in size. On the concentrate (hashish) side, there are usually several options; some classic hard-pressed imports. The flower (weed) side tends to be more robust, usually featuring a decent mix of recognized city favorites. Pricing here tends to be a bit more reasonable than in the center of the city as well, as expected of a shop that caters more to local students and residents. Worry not if you are a visitor to the city. Papillon sees its fair share of tourist traffic too. This tends to be a welcoming place. We found quite a diverse crowd during our visits.

There are also plenty of juices, sodas, and other drinks and snacks on the menu here. They make some pretty good coffee too.

Van der Helstplein, Amsterdam Zuid

COFFEESHOPS

SHOP FEATURES

SHOP HOURS:
Daily:
10:00am-8:00pm

PARADOX

ADDRESS: Eerste Bloemdwarsstraat 2R, Amsterdam (Centrum)

MAP IT

Paradox Coffeeshop is located on Eerste Bloemdwarsstraat (the first cross street of Bloemstraat), just west of the central canal ring. This coffeeshop resides on a largely residential block in the Jordaan district. The neighborhood and main streets that surround Paradox are often very busy. The block that Paradox is found on, however, is generally much more quiet. As such, this shop can be a nice respite from the hustle and bustle of Amsterdam.

The Shop

The interior of Paradox is chill and artsy. When you walk in, you will immediately notice that they feature the work of local artists. A unique feature here is the enormous cartoon that stretches along the wall on the left. It is fun and upbeat. Next, perhaps the oldest feature in the room, is the exposed brick (opposite wall) which gives Paradox an urban-industrial yet warm atmosphere.

This coffeeshop is a true "chill out" place. The furniture is comfortable (especially the couches) and the music is hip (we think so anyway) - management makes an effort to keep the customers happy. If you are up for a game, look around. Backgammon, chess, and others are available. Want a snack? They have everything from milkshakes to chocolate chip cookies, and of course, a diverse assortment of coffees, teas, juices, soft drinks, and other treats. A testament to how celebrated this place is, is the local clientele. Though Paradox is very popular with tourists, you are likely to find just as many Jordaan locals hanging out here.

The Menu

The cannabis menu is not extensive at Paradox. They usually have less than ten strains of weed (flower), and maybe half that on the hashish (concentrate) side. Though the stock is limited, we have found the quality to be very good. They sell pre-rolled joints, both mixed and pure. We generally do not recommend pre-rolls as they are sometimes made from the lowest quality stock. We have not noticed that issue, however, at Paradox.

This shop is also well known for its cake edibles. However, you should be warned. They put a full gram of cannabis in each piece. In case you are unaware, that is quite a lot. These are STRONG, far more potent than you generally see in Amsterdam. We advise consuming just a little at first if you are not used to higher-dose edibles. Also, if your preferred method of consumption is vaping, this coffeeshop also features a pair of Volcano vaporizers. This makes Paradox a great Vapor Lounge too. We highly recommend this coffeeshop if that is your thing.

COFFEESHOPS

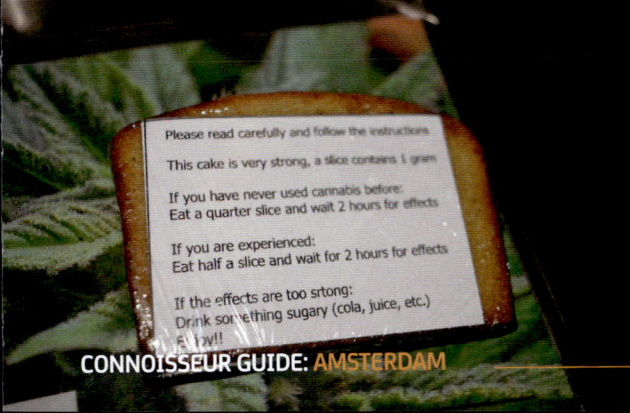

CONNOISSEUR GUIDE: AMSTERDAM

COFFEESHOPS

SHOP FEATURES

SHOP HOURS:

Daily:
10:00am-1:00am

POPEYE

ADDRESS: Haarlemmerstraat 63, Amsterdam (Centrum)

MAP IT

Popeye Coffeeshop takes its name from the classic comic strip character "Popeye the Sailor Man". His image, along with that of beloved Olive Oyl and nemesis Bluto, can be found on the shop's three large, front windows. Popeye himself is also on the neon sign out front. Instead of holding a can of spinach, however, he is puffing on a big green water pipe. While Warner Brothers (distributor of the copyrighted work) might not appreciate a coffeeshop using the likeness of the character, they do not have any claim to it since the original Popeye comic strips entered public domain in the EU back in 2009.

The Shop

The interior is quite warm and welcoming. It is not large, but does have three distinct levels. The main floor has some chair and bench seating, as well as the counter for ordering cannabis, drinks, and hot food. There are additional seating areas on an elevated platform towards the back of the shop, as well as downstairs. One thing to note - while the cartoon characters can be found on the windows and menus, they are not really seen elsewhere in the shop. Furthermore, the décor is more of a cross between Indian and abstract art and makes for a very comfortable setting.

The Menu

The cannabis menu at Popeye Coffeeshop is fairly large.

In the weed section you will find a broad list of strains. There are many contemporary items here, which sit alongside traditional Amsterdam favorites. The hash selection is smaller, but still robust. The items are mainly imported pressed hashes from the usual places such as Morocco, India, and Nepal. You are also likely to find Nederhash here as well, also known as high potency bubble hash. Pricing can also be quite reasonable depending on what you order, but expect to pay for several "premium" choices.

Popeye also has a large breakfast menu, which is not common among Amsterdam coffeeshops. As one might guess, it can be especially popular in the mornings, serving eggs, pastries, and even a full English breakfast, to enjoy with your smoke.

Popeye Coffeeshop fits in nicely with the surrounding "trendy" neighborhood. Haarlemmerstraat is home to some of the city's higher-end coffeeshops, which tend to offer larger menus and more services to their customers. In this regard, Popeye does a good job of keeping pace with the competition.

King's Day Celebration

COFFEESHOPS

SHOP FEATURES

SHOP HOURS:

Daily:
7:00am-1:00am

PRIX D'AMI

ADDRESS: Haringpakkerssteeg 3, Amsterdam (Centrum)

MAP IT

Prix d'Ami Coffeeshop is located on Haringpakkerssteeg (Herring Packers Alley). It would be hard to describe this street as anything but an alley. It is short and narrow. Even so, it can be quite busy with travelers. Haringpakkerssteeg connects the Damrak, a main artery into the city center, with Nieuwendijk, an extremely popular shopping street.

The Shop

It is difficult to tell from the outside, but Prix d'Ami is massive. It is, in fact, the largest coffeeshop in Amsterdam. It can probably hold a couple hundred people, if not more. This shop exists on three floors, and has a total of six separate rooms. The décor is modern and carried throughout. Where there is seating, you will find either plush silver leather couches and stools, or wooden benches with silver leather cushions. The color palette, consisting of silver and purple, is quite pleasing, . We would definitely describe Prix as more of a marijuana nightclub than a traditional Dutch cannabis bar.

This coffeeshop is rich on amenities. For starters, it is the only shop with a 3D movie lounge, located in a room on the top floor. This is a nice touch for those who just want to watch something (usually weed-themed) and chill out. They have a billiards hall in here as well. If you are into music, check their schedule. On many evenings they have a live DJ.

How about food or drink? They have wait staff, servicing each room, ready to assist. It is of note that the menu options are quite broad on both counts. For beverages, you can order just about anything you can think of including sodas, coffee, fresh mint tea, hot chocolate, juices, and smoothies. The food menu is equally impressive, offering a full range of sandwiches, toasties, paninis, salads, pizzas, gourmet burgers, some entrées, and desserts. Visit Prix d'Ami Coffeeshop in the morning, and you will find they also serve eggs and pancakes, as well as a full English breakfast.

The Menu

With regard to cannabis, Prix d'Ami has an extensive menu. They offer the greatest variety on the weed-side, where you will typically find listed upwards of a dozen strains. The selection here includes a few traditional old-school favorites, but mainly contemporary items. There are several choices on the hashish-side, usually traditional pressed items from places like Afghanistan, Morocco, and Nepal. In addition, they offer a variety of pre-rolled pure and mixed joints, and space cakes.

COFFEESHOPS

CONNOISSEUR GUIDE: AMSTERDAM

COFFEESHOPS

SHOP FEATURES

SHOP HOURS:

Sun-Thurs:
9:30am-12:00am

Fri-Sat:
9:30am-1:00am

REEFER

ADDRESS: Sint Antoniesbreestraat 77, Amsterdam (Centrum)

MAP IT

Reefer Coffeeshop is found on Sint Antoniesbreestraat (St. Anthony's Broad Street). It is located south of Nieuwmarkt, right near Rembrandthuis (Rembrandt House). This area of the city feels a touch more residential than the very center of Amsterdam, with a few more trees and a bit less traffic. Still, this is a popular shopping district, and boasts many small boutiques and specialty shops.

The Shop

Reefer is hard to miss if you are looking for it. Two large red neon signs serve as beacons for finding the place. The décor at Reefer is quite traditional for a Dutch coffeeshop. Polished wood dominates the interior. This establishment is reminiscent of a craft brewery, or perhaps a neighborhood bar or restaurant. Although not especially large, there is ample room here. Reefer exists on a split level layout. Most seating is found on the main floor and on an elevated balcony above.

Below, you will find the bar for ordering cannabis products, as well as a variety of drinks and snacks. Overall, the vibe is chill. This shop seems to be quite popular with locals, who may prefer the absence of frills which cater to tourists. That is not to say this coffeeshop is for locals only. To the contrary, you are likely to find a diverse crowd here.

The Menu

Reefer tends to have a small-to-moderate sized cannabis menu, with a fair selection of both weed (flower) and hashish (concentrate) options. While they do not seem to keep up with trendy strains and the latest cup winners here, they do seem to focus on quality. They also appear to be a more value-centered coffeeshop, catering more to locals, who are much more likely to be price-conscious.

Rembrandt House Museum

COFFEESHOPS

SHOP FEATURES

SHOP HOURS:

Daily:
9:30am-12:00am

RELAX

ADDRESS: Binnen Oranjestraat 9, Amsterdam (Centrum)

MAP IT

Relax Coffeeshop is located on Binnen Oranjestraat (Orange Interior Street), in the city's famous Jordaan district. The Jordaan is a very popular part of the city, known for its picturesque canals and historic buildings. Most streets see a great deal of foot traffic. While Relax is not an exception, it does reside on a small side street, in a quieter and more residential neighborhood. The atmosphere here is somewhat more relaxed, which perhaps ties into the meaning behind the name of the coffeeshop. Just a block to the north is Haarlemmerstraat, however, which is perhaps among the busiest streets in the area.

The Shop

The décor of Relax is very traditional for a Dutch coffeeshop. You will not find a lot of frills here. Instead, it is like your average neighborhood bar. Between the tables, chairs, leather-topped benches, flooring, bar, and wall trim - there is a lot of wood inside. The shop is clean, comfortable, and well maintained. Relax does sit on the corner of its block, which is a nice feature. It allows the place to have two large windows in front, one on each side. These let in a lot of light, which makes this place feel very open and warm. It also makes it feel a bit larger than it actually is.

The Menu

Relax has a digital cannabis menu. On this you will find a moderate number of flower (weed) and hashish (concentrate) varieties. On the weed-side, they tend to favor old-school genetics here. For hashish, traditional pressed imports. They also offer many of their cannabis products in pre-rolled joints. If you prefer vaporization to smoking, they also have a Volcano vaporizer available for use.

In addition to cannabis products, one will find a long list of basic drinks and snacks. They also make some decent coffee, for sure.

COFFEESHOPS

COFFEESHOPS

SHOP FEATURES

SHOP HOURS:

Daily:
8:00am-1:00am

RELAX ZUID

ADDRESS: Vechtstraat 9, Amsterdam (Zuid)

MAP IT

Relax Zuid coffeeshop is found on Vechtstraat, in the Ijsselbuurt neighborhood of Amsterdam South (Zuid). This is a quiet residential area on the Amstel River, which is mainly occupied by a mix of contemporary and historic multi-floor apartment homes. Relax is just a block from the Amstel canal, and not far from the lively De Pijp section of the city. In contrast, however, there are not a lot of businesses here. Ijsselbuurt is the type of place you may take a stroll to when you want to get away from the crowds for a while. We would say the name of this coffeeshop is appropriate.

The Shop

This coffeeshop was formerly known as Het Wolkje, or "The Cloud" in English. It was a no-frills take-away-only location, which hosted a modest cannabis menu, and catered mainly to local residents. It has since been taken over by new management, specifically the owners of Relax Coffeeshop in Amsterdam Centrum. They have rebranded the shop as Relax Zuid (South). With the takeover, the place has been completely remodeled, and the cannabis menu greatly expanded. There is little in here to recognize from the previous establishment.

The new Relax location looks a lot like a small USA cannabis dispensary... perhaps with a hint of spa to it. There is a lot of light-colored wood inside, which is accentuated by the tile flooring and soft hanging lights. Cannabis products are neatly on display behind the counter in glass jars. It all feels very clean and modern. While the room is open for customers now, it is not really a smoking lounge. Rather, you will find a couple of stools and counters/tables in here, more than suitable for you to stop and roll a joint at. You can order a coffee as well, though you will probably end up hanging out somewhere else.

The Menu

The Cannabis menu at Relax Coffeeshop is decidedly larger than its predecessor. On the weed-side, you will typically find more than a dozen strains. The genetics here will range widely, from low potency imports usually reserved for cannabis newcomers, to the types of high-THC varieties you tend to find in USA dispensaries. In-between, you will notice recognized Amsterdam classics. The quality is generally very good. The hashish menu is smaller, though also tends to have a nice selection. These range from traditional imports, to more potent domestic isolator (nederhasj) varieties. Relax has also been working with a good supplier for their edibles as of late. They are not only tasty, but also especially potent. Eat a half or quarter of something first, if you are new to edibles.

Relax
COFFEESHOP
AMSTERDAM

Analysis Report
Batch # 183871
Client Relax, Amsterdam
Date 21st September, 2018
Sample Material Strawberry Banana Kush
Test Method HPLC
Test Type Full Spectrum
Test Environment 19.5 °C / 57% Hum
Cannabinoid Content
THC 0.97
THC (a) 20.11
THC - V 0.37
CBN 0.01
Total THC* 18.61
CBD 0.09
CBD (a) 0.38
CBG 0.66
CBC 0.07
Total CBD* 0.42
Terpenes
mg/g
Beta-Caryoph 0.74
Alpha-Pinene 1.08
Beta-Pinene 0
Myrcene 0.83
Limonene 0
Camphene 0
Geraniol
Linalool
Terpinolene
Eucalyptol
Humulene

Relax

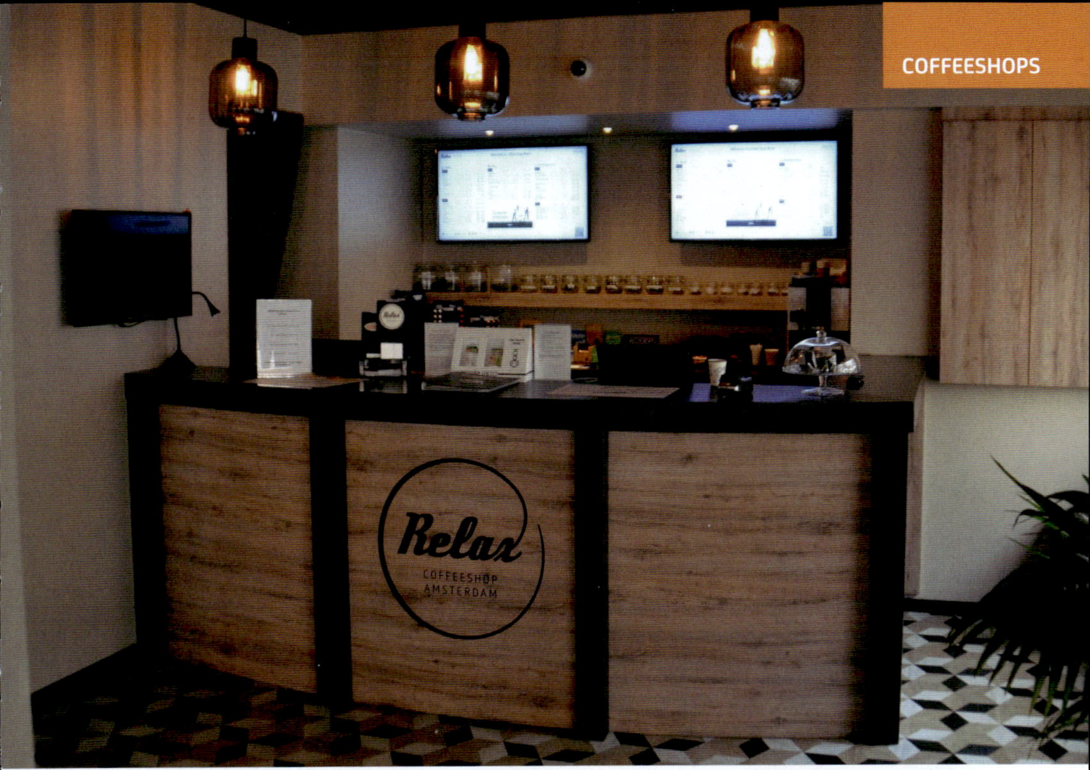

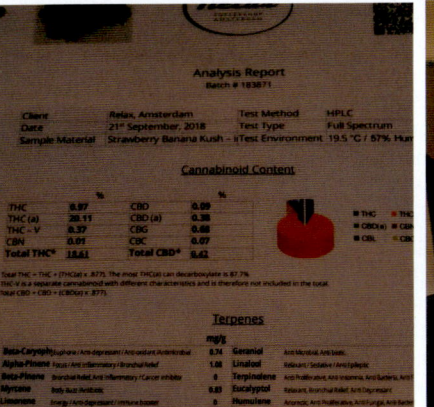

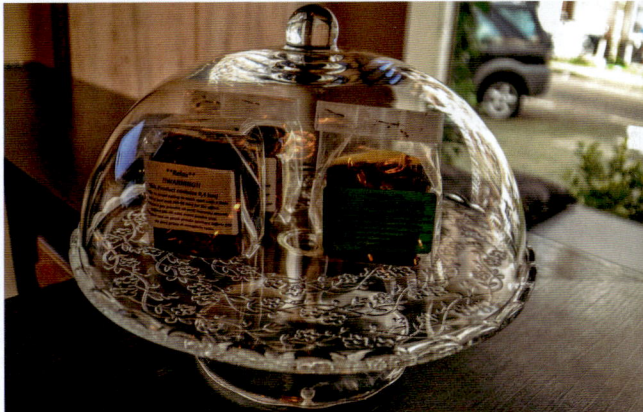

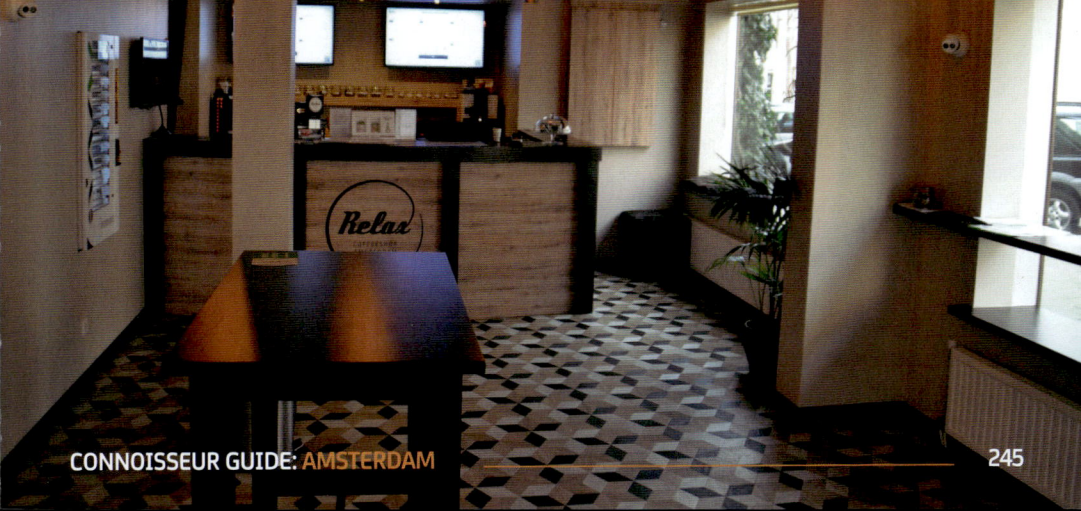

COFFEESHOPS

SHOP FEATURES

SHOP HOURS:

Mon-Fri:
6:00pm-1:00am
Sat-Sun:
7:00pm-1:00am

RESIN

ADDRESS: Hekelveld 7, Amsterdam (Centrum)

MAP IT

Resin Coffeeshop is located on Hekelveld, a small square just a short walk south from Centraal Station. It is found at the north end of Spuistraat, where the street forks off from Martelaarsgracht (Martyrs Canal). Like most parts of Amsterdam, there is a lot of history here. One important event is memorialized on a stone and bronze monument, which can be found to the southeast of the shop. It is a tribute to Annick van Hardeveld, a courier for the Allied Resistance who was shot and killed by the Grüne Polizei at this location in 1945. This is a busy part of the city so do not let the hustle and bustle cause you to overlook the rich history and architectural beauty of this area.

The Shop

In the front of Resin is a small room with counter for ordering. This part of the shop is not particularly special. However, behind it is a large partitioned-off lounge, which we would say is. This part of the shop is artsy and extremely chill. In fact, we included Resin coffeeshop amongst our list of favorite establishments when it comes to layout and décor. The first thing that jumps out are the colors: lime green and brown. Long wood and leather bench seating lines much of the room. There are "tiered level" bench seating in the back, and small brown stools and tables throughout.

You will find beautifully hand-painted artwork depicting nature scenes wrapped-around the shop. Among it are prominent figures in the cannabis world, such as Bob Marley and Snoop Dogg. The music tends to be upbeat but chill - a mix of reggae, classic rap, and modern hip-hop. Both artists come up with some frequency. The lounge also features a small balcony section, which you will find at the top of a narrow tall staircase. You can look down into the main room from here…a room we would describe as "Miami night club" inspired. The back of the room also has an indoor swing. We are pretty sure this is the only coffeeshop in Amsterdam with one which makes this quite an unusual feature.

The Menu

The cannabis menu tends to be a fairly even split between weed and hashish (concentrate) products here, roughly about ten of each. The weed items are likely to be a mix of contemporary strains, and the old-school varieties the locals favor. Though they do stock a good variety of weed, the shop has a stronger reputation for hashish. On this side of the menu you will likely find a variety of imported pressed hashes, and stronger local isolates. They also sell pre-rolled joints and space cakes here, if you are looking for something a bit simpler to use.

COFFEESHOPS

CONNOISSEUR GUIDE: AMSTERDAM

COFFEESHOPS

SHOP FEATURES

SHOP HOURS:

Sun-Thurs:
8:00am-1:00am

Fri-Sat:
8:00am-2:00am

RICK'S COFFEESHOP

ADDRESS: Oudezijds Voorburgwal 252, Amsterdam (Centrum)

MAP IT

Rick's Coffeeshop is located on the Oudezijds Voorburgwal, just to the south of Damstraat. This shop rests just outside the city's famous Red Light District, with Damstraat being one of the main thoroughfares in and out. There is a great deal of activity in this neighborhood, and likewise many restaurants, boutiques, and coffeeshops for visitors to choose from. In an area with so many coffeeshops, Rick's Coffeeshop stands out as a unique place.

The Shop

The shop itself is fairly basic. Not a lot of frills here, though it is known for having unusual bench seats from an old bus on the inside. It does make for an interesting place to hang out. There are even racks overhead if you want to rest your stuff, though perhaps it is not the best idea. Placing something out of visual contact before getting high is just not a good idea. For many, it will most certainly lead to leaving it behind. That risk aside, most customers take their purchases outside anyway.

It is here that we find Rick's two most notable features. The first thing that makes Rick's interesting is the outdoor seating. In addition to tables and chairs directly in front of the window, Rick's also has a nice stretch of seating on the other side of the street, directly on the canal. There are wide tables and chairs here, with some umbrellas for shade. This is a perfect place to sit and watch the boats and people go by. Not many coffeeshops offer such prime seating.

The second feature is the sister business next door, Rick's Café. This place serves alcohol, and shares canal-front seating with the coffeeshop. This smoke-friendly bar was created out of necessity years ago, when the city banned alcohol from coffeeshops. Ricks used to serve both. Instead of choosing, they moved the cannabis operation next door. Though two separate establishments, customers often purchase cannabis at the coffeeshop, and hop over to the café to chill.

SHOP FEATURES

COFFEESHOPS

SHOP HOURS:

Daily:
9:00am-12:00am

MAP IT

RISKY BUSINESS

Bos en Lommerweg 163-A, Amsterdam (West) **:ADDRESS**

Coffeeshop Risky Business is located in the Landlust section of Amsterdam West. Named after an old farm in the area, this neighborhood is just to the south of Westerpark, among the city's more popular green areas and event spaces. This is a largely residential part of the city, and having been developed during the 1930's, does not quite have the architectural history of the Centrum. However, it is still quite beautiful.

The Shop

Once there was a small smoking lounge open here. These days, Coffeeshop Risky Business serves as a take-away only establishment. Inside this shop you will find a large waiting room and a counter, where you can order cannabis products. They cater mainly to local residents here, who stop in for a quick purchase before going on with the rest of their day or evening.

The Menu

The cannabis menu at Risky Business is fairly modest in size. This, of course, is typical of shops outside the more touristy areas. On the weed-side, they typically stock old-school strains; items like white widow, amnesia, hazes. These are the types of products locals have become most familiar with and also made Amsterdam so famous. For many, a favorite strain is like a favorite brand of beer.

On the hashish-side of the menu, you can expect to see a few options. These will be imported pressed varieties, mostly from Morocco. Pricing tends to be reasonable here compared to many shops in the city center, presumably given the focus on local repeat customers.

CONNOISSEUR GUIDE: AMSTERDAM

COFFEESHOPS

SHOP FEATURES

SHOP HOURS:
Daily:
9:00am-1:00am

ROCK IT

ADDRESS: Nieuwmarkt 12, Amsterdam (Centrum)

MAP IT

Rock It Coffeeshop is located on Nieuwmarkt (New Market) square. This section of the city has a high density of businesses including restaurants, cafés, bakeries, and of course, coffeeshops. There is a lot of history here. In the center of the square you will find a 15th century building known as the Waag ("Weigh House"). A long time ago, when Amsterdam had an outer wall, this was one of the entrance gates. It served many purposes after, even hosting a guillotine at one point. Inside today, you will find a posh restaurant. The Nieuwmarkt is one of the most popular spots with visitors to the city. Likewise, the area is usually quite crowded.

The Shop

The inside of this coffeeshop is not what most people expect. Given its name, a theme along the lines of Hard Rock Café would seem in order... a shop plastered with rock-and-roll posters and memorabilia. Instead, you will find a contemporary lounge that feels more like an urban coffee house or café. Green and brown colors dominate the interior, providing an earthy vibe. There is tribute to influential musicians here, but it not necessarily a collection of rock icons. The music décor seems more like an accent than a focal point for the main theme of the shop.

Rock It is split into two levels. On the main floor is the shop's ordering counter. Here, you can purchase cannabis, along with some basic refreshments. Once you have made your purchase, you can head upstairs to the lounge. The area is quite comfortable. Long padded benches run the length of most walls, with small chairs and stools provided for additional seating. Modern light fixtures and exposed wooden beams solidify a contemporary urban vibe here. If you prefer fresh air though, you can also find several sets of tables and chairs in front of the shop. This is prime seating if you like to watch the crowds go by.

The Menu

The cannabis menu at Rock It coffeeshop is substantial in size. For weed, you can typically find more than a dozen strains. These are usually a mix of old and new genetics. For hashish, they have a smaller but still fairly large selection of pressed imports. They also sell pre-rolled joints and edibles. When it comes to pricing, remember this is a major tourist area so you are likely to pay a bit more. Aside from cannabis, they make decent coffee, and have a pretty standard selection of drinks and snacks.

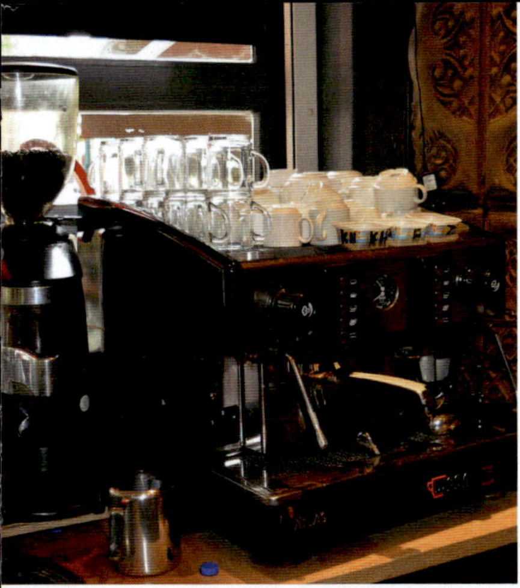

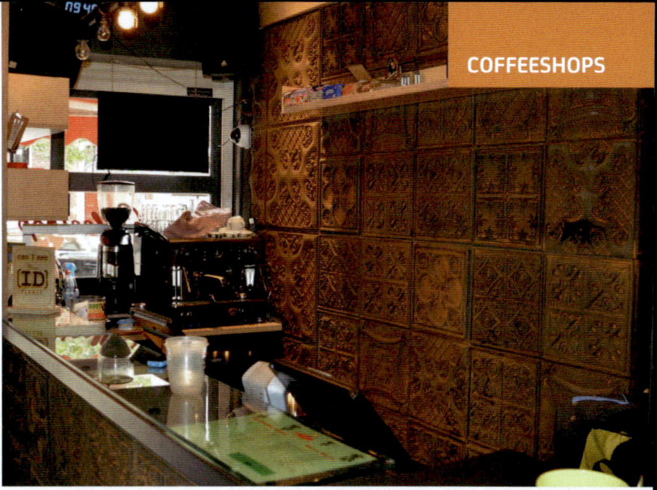

A MAN WHO
STANDS FOR
NOTHING
WILL FALL FOR
ANYTHING.

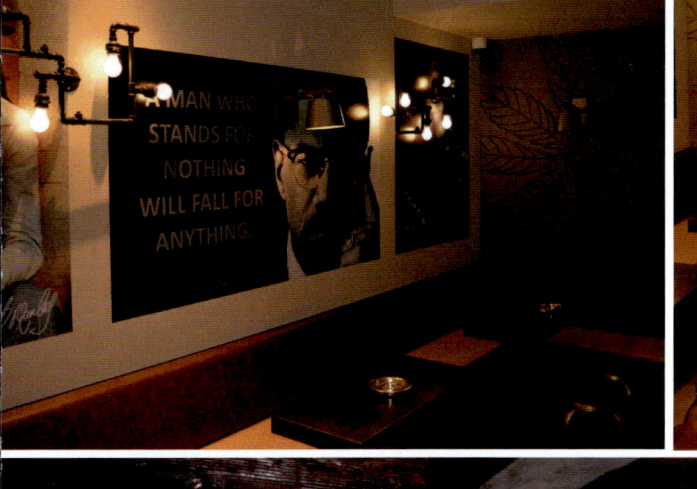

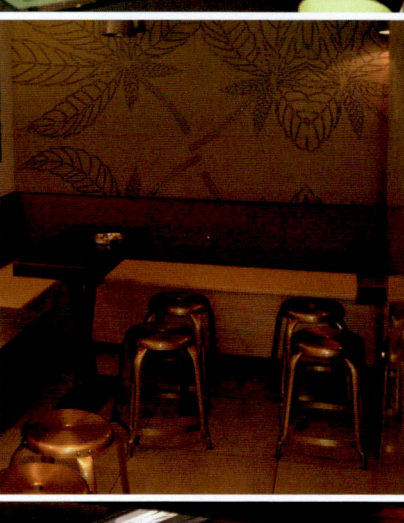

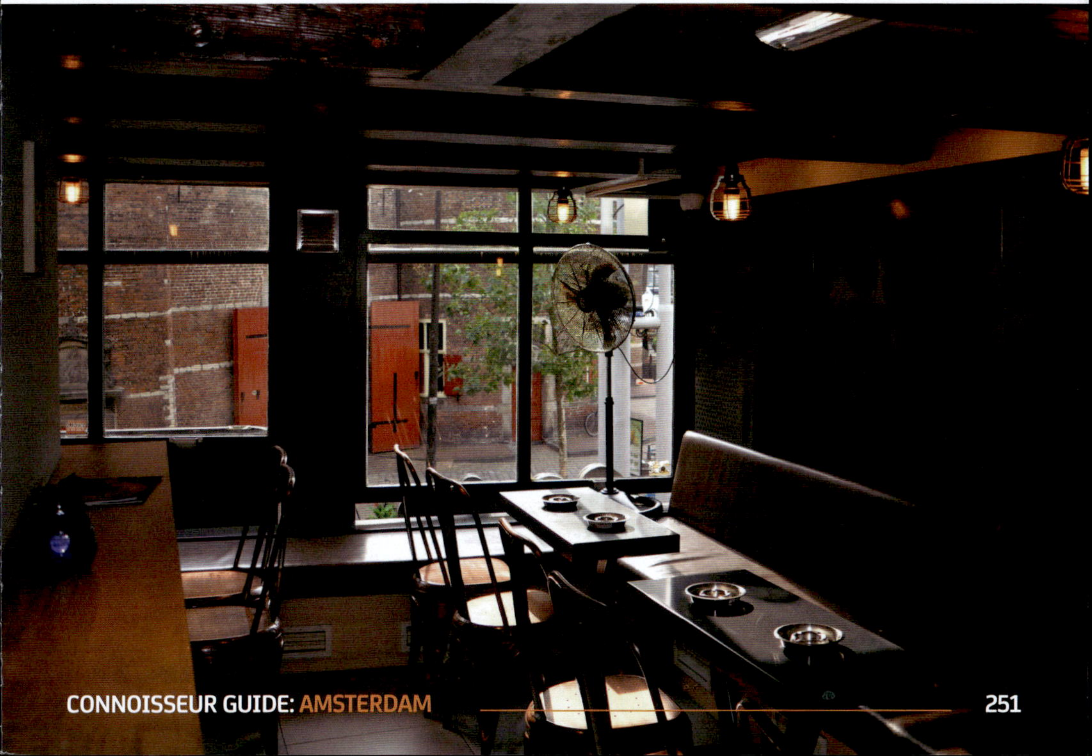

COFFEESHOPS

SHOP FEATURES

SHOP HOURS:

Sun-Thurs:
11:00am-12:00am

Fri-Sat:
11:00am-1:00am

ROCKLAND

ADDRESS: Raadhuisstraat 8, Amsterdam (Centrum)

MAP IT

Rockland Coffeeshop is found on Raadhuisstraat (Council House Street). This coffeeshop is very close to Dam Square and the Royal Palace, just a few blocks to the east. Walk a little to the south, and you will find the famous shopping district referred to as "The Nine Streets". These are among the most iconic tourist destinations in the city. Those aside, this is the heart of the Canal Ring. You will find no shortage of things to do and see in the surrounding neighborhood.

The Shop

One of the first things you notice as you walk up to Rockland is a strip of tables and chairs out front. They have a substantial section of outdoor seating here. If one of the things you love to do is people watch, you will find an exceptional vantage point here. Grab some coffee, sit back, and smoke a joint. A hundred people will have passed by you in no time, as they rush in and out of the city center.

Rockland Coffeeshop is found on the basement level of its building. As you pass the outdoor seating, you step down into this single room shop. While not large, the inside is quite contemporary in its décor. The color theme in here is a mix of wood and red. Comfortable red leather topped benches run along the walls, with pull-up leather (black) stools in front. The shop is clean, well-lit, and has the feeling of a contemporary coffee bar or bakery. It is cozy.

The Menu

This coffeeshop generally has a moderate to large cannabis menu. The options tend to favor the flower (weed) side, though their hashish offering is sizable as well. They tend to favor traditional strains and products here. The genetics on the flower-side are largely old-school favorites, though you may find a contemporary item or two as well. For hashish, most of the menu will be imported pressed items from Morocco and other common source regions. However, they do tend to stock a more potent nederhasj (Isolator) or two. Pre-rolled joints and a basic Space Cake round out the menu.

COFFEESHOPS

COFFEESHOPS

SHOP FEATURES

SHOP HOURS:

Daily:
8:30am-1:00am

ROOKIES

ADDRESS: Korte Leidsedwarsstraat 145-147, Amsterdam (Centrum)

MAP IT

Rookies Coffeeshop is located on Korte Leidsedwarsstraat, one of the main streets crossing the Leidseplein (Leiden Square). This is a consistently busy area of the city, with a great many restaurants, boutiques, and other small shops to enjoy.

The Shop

Rookies coffeeshop was opened in 1992. In a market that was long since established, the owners were said to be the youngest in Amsterdam at the time, hence their adoption of the name "The Rookies".

This coffeeshop is a bit larger than it seems from the outside. Though existing only on one level, the building it is in is quite long. The inside is also wide enough to be divided. The left side of Rookies is dominated by a large bar/counter. There is plenty of seating in here, mainly in the form of pull-up stools, along with additional table and chairs. To the right side of the shop is a glass-enclosed smoking lounge. The is the main lounge area of Rookies, with many wall-mounted tables and chairs. The two sides provide a lot of seating room. This shop can hold close to a hundred people at capacity.

The décor of Rookies Coffeeshop is fairly traditional for a Dutch coffeeshop. There is a lot of wood in here. The floor, tables, wall treatments, and counter all seems to blend in together. The decorations are modest, but fun. You will notice a lot of old pictures, posters, and other bits of coffeeshop memorabilia up on the walls. The best way to describe Rookies is to say that it appears very much like a neighborhood bar. Actually, until the city banned the sale of alcohol in coffeeshops, they were. At one time, both cannabis and alcohol were served here.

The Menu

The cannabis menu at Rookies is not extensive, but carries an ample variety of both weed (flower) and hashish (concentrate) options. The cannabis is stated to be "100% Bio", which we take to mean is grown with natural soil and fertilizers. Those interested in marijuana edibles may want to try their space cakes, which can be a cut above many competitors.

COFFEESHOPS

CONNOISSEUR GUIDE: AMSTERDAM

COFFEESHOPS

SHOP FEATURES

SHOP HOURS:

Daily:
9:00am-12:00am

ROOTS

ADDRESS: Hoekenrode 14, Amsterdam (Oost)

MAP IT

Roots Coffeeshop is a new addition to Amsterdam's cannabis scene. It opened in the summer of 2017, in Amsterdam-Zuidoost (Southeast). It is right near Amsterdam Arena. This section of the city is a bit removed from the old city center, and is actually quite newly developed. The neighborhood hosts a lot of commercial activity, mixed with many modern large block apartment buildings. There are no other coffeeshops in the immediate area, making Roots the sole neighborhood option for cannabis, if you live or plan on staying in this part of the city.

The Shop

Inside Roots Coffeeshop, one will find a decidedly contemporary establishment. Its hardwood floors, polished light-colored wood furniture, and an overall black, white, and wood scheme for décor make the place feel more like a modern office than a coffeeshop. The newness of its construction is quite visible. This shop also has a lot of glass, creating a very open, bright, and clean feeling which only adds to the office vibe. Large cushion-topped benches, chairs and tables provide plenty of seating in the back. Though perhaps unconventional, Roots can be a highly comfortable place to chill.

The Menu

The cannabis menu is fairly large at Roots Coffeeshop, especially considering this is an isolated location for the area. On the weed-size, expect to find a dozen items or so. They have a lot of traditional strains here, old school Amsterdam favorites… though you may still encounter some contemporary USA genetics, such as Kush hybrids. The hashish menu is smaller, but still quite sizable. The items are traditional pressed imports. They also have space cake, and plenty of pre-rolled joint options here, if preferred. List is largely a locals' shop. Pricing can be quite reasonable here compared to what you will find in the city center.

Beyond cannabis, they have coffee, tea, hot toasties, and a standard selection of juices, soda, and basic snacks on the menu.

COFFEESHOPS

CONNOISSEUR GUIDE: AMSTERDAM

COFFEESHOPS

SHOP FEATURES

SHOP HOURS:
Daily:
7:00am-1:00am

ROXY

ADDRESS: Gerard Doustraat 188, Amsterdam (Zuid)

MAP IT

Roxy coffeeshop is located on Gerard Doustraat, in a lively section of Amsterdam-Zuid (South). This establishment is close to Albert Cuyp Markt, which is the largest outdoor market in the Netherlands. Here you will find hundreds of vendors offering everything from trinkets to fresh vegetables. Beer, coffee, food; it is all here. This place can be a lot of fun. Naturally, the market is a popular draw with city visitors. We do highly recommended stopping by if you are considering a trip to this coffeeshop.

The Shop

Coffeeshop Roxy has a very upscale feel to it. The place looks more like a trendy restaurant or small art gallery than a traditional Dutch coffeeshop, which is typically more austere. The seating here is all black leather. It comes in the form of comfortable chairs, pulled next to matching black tables. There is also an elevated seating area in one corner with plush leather benches. It has a bit of a private "VIP section" feeling. The dark wood and furniture in this shop all visually contrasts with the white walls and vibrant accent lighting. It is a posh contemporary look. While not expansive, the Roxy still comes across as spacious. The open layout of this place probably makes it appear larger.

The Menu

The cannabis menu here is substantial in size. You can expect to find more than a dozen strains of weed. This will be a lot of traditional old-school varieties, but mixed in, some contemporary USA genetics. The have roughly half this selection on the hashish (concentrate) side. However, do not let this discourage you. The Roxy has a reputation for quality hashish. They tend to keep the quality tight, in our experience. They also have pre-rolled joints; quite a lot of them. Just about any strain on the menu. Some basic space cakes too.

If needed, the Roxy also has a solid selection of smoking accessories such as pipes, bongs, grinders, and vaporizers. While most coffeeshops have the basics for use, a surprising portion do not stock a lot of this stuff for sale. No need for a trip to the headshop here.

Like most coffeeshops, the Roxy serves a selection of hot and cold drinks. This includes teas, coffee, and soda. The coffee is pretty good here. They also have a small selection of basic snacks likes chips and candy. There is enough here to stave off the munchies for a little while, but not enough to take the place of a meal. For that, we suggest a break at one of the many local restaurants, or of course, the Albert Cuyp Markt.

COFFEESHOPS

CONNOISSEUR GUIDE: AMSTERDAM

COFFEESHOPS

SHOP FEATURES

SHOP HOURS:

Daily
8:00am-12:30am

RUSLAND

ADDRESS: Rusland 16, Amsterdam (Centrum)

MAP IT

Rusland Coffeeshop is located in the old city center known as De Wallen ("The Walls"). It is outside the Red Light District near the southern edge, not far from Dam Square. Rusland is actually found on the street of the same name. The word in Dutch translates into "Russia". This is something the shop seems to have embraced with great enthusiasm. For this is the city's only Russian-themed coffeeshop. This is a fact made obvious with the shop's logo, which incorporates the traditional Russian hammer and sickle.

The Shop

Rusland has the distinction of being the second coffeeshop in Amsterdam (though it holds license #001). There is a bit of history so let's explain. The first was Mellow Yellow which opened in 1972. Rusland opened its doors on April 30, 1975. The Bulldog 90 opened in December of 1975 which would make it the third coffeeshop. However, and this is where it gets murky, Bulldog sold weed when it was a sex shop in 1974 making it to some, the second coffeeshop to operate in Amsterdam.

Today, Rusland stands as the oldest coffeeshop in the city after Mellow Yellow closed its doors due to new zoning requirements in 2017. Though the shop has not moved, the interior of Rusland has changed a lot over the years. It began as a really small place on one level; very basic.

Now Rusland in its current form is anything but. It now has a split-level interior that is luxurious and spacious. The décor is beautiful. The front of the shop has the appearance of a gourmet bakery or coffee/tea shop. Further in, the upper seating area is plush with comfortable leather benches. Downstairs is the shop's named "Poetin Lounge". This area has additional seating, a large glass display case full of bongs and souvenirs, and an enclosed smoking room. A large oil painting of the Russian leader sits at the entrance.

Rusland is one of the nicest shops in the city when it comes to décor, and hosts a warm, chill atmosphere.

The Menu

The cannabis menu is very good here. On the weed-side they usually have a dozen strains or so; some contemporary, some old school. They are perhaps better known for their hashish, which tends to be excellent. They really seem to like imported soft dark hashes here, but also have some higher potency domestic isolators too. They have a big selection, and really keep the quality up. Decent edibles too.

COFFEESHOPS

SHOP FEATURES

SHOP HOURS:

Daily:
10:00am-1:00am

RUTHLESS

ADDRESS: Hoofdweg 174, Amsterdam (West)

MAP IT

Coffeeshop Ruthless is located on Hoofdweg, in a largely residential part of Amsterdam West. It is right on the eastern side of Rembrandtpark (Rembrandt Park), one of the city's most popular green areas. The street name Hoofdweg actually translates into "highway" in English. Likewise, it is a wide main road for this section of Amsterdam. Still, the area is quieter than the city center. Residences dominate the streets here, with businesses dotted along the ground level.

The Shop

There is a small pick-up area in the front of Coffeeshop Ruthless. After making a purchase, you may proceed through the side door to the shop's smoking lounge. The décor in here is best described as contemporary. Seating is mainly in the form of large red and black leather benches, very plush and comfortable. There are also some pull-up leather stools at the counter. The color scheme is a strong mix of red and black. It makes the place feel a bit like a small Asian restaurant. You half expect to order Pho or Pad Thai with a side of weed.

The Menu

The cannabis menu is moderate in size at Coffeeshop Ruthless. Further, it tends to strongly favor weed, with a number of options. Expect to find more than a dozen different strains. These tend to be a mix of both old-school favorites and contemporary USA strains. The hash menu usually has a few options at best. These are imported pressed varieties, from common source countries like Morocco. They also have a few pre-rolled joint (weed and hashish) options, if preferred. Note that Coffeeshop Ruthless has a glass-enclosed smoking lounge in the back. As such, tobacco consumption is permitted here.

SHOP FEATURES

COFFEESHOPS

SHOP HOURS:

Mon-Fri:
10:00am-12:00am
Sat-Sun:
10:00am-1:00am

MAP IT

SENSEMILLIA

Gillis van Ledenberchstraat 135 HS Amsterdam (West) **:ADDRESS**

Coffeeshop Sensemillia is located in the Frederik Hendrikbuurt section of Amsterdam West. This neighborhood is next to the Jordaan, one of Amsterdam's more desirable and picturesque residential neighborhoods. Though Frederik Hendrikbuurt is also largely residential, this coffeeshop does sit on the main s105 motorway. As such, the immediate area around this shop is quite busy.

The Shop

Coffeeshop Sensemillia uses a variant of an obvious cannabis term for its name. Sinsemilla is, of course, seedless marijuana, a necessity if you want high THC plants. Though Sensemillia is an old brand in Amsterdam, the inside of this shop has a contemporary feel to it. The color scheme is white with lime green; the walls painted with large leaf patterns. The front room is bright, open, and clean.

This shop mainly serves as a take-and-go location for local residents. However, there are a couple of tables, a soda machine, and a coffee machine in here. You can prep a drink and a smoke before you leave.

The Menu

The cannabis menu at Coffeeshop Sensemillia is robust. The options largely favor the weed-side, with typically well more than a dozen strains available. As a shop that caters largely to locals, there are a lot of old-school genetics here: like White Widow, Amnesia, Haze. However, they do also bring in some contemporary strains from time to time. Expect a couple of options. The hashish-side of the menu is much smaller, usually just several items. These are standard imported pressed varieties, though the quality is often very good in our experience.

COFFEESHOPS

SHOP FEATURES

SHOP HOURS:

Sun-Thurs:
10:00am-12:00am

Fri-Sat:
10:00am-1:00am

SENSEMILLIA OSDORP

ADDRESS: Meer en Vaart 177/B, Amsterdam (West)

MAP IT

Sensemillia Osdorp Coffeeshop is located in the western suburbs of Amsterdam, one of the most beautiful and lush areas of the city. It actually has the distinction of being the westernmost shop that is still within city limits. It is also found on one of the most stunning properties, resting on the very edge of Sloterpark. This is a large and beautiful park with many walking trails, and one of the biggest lakes in the city, Sloterplas.

The Shop

Sensemillia Osdorp is found on the upstairs of a modern standalone building right on the lakefront, above an upscale restaurant called the Grand Café. There is also a Cantonese restaurant in the same building. The surrounding town is a bit more spread out than you would expect of Amsterdam, and nothing short of charming.

The shop itself is fairly standard for a Dutch coffeeshop, minus one very unique feature. Once you pass the counter and head to the back of Sinsemilla Osdorp Coffeeshop, you will find an outdoor terrace. This is the smoking area. There is a stunning view of Sloterplas on one side of the terrace. Unfortunately, the terrace just has the feeling of unrealized potential with just a few chairs and an ashtray. Furthermore, there is a thick sheet of acrylic over the opening where you view the beautiful lake. We are unsure of the reason for it but it would undoubtedly be a much nicer view without it.

The interior of the shop is a bit more inviting, with hardwood floors, high ceilings, and ample natural lighting. No smoking is allowed in here, however.

The Menu

Sensemillia Osdorp has an extensive cannabis menu. They are mainly focused on their weed selections, with just a few types of hashish to round it out. The shop carries a mix of old Amsterdam favorites (such as Amnesia and White Widow), and more contemporary trending strains. Pricing seems to be fairly reasonable, certainly more so than you generally find in the city center. Beyond the cannabis offerings at Sensemillia Osdorp, there is a limited selection of hot and cold drinks. They do not serve food. Then again, sitting above two restaurants provides ample opportunity for customers to have a delicious meal during their visit.

Waterfront at Sloterpark, Amsterdam West

COFFEESHOPS

SHOP FEATURES

SHOP HOURS:

Mon-Thurs:
9:00am-11:00pm

Fri-Sat:
9:00am-12:00am

Sun:
10:00am-11:00pm

SIBERIË

ADDRESS: Brouwersgracht 11, Amsterdam (Centrum)

MAP IT

Siberië Coffeeshop sits canal-side on Brouwersgracht, just to the southwest of Centraal Station. It is also very close to the bustling avenue of Haarlemmerstraat, where you will find many boutiques and restaurants, and a few of the city's higher-end coffeeshops. Though Siberië sits in close proximity to these busy areas of the city, comparatively speaking, it is on a fairly quiet side street.

The Shop

The shop interior is best described as modern in appearance. While Siberië may have traditional wooden floors, tables, and chairs, these are complimented by some funky light fixtures, a large curved counter, local artwork, and a touch of neon.

As you walk in, you will also notice that Siberië is divided into two sections. In the front is a seating area and smoking room, which has a few large tables on the right side, opposite a small table for two. A glass door partitions this area from the main room, where you will find the counter and additional table and bench seating.

Siberië has several features that make it stand out. One is the large set of double doors in front. These are opened when the weather is warm, providing an open and airy feeling to the shop, particularly the front seating room. At times, they will have additional tables and chairs outside.

On a sunny afternoon, Siberië Coffeeshop can be one of the nicest places to go sit, unwind, and watch the boats go by. It is also one of the more serious "coffee" coffeeshops. By that, we mean they actually serve gourmet coffees and teas.

The Menu

Siberië coffeeshop has an excellent cannabis menu, which brings us to another notable feature of this shop. It is one of only a few in the city providing lab test reports. Many claim THC percentages, but do not have supporting documentation. Here, you will find a set of laminated reports near the register. They not only show the THC percentage of the given weed or hashish item, but also a full cannabinoid profile. The few exceptions tend to be special menu items, which change with regularity.

The menu itself is also quite extensive, with approximately two dozen selections. The weed strains are generally modern and trendy, while the traditional pressed hashish imports are from places like Morocco, India, Nepal, and Tibet. Pricing is quite reasonable here as well, especially compared to other connoisseur shops in the area.

COFFEESHOPS

CONNOISSEUR GUIDE: AMSTERDAM

COFFEESHOPS

SHOP FEATURES

SHOP HOURS:

Daily:
7:00am-1:00am

SMOKE PALACE

ADDRESS: Linnaeusstraat 83 HS, Amsterdam (Oost)

MAP IT

Smoke Palace coffeeshop is located on Linnaeusstraat, in the Dapperbuurt neighborhood of East Amsterdam. This is just a beautiful corner of the city. It is a bit away from the center so it is less crowded, and mostly residential. Tree-lined streets and beautiful historic architecture define the area. Even better, Smoke Palace sits right next to Oosterpark ("East Park"). This is a shady serene oasis we highly recommend you consider taking a stroll through.

The Shop

We will begin by pointing out that Smoke Palace is among the largest and more luxurious coffeeshops in the city. Before even getting inside you will notice a large section of outdoor seating. This alone has the amount of seating found at most coffeeshops. The area is separated from the street by a partition so it does feel intimate. It is also packed with plants, wooden crate-style bench seating, and umbrellas to provide shade. It almost feels beachside. On a beautiful sunny day, this spot is hard to beat.

As you step down to enter Smoke Palace, you find an equally impressive interior. The shop is large, and clearly, a great deal of time and thought was spent on the décor. Custom tile and woodwork are featured on the walls and counter throughout much of the shop. The flooring in the main lounge area is beautiful, polished hardwood. The tables and modern stools add a contemporary element. Tie in some mirrors and track lighting, and you have a place that looks much more like a nightclub than a coffeeshop.

The Menu

The cannabis menu at the Palace is moderate-to-large in size. It tends to favor the weed (flower) side with regard to diversity. They may have about a dozen strains here, often a mix of recognized favorites and new genetics. The hashish menu tends to be smaller, though still formidable compared to many shops. They also have a large selection of pre-rolled joints.

In addition, this is a full-service shop. A wide array of coffees, teas, sodas and other drinks, snacks, and even a few quick hot foods are available for order. This shop is not only inviting, but has plenty to offer to keep you comfortable if you plan on parking yourself here for a while.

COFFEESHOPS

CONNOISSEUR GUIDE: AMSTERDAM

COFFEESHOPS

SHOP FEATURES

SHOP HOURS:
Daily:
10:00am-1:00am

SMOKEY

ADDRESS: Rembrandtplein 24, Amsterdam (Centrum)

MAP IT

Coffeeshop Smokey is located in Rembrandtplein (Rembrandt Square), an area of the city known for its restaurants, bars, and active nightlife. It is upbeat, loud, and active - a large draw for tourists. Smokey appears to fit into this neighborhood quite well.

The Shop

As soon as you enter, you will notice that this is not a typical Dutch coffeeshop. Far from quiet and relaxed, the vibe of this establishment is fast and loud. Smokey is most reminiscent of a theme restaurant; think the Hard Rock Café or Planet Hollywood. There are a lot of colorful lights and decorations hung about, classic rock or contemporary music is heard playing over the speakers, and the place is usually packed full of tourists and waitstaff alike.

The Menu

Coffeeshop Smokey has a large selection of cannabis products, both on the flower (weed) and hashish-side of the menu. Instead of providing the traditional paper menu, you will find a glass display case here. Found on the left side of the shop when looking in, all of their offerings are on display so that you can examine them before purchase.

type of shop you visit with a group of friends for some smoke, drink, and food. Note there is also outdoor seating, if you and your group would like to enjoy some fresh air.

As expected, there is also no shortage of food and drink options here. Smokey is not really an ideal grab-and-go establishment for connoisseur cannabis. Rather, it is the

CONNOISSEUR GUIDE: AMSTERDAM

SHOP FEATURES

SHOP HOURS:
Daily:
9:00am-1:00am

COFFEESHOPS

MAP IT

SOFTLAND
Spuistraat 222, Amsterdam (Centrum): **ADDRESS**

Coffeeshop Softland is found on Spuistraat ("Lock Street"), to the southwest of Dam square. Spuistreet is a main thoroughfare leading in-and-out of Amsterdam Centraal. Consequently, this street sees a lot of traffic. There is an abundance of stores and restaurants on both sides. If you visit the city center, there is a good chance you will find yourself on Spuistraat. Softland is hard to miss when you do. The large neon sign out front featuring the now tech-savvy symbol "@" is very attention getting.

The Shop

As expected, this shop offers internet access. Note, however, there may be a charge for its use. Softland is a theme coffeeshop. It will feel like you are entering a spaceship when walking into this establishment. We liken it to the Ripley Scott movie Alien. The room is long, and the floor is metallic. Your steps reverberate, making it feel like you are stepping on an elevated platform.

Large, silver air conditioning ducts overhead run nearly the length of the "ship", and frame the mural on the ceiling, which features the spaceship's overhead paneling. There appears to be a portal in the center of this painting. Perhaps it leads to the level above? Murals and molding on the walls, trippy light fixtures, and custom tables and counter all add to the effect. A large sidewalk outside also provides ample room for some additional outdoor seating, which they sometimes take advantage of on sunny afternoons.

The Menu

The cannabis menu at Coffeeshop Softland is moderate in size, though has a fairly diverse selection of old and contemporary weed (flower) strains. They also stock a decent number of hashish varieties, mainly pressed imports from Morocco. Beyond the basic cannabis options, they also serve coffee, tea, and a standard selection of basic drinks and snacks.

COFFEESHOPS

SHOP FEATURES

SHOP HOURS:
Daily:
10:00am-12:00am

SOLO

ADDRESS: Korte Koningsstraat 2, Amsterdam (Centrum)

MAP IT

Solo Coffeeshop is located on Korte Koningsstraat (Short King Street), to the east of Nieuwmarkt Square. This neighborhood is much more quiet than that to the west. Solo has a similarly comfortable and relaxed vibe to it, so this coffeeshop fits in well with its neighbors.

The Shop

The décor inside Solo coffeeshop is best described as "upscale pub". There is a lot of dark wood, generally well maintained and polished. Several booths are found on one side of the shop, which provide restaurant-style seating for small groups. There is a long bar on the other, which has pull-up leather topped stools in traditional bar style.

The best seating in the shop is perhaps found near the front. On nice days the shop will often open up one of the wide, front windows. If you are sitting directly beside it, you will have a table that feeds directly to the outside. This allows you to take in the city, fresh air, and sunshine while indoors. This feature would place Solo on the "coolest coffeeshop seating" list were we to have one.

The Menu

Solo Coffeeshop has a fairly large selection of cannabis products on its menu. The most diverse variety is found on the flower (weed) side, though the shop also seems to carry a nice variety of imported and domestic hashish products. They also serve space cakes, and have a small assortment of pre-rolled joints. Additionally, one will find a pretty decent selection of coffees, teas, and other drinks here.

COFFEESHOP
SOLO
PETER TOSH
LEGALIZE IT

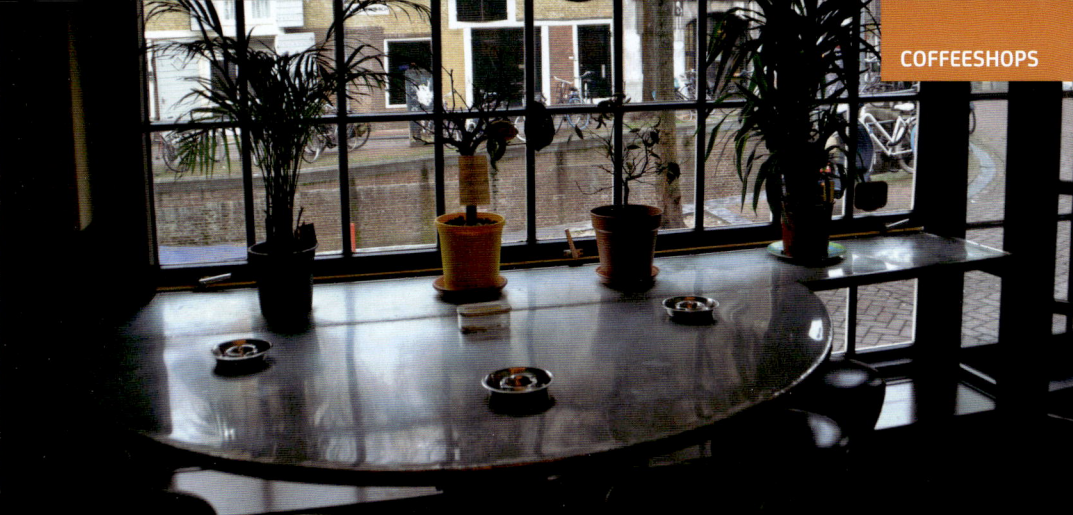

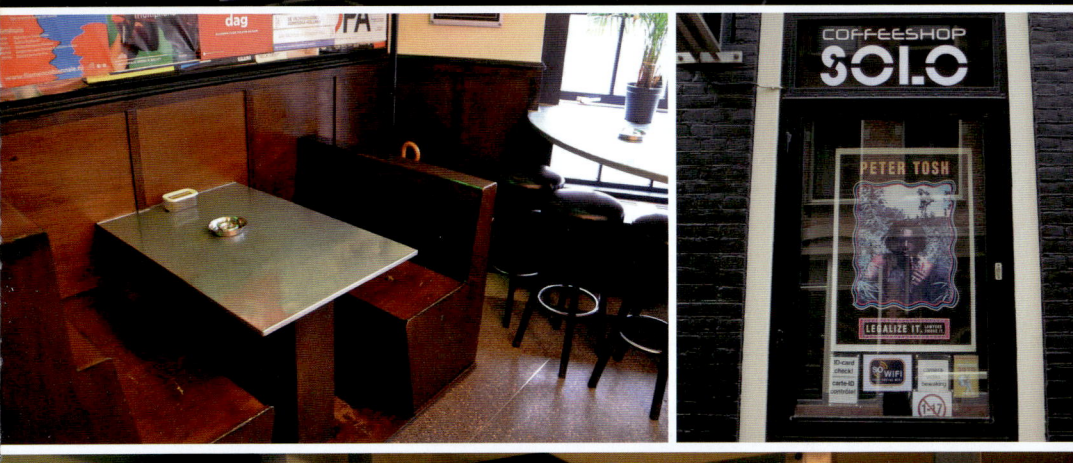

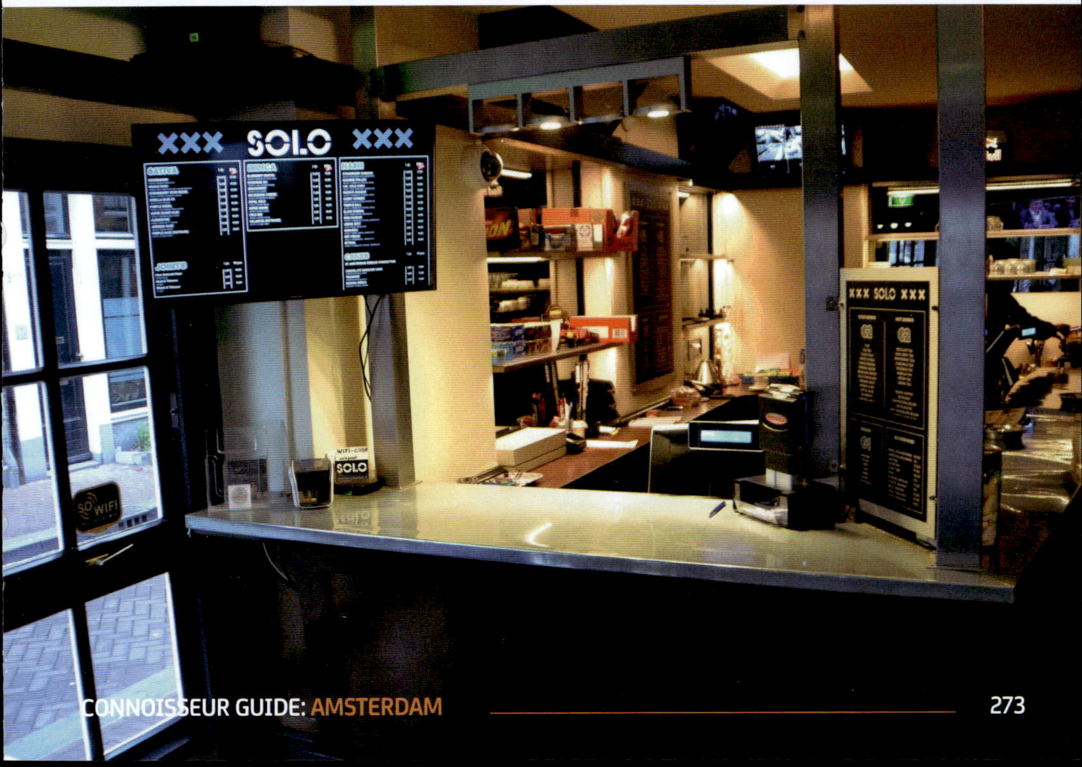
XXX SOLO XXX
SOLO
XXX SOLO XXX

COFFEESHOPS

SHOP FEATURES

SHOP HOURS:
Daily:
7:00am-1:00am

SPEAKEASY

ADDRESS: Eerste Oosterparkstraat 47, Amsterdam (Oost)

MAP IT

Speakeasy coffeeshop is located on Eerste Oosterparkstraat, in Amsterdam Oost (East). This is a more residential area of the city, less packed with hotels and tourists. The shops in this part of the city tend to cater largely to locals, and be a bit more down-to-earth. However, Speakeasy, is likely going to be more upscale than you expect.

The Shop

This shop was originally founded in 1982, but at a different location in the Red Light District. It stood there for more than twenty years. However, they were forced to close down in 2013 due to changes in city zoning regulations. Luckily, this shop was permitted to find another home in Amsterdam Oost. Moving to a new location allowed Speakeasy coffeeshop to rebuild from scratch. They seemed to have embraced this opportunity.

The interior of the new space is a well designed mix of contemporary and classic. On the one hand, you have brushed leather seats, tiled walls, polished wood, and a flat screen television. On the other, you will find collages of framed pictures that pay homage to prohibition-era gangsters. It is a little bit of history which relates at some level to all cannabis businesses. The shop is interesting, as much as it is comfortable and accommodating. They also invested in a fancy commercial cappuccino machine, so expect to find quality coffee/hot drinks here.

The Menu

The cannabis menu here is modest in size. Usually we find less than a dozen items of mixed weed and hash. However, sometimes that means the shop is keeping tight control over their inventory. To that, you will notice a microscope on the counter - a good sign. This is usually an indication that you are in a connoisseur shop, where they encourage customers to inspect their offerings very closely. Under a microscope you can often see things that would otherwise go unnoticed, such as broken or malformed trichomes, or bug excrement. Not many shops invite you to examine their inventory for fear you will discover such things in your purchase. We applaud shops like Speakeasy that do this!

COFFEESHOPS

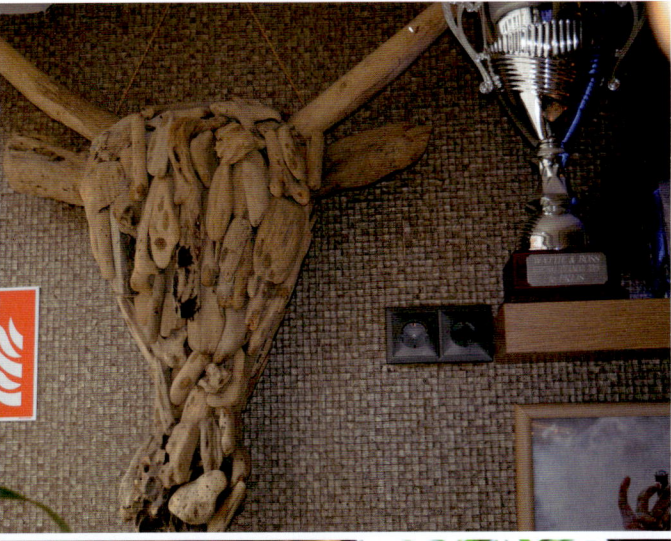

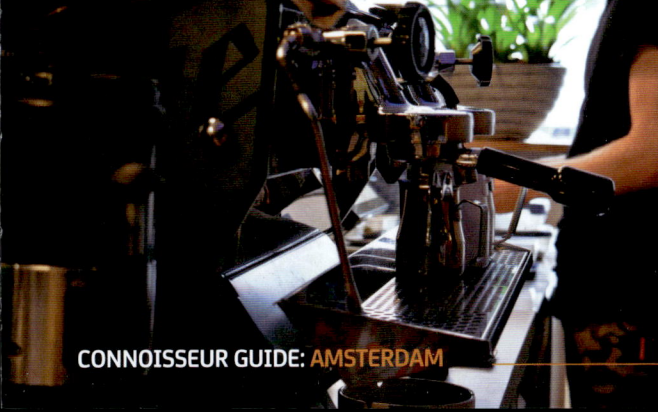

CONNOISSEUR GUIDE: AMSTERDAM

COFFEESHOPS

SHOP FEATURES

SHOP HOURS:
Daily:
8:00am-1:00am

STONE'S

ADDRESS: Ruysdaelkade 145, Amsterdam (Zuid)

MAP IT

Stone's Coffeeshop is located on Ruysdaelkade, a long street the runs beside the boerenwetering canal. It is in the Oude Pijp (Old Pipe) section of Amsterdam, a lively multicultural area of the city that is also home to Albert Cuypmarkt, Sarphatipark, and the major tourist draw that is The Heineken Experience. Stone's is located in a busy part of the Oude Pijp, which is also home to a small red light district.

The Shop

Stone's Coffeeshop is a long-standing brand in Amsterdam, which established itself in the main Red Light District (De Wallen). Its original coffeeshops, however, have since been de-licensed, due to changes in zoning regulations, and now operate as a pub and café. This location in Amsterdam Zuid is their newest, and unfortunately, only remaining coffeeshop. Its building was actually the former home to the Kabouter Coffeeshop. The change to Stone's occurred sometime in 2014.

Inside this coffeeshop, one will find a basic but contemporary décor. The place is bright, warm, and inviting. There is not really a smoking lounge here, though. Stone's is a small establishment. They are operating mainly as a take-and-go location at this time. There is a counter in front of the window, so a small area is available for prepping your smoke before you head out the door.

The Menu

Though a "carry out" coffeeshop, Stone's is generally regarded as a quality establishment. They have a fairly large cannabis menu, which typically includes a good variety of both flower (weed) and hashish options. The strains on the weed-side are mainly old school; recognized Amsterdam favorites. They will stock a bit of modern genetics though as well. For hashish, they have a small selection of traditional imports. Most of the time they will also stock at least one variety of more potent domestic nederhasj (Isolator).

Being a bit out of the city center, and noticing a lot more "locals" business, pricing here also tends to be more reasonable than its counterparts in Amsterdam Centre.

Street Art
NDSM Warf

COFFEESHOPS

SHOP FEATURES

SHOP HOURS:

Mon-Sat:
8:00am-1:00am

Sun:
8:00am-12:00am

SUPER SKUNK

ADDRESS: Prinsengracht 480, Amsterdam (Centrum)

MAP IT

Super Skunk Coffeeshop is located on Prinsengracht (Prince's Canal), close to the Leidseplein. This square is one of the city's hotspots, known especially for its active nightlife. While Super Skunk sits just a bit to the north, it is also in a very busy spot, and sits directly on one of the city's most famous canals.

The Shop

This coffeeshop was once known as Tops. It has since changed its name to Super Skunk, and now has a sister shop of the same name in De Pijp (The Pipe) section of Amsterdam. The building that houses Super Skunk is longer than average for the city center. This provides a bit more room than is typical for the tall narrow architecture of Amsterdam. As such, while not exactly large, this is not a small coffeeshop either.

The décor inside is contemporary and impressive, and the shop has a decidedly "upscale lounge" feel to it. Super Skunk is split into two lounge areas. The front has the counter, which is best described as a futuristic glowing cube. There is a lot of polished wood, tables and stools for seating, and some cool accent lighting.

If you go on further into the back, you will find a glass-enclosed smoking room. Here, the shop shifts to more of an artsy Arabian theme. There are plush couches and stools, wooden coffee tables, brass fixtures, and funky lighting all around the room. If you prefer an al fresco experience, Super Skunk also has a nice big sidewalk out front. They take advantage of this fully by placing out tables and chairs for patrons to enjoy.

The Menu

Super Skunk Coffeeshop has a fairly large cannabis menu, with a decent variety of both flower (weed) and hashish (concentrate) options. They also serve gourmet coffees and teas in here, along with a full compliment of drinks and a selection of basic foods, desserts, and snacks... a bit more than you find at most.

CONNOISSEUR GUIDE: AMSTERDAM

COFFEESHOPS

CONNOISSEUR GUIDE: AMSTERDAM

COFFEESHOPS

SHOP FEATURES

SHOP HOURS:

Mon-Sat:
8:00am-1:00am

Sun:
8:00am-12:00am

SUPER SKUNK DE PIJP

ADDRESS: Daniel Stalpertstraat 78, Amsterdam (Zuid)

MAP IT

Coffeeshop Super Skunk is found in De Pijp ("The Pipe") section of Amsterdam South. This is one of the more trendy parts of the city. Nearby you will find the famous Albert Cuyp Market, and no shortage of busy restaurants, shops, boutiques, and bars. Likewise, the area can be quite lively with younger crowds, especially in the evenings. This Super Skunk shop is actually the second for this brand, the other (original) being located just behind the Leidseplein.

The Shop

The inside of Coffeeshop Super Skunk is fairly contemporary. In the front of the shop you will find an open and airy room. There are bar stools lining a brightly lit ordering counter; very funky. Around the room, several high-top tables and leather-topped stools. The place feels a bit like an upscale café or hotel lobby bar. There is also a small back room, where you will find four massage chairs. We must say, a joint and a fifteen minute massage is a great way to rejuvenate. This shop does not provide a massage therapist, though, so you are out of luck there.

The Menu

The cannabis menu at this Coffeeshop Super Skunk is similar to their original location. In size, it is quite robust. They are big on weed here. We found close to two dozen strains on order. Expect a strong collection of old-school Amsterdam genetics, combined with a few contemporary strains with genetics coming from West Coast USA. The hashish-side of the menu is also fairly large; usually holding nearly a dozen items. Like most coffeeshops, these are mainly imported pressed varieties from Morocco and other common source countries. However, you are likely to find a more potent domestic nederhash (isolator) option or two as well. They also have space cakes and muffins, which are served in both "strong" and "light" varieties. You have options, depending on your tolerance.

SHOP FEATURES

COFFEESHOPS

SHOP HOURS:

Daily:
9:00am-1:00am

MAP IT

'T KETELTJE

Marnixstraat 74-HS, Amsterdam (Centrum) **:ADDRESS**

'T Keteltje coffeeshop is located toward the north end of Marnixstraat, at the western edge of Amsterdam Centrum. It is also at the edge of De Jordaan, a quieter residential neighborhood known for its beautiful old Dutch buildings, upscale modern boutiques, and high real estate prices. Located only a minute's walk west to the Singelgracht canal, there is no shortage of scenery to enjoy while walking around this district with a joint.

The Shop

'T Keteltje fits well into the Jordaan neighborhood. On the one hand, it feels more traditional than many of the shops in the city center. At the same time, however, it has a decidedly upscale feel to it. A great deal of wood is incorporated into the décor of this shop. As you walk in, you immediately notice a tall, large front counter. It is hand made of thick and beautifully polished interconnected planks. The front room is also adorned with several wood sculptures, and a great deal of additional wood trim. Look down. The flooring is also made of large planks of polished hardwood. Additional fixtures like digital menus, a commercial cappuccino machine, and stone tiling only add to the upscale feel.

The back of 'T Keteltje has an enclosed smoking lounge. As with the front of the shop, the feeling here is polished and upscale. There are wooden tables and comfortable bench and stool seating. In the center of the smoking lounge is a billiards table, along with a large TV hung on the back wall. Artwork, track lighting, loft-style air-conditioning vents, and contemporary colors all make this room inviting and comfortable.

The Menu

This shop generally has a large cannabis menu, with ample varieties of both weed (flower) and hashish. The weed is largely old-school. The hashish, traditional pressed imports. They also have a nice selection of gourmet coffees and teas, as well as other drinks and snacks to keep you comfortable during your visit.

CONNOISSEUR GUIDE: AMSTERDAM

COFFEESHOPS

SHOP FEATURES

SHOP HOURS:

Daily:
10:00am-10:00pm

'T OOIEVAARTJE

ADDRESS: Ooievaarsweg 10-HS, Amsterdam (Noord)

MAP IT

Ooievaartje is found just a bit behind Centraal Station, in the less-congested Noord section of Amsterdam. The surrounding neighborhood is largely residential here, so it is decidedly more tranquil. Many of the streets are lined with historic apartment buildings and small homes. There are many businesses too, among them many local gems. It is not a bad place to do some wandering around.

The Shop

The name of this shop translates into "The Stork" in English. 'T Ooievaartje actually borrows this name from the street it is found on. However, this coffeeshop takes its avian connection quite seriously. Once you step inside, you will be engulfed by a tropical jungle theme. Paintings cover the entirety of the walls, and even the ceiling! The art is well done.

The seating room in the front feels like a living room. The couches are comfortable and good for relaxing. Just past the first seating area is the counter, where in addition to the usual array of cannabis offerings, they also offer a variety of pipes, grinders and other smoking accessories.

In the back of the shop, you will find the smoking lounge. Here, there is an unusual feature which separates Ooievaartje from virtually all others in the city. 'T Ooievaartje has pigeon coops fixed into the building, with clear plexi-glass windows giving you a view right into the bird cages. It can be mesmerizing watching the birds after the effects of cannabis kick in. Just do not tap on the windows.

The Menu

The cannabis menu at Het Ooievaartje is considerable in size, considering this is a place for locals. For weed, expect a dozen or more items. The strains are a mix of contemporary genetics, such as Kush hybrids, with some long established favorites like White Widow and Cheese. The selection is also fairly contemporary on the hashish-side. There are a lot of pressed imports, with some being highly flavorful Moroccan block hashes. They also stock some more potent domestic isolator (nederhasj) varieties, which are less common outside the city center.

There is a large assortment of sodas, juices, and other beverages here, and some basic snacks if you need. The coffee is, in particular, pretty good here.

COFFEESHOPS

COFFEESHOPS

SHOP FEATURES

SHOP HOURS:

Daily:
9:00am-12:30am

TERMINATOR

ADDRESS: Admiraal de Ruijterweg 104, Amsterdam (West)

MAP IT

Terminator Coffeeshop is located in the De Krommerdt ("The Curves") section of Amsterdam-West. This is a largely residential neighborhood, with wider streets and more trees than you generally find in the centrum. Several main roads do cross through the area though, bringing with it a fair share of businesses and outside traffic. As such, it can still be quite busy here at times.

The Shop

Terminator Coffeeshop is named after the famous 80's movie of the same name. They borrow some graphics from the film, but do not go too overboard with it. If we had to make a comparison, we would say this place feels like an artsy university dormitory. There is a large lounge in the back of the shop. It has hardwood floors, contemporary wood furniture, and wood trim, which contrast with vibrant airbrushed artwork on the walls. The room is pretty cool - open and warm.

There is also a separate glass-enclosed area in the back of the shop. Here, tobacco (mixed joint) smoking is permitted. There are plush leather-topped benches, and several small tables. Whereas some shops only have a small bare room to meet the minimum requirements for a tobacco smoking area, this shop has made a tobacco lounge that is inviting and comfortable.

The Menu

As a shop that caters largely to local residents, the cannabis menu is small at Terminator. Still, they carry several different types of weed and hash, usually a fairly even split. On the weed-side of the menu, it is old-school genetics. For hashish, pressed imported varieties. They also offer some very tasty edibles (space brownies). The shop clearly takes pride in these.

Though they do not offer a lot by way of food otherwise, you can find some basic drinks (soda, juices) and pre-packaged snacks in vending machines.

SHOP FEATURES

COFFEESHOPS

SHOP HOURS:

Daily:
8:00am-1:00am

MAP IT

THE BORDER

Amstelveenseweg 1160, Amsterdam (Zuid) **:ADDRESS**

The Border Coffeeshop is an apt name given the location of this shop. It sits at the very southern edge of Amsterdam. Just across the intersection to the south, you will see a sign for Amstelveen, the next city. Directly to the west is also the beautiful and very large Amsterdam Bos, or "The Woods of Amsterdam." This park is a very interesting destination in its own right. It has a forest, several long running and biking trails, and a canal with a myriad of serene winding waterways throughout.

There is even a working farm here. Come at the right time, and you may run into a massive Schotse Hooglanders (Red Highland Cow) grazing openly in a field. You will also find Kersenbloesempark ("Cherry Blossom Park"), which is home to four hundred Japanese sakura trees. These were planted in 2010 to commemorate the 400-year relationship between The Netherlands and Japan. When the sakuras bloom in spring, it is one of the most amazing sights in the city.

The Shop

The Border is a takeaway only coffeeshop. Although there is no lounge here, the décor is quite posh. You may not be able to stick around after a purchase, but you do leave feeling like you have been to a higher-end establishment. The majority of their customers are local, so this buy-and-fly setup probably works well for its location.

The Menu

Visitors will find an interactive touchscreen menu at The Border, which lists their available weed and hash selections. The menu is fairly extensive, larger than what you typically find at a "locals" shop so far out of the city center. The expansiveness of the cannabis menu at The Border Coffeeshop is mirrored by a large assortment of pipes, grinders, vaporizers, and vaporizer accessories. The feeling is that this coffeeshop wants to be your quick one-stop shop for everything needed for smoking. In that regard, they seem to have been successful.

COFFEESHOPS

SHOP FEATURES

SHOP HOURS:

Daily:
10:00am-1:00am

THE DREAM

ADDRESS: Witte de Withstraat 30-A, Amsterdam (West)

MAP IT

Coffeeshop The Dream is located in De Krommerdt (The Curves) section of Amsterdam West. It is not far from Rembrandtpark, one of Amsterdam's most lush green areas; just a moderate walk to the west. This is a largely residential neighborhood, which does not see a great deal of tourist traffic compared to the city center. As such, The Dream largely caters to local residents, though all are welcome here.

The Shop

The Dream is a fairly traditional Dutch coffeeshop. The décor in the smoking lounge is basic, not a lot of frills. Stools, chairs, and a couple of comfortable leather benches provide seating. It is a place to get some smoke and hang out. Simple. This is not a tourist-oriented shop. The key feature here is likely the billiards table. There is also a beautiful garden area in the back, if you are looking for a little fresh air and peace.

The Menu

The cannabis menu at Coffeeshop The Dream is modest in size. On the weed-side of the menu, expect half a dozen options, give or take. These are largely going to be old-school strains… local favorites such as Amnesia, White Widow, Haze hybrids. The hashish-side is much smaller; usually just a couple of options here. These are most often traditional pressed imports from Morocco.

If you are hungry, they do offer a handful of snack options at The Dream. In addition, they have a decent variety of hot and cold beverages. While not a gourmet food and drink type of place, they offer enough to satisfy the munchies.

Autumn in Rembrandtpark

COFFEESHOPS

SHOP FEATURES

SHOP HOURS:

Daily:
7:00am-12:00am

THE NOON

ADDRESS: Zieseniskade 22, Amsterdam (Centrum)

MAP IT

The Noon Coffeeshop is located on Zieseniskade, in the southwestern part of the canal ring. It is close to the Rijksmuseum, home to some of the most famous Dutch paintings, which is found just on the other side of the s100 motorway. The immediate surroundings are just a bit more residential, and runs at a slightly slower pace than you see in the middle of the centrum. Still, there is a lot happening around here, making it a great part of the city to walk around.

The Shop

This establishment is not expansive. The Noon is made up of one room, occupying one floor. However, the space is open, and feels larger than it is. The décor inside is decidedly artsy. The walls are covered with beautiful hand-painted murals, some of which run the full length and height of the wall. Seating is mainly in the form of wide, leather-topped benches here, which are fronted by polished wood tables. The room is very comfortable, with a relaxed and welcoming feel to it - a great place to hang out and smoke.

The front of the building has a lot of glass. This lets in a good amount of natural light. On warm days, the wide front window is often open as well. This provides a ton of fresh air, as well as a sense of connection to the outside. While The Noon may be in an area of the city that sees a great deal of tourist traffic, this is a coffeeshop popular with locals as well. On many afternoons, it can be quite crowded at The Noon.

The Menu

This place has a reputation for quality cannabis, and at one time the shop was active in competitions. They are most known for their blueberry strain, something they have cultivated since the 1990s. Combine this with more reasonable pricing compared to other shops in the city center, and we can understand its draw with Amsterdam residents. Do not let this dissuade you. The Noon sees its fair share of travelers, many of whom are looking for a taste of their famous Blueberry.

COFFEESHOPS

SHOP FEATURES

SHOP HOURS:

Daily:
10:00am-1:00am

THE OLD CHURCH

ADDRESS: Amstel 8, Amsterdam (Centrum)

MAP IT

The Old Church coffeeshop is located on Amstel, near the top of the Amstel canal, where this busy waterway feeds into the Rokin. The Mundtplein ("Mint Square") is just to the south. This is a very busy part of Amsterdam centrum, with a high density of small shops, boutiques, restaurants, pubs, and nightclubs. Kalverstraat, a main shopping street in Amsterdam, also terminates here. Likewise, the area can be quite crowded, teeming with activity.

The Shop

This shop takes its name from the Oude Kerk (Old Church), a famous historical church and architectural landmark found in the Red Light District. The Oude Kerk is a popular tourist attraction, and The Old Church Coffeeshop once sat right next to this famous building. This provided a steady draw of customers. This original location, however, has since closed. The new shop (formerly The Old Church 2) took over the name of the original location, although it is found in a much different part of the city.

The interior of this shop is far from what you would expect with a name like Old Church. Instead of being "old", the décor in here is quite modern. One of the most notable features is an exposed brick wall, which is tastefully framed with metal and wood trim. This is complimented by hanging lights, polished wood tables, and leather-topped benches and stools. There is also some stunning artwork hanging on the walls depicting famous counterculture figures like Bob Marley and Jimi Hendrix. This all combines to give The Old Church Coffeeshop the feeling of a small but trendy urban coffee house, or high-end restaurant.

The Menu

The cannabis menu at the Old Church is substantial. On the weed-side, expect to find close to two dozen strains on order. There is a good mix of old and new here. You will find established Amsterdam favorites like White Widow and Amnesia, side-by-side with modern hybrids like Kosher Kush and LA Confidential. The hashish-side of the menu is similarly impressive. Though the selection is smaller, they carry both traditional imports, and a variety of stronger Dutch neder-hasj (isolator) varieties. Like many shops, pre-rolled hash and weed joints round out the selection.

Aside from cannabis, they also make some very good coffee here. The selection includes the basics such as latte, cappuccino, espresso, Americano etc., along with a couple of their own specialty coffees. There is also fresh mint tea, and a wide selection of soda, energy drinks, and juices. Some desserts and basic snacks can be found here too.

SHOP FEATURES

COFFEESHOPS

SHOP HOURS:
Daily:
10:00am-12:00am

MAP IT

THE OTHERSIDE

Reguliersdwarsstraat 6, Amsterdam (Centrum) **:ADDRESS**

The Otherside Coffeeshop is located in Amsterdam Centrum, close to the famous Amsterdam floating Flower Market ("Bloemenmarkt"). It resides on Reguliersdwarsstraat, which is known as Amsterdam's famous gay street. This is a hotspot for city nightlife, with an ample selection of LBGT (gay-friendly) pubs, nightclubs, cafés, and other businesses. If you are in the city to enjoy the scene, you will undoubtedly come across this coffeeshop.

The Shop

This establishment is one of two well-known LGBT coffeeshops in Amsterdam. The other is Free I, which is located towards the other end of Reguliersdwarsstraat. For any visitors unaware, there are a couple of conspicuously placed rainbow flags and a sign reading "Gay St." behind the counter making sure the point is not lost. The Other Side is not a gay-only establishment, by any means. All visitors are welcome here, regardless of orientation and identity.

The front of this shop is the smoking room. It is not particularly large, but open and comfortable nonetheless. The décor is a bit contemporary, a bit artsy. Faux granite tables, leather-topped stools, oversized portraits, and a mix of abstract and chandelier-style lighting all add to the ambiance of this place.

Towards the back, one will find the ordering counter. Here you can purchase cannabis, coffees, or from a selection of basic drinks and snacks. Overall, we would say that The Otherside is a chill place with an upbeat vibe.

Note that they maintain this shop as a WiFi Free zone. As they have a sign explaining, The Otherside is a place where you are expected to "Have a break. Talk to your neighbor. Dare to be WiFi free."

The Menu

The cannabis menu here is moderate in size. On the weed-side, they carry a little less than a dozen options. The strains are mainly locally grown, with old-school genetics. You might also find an import or two from Thailand or Jamaica. These will be very weak, however, and are recommended only for beginners. The hashish-side of the menu is a bit more substantive. They like traditional pressed imports here. Additionally, they do not favor any particular source country, so expect high product diversity. Pre-rolled joints, both pure cannabis and tobacco mixed, round out the menu.

COFFEESHOPS

SHOP FEATURES

SHOP HOURS:

Mon-Fri:
9:00am-1:00am
Sat:
7:00am-1:00am
Sun:
7:00am-12:00am

THE PLUG

ADDRESS: Nieuwezijds Voorburgwal 132, Amsterdam (Centrum)

MAP IT

The Plug Coffeeshop is found on the busy street of Nieuwezijds Voorburgwal ("New Side Front Bastion Wall"). It is just a bit south of Centraal Station, towards the west side of the canal ring. This is one of the newest shops in Amsterdam, technically speaking. For a long time it was known as Utopia, but changed hands in early 2018. Interestingly, the new owner also runs The Plug cannabis club in Barcelona, which is well known for its connoisseur products. As it was explained to us, the owner always wanted to have a coffeeshop in Amsterdam. Now, he finally does.

The Shop

The inside of The Plug has a long lounge area. The décor has been updated quite a bit since changing ownership. The walls are dark with a modern pattern and texture. Seating is in the form of large comfortable leather benches; restaurant booth-style. Grab a booth, and you will have ample room to spread out. Soft accent lighting provides a notable "posh pub or nightclub" feel to this coffeeshop, though it admittedly is too small to pack in a crowd. In the back is a large bar area for ordering cannabis products, as well as basic refreshments.

Large windows in the front allow ample light to enter. While this shop can be a bit dark at night, it can be quite bright and open during the day. Outside, one will also find a large white picnic table. When the weather is nice, this can also be a great spot to chill, take in some sun and fresh air, and watch the local activity. This part of the city can be quite busy. In our experience the atmosphere at The Plug is relaxed, the music chill, and the shop clean and well-maintained.

The Menu

The cannabis menu at The Plug coffeeshop is fairly large. On the weed-side, you may find as many as two dozen strains. They carry many contemporary USA genetics too. Think Kush strains, Gorilla Glue. They also have a high priced "Special" section for California imports. The hashish side of the menu is much smaller, but has a nice mix of imported and more potent domestic ice-hash (Nederhasj) varieties. They also have pre-rolled joints, and edibles such as muffins and brownies. The quality, particularly of their flower, has been exceptional thus far, warranting The Plug recognition as a connoisseur establishment. As always, we will continue to keep an eye out to see if they are able to maintain the high quality standards they have set thus far.

COFFEESHOPS

SHOP FEATURES

SHOP HOURS:
Daily:
9:00am-11:00pm

THE POINT

ADDRESS: Derde Oosterparkstraat 73, Amsterdam (Oost)

MAP IT

The Point Coffeeshop is located on Derde Oosterparkstraat, in a heavily residential part of Amsterdam Oost (East). The name of this street translates essentially into "Third Eastern Park Street", referencing its proximity to Oosterpark ("Eastern Park"). Eastern Park is a large and beautiful green area, with both a natural lake and man-made pools. It is arguably the most poplar park in this section of the city, and well worth a visit if you are in the area. The wider neighborhood around this shop is also quite beautiful. It is a great place to walk around if you like quiet side streets, and small outdoor cafés.

The Shop

The owners of The Point Coffeeshop are from Ghana. This is proudly displayed on their red, green and yellow sign out front, as well as a national flag they have hung behind the ordering counter. Their establishment is a locals' shop, which primarily serves as a take-and-go location. Residents in the area generally just pop in for a quick cannabis purchase. However, they do have a small seating area at this shop, which features a couple of comfortable old couches. When the lounge is occupied, you can usually find a handful of shop regulars here. If it is open and you need a place for a short rest, you will probably find it suitable.

The Menu

The cannabis menu is fairly robust here, especially when you consider they are a shop that caters almost exclusively to locals. Strain hunters visiting the city almost never find this place. On the weed-side, expect to find roughly a dozen strains on most days. The genetics are mainly old-school, but notable with the choice of recognized favorites. The hashish-side of the menu tends to be short; just a few traditional pressed imports.

They sell cannabis in pre-weighed bags here, which keep the transactions simple and fast. Pricing on both weed and hashish tends to be reasonable at this shop, which is more common with those businesses that service mostly local repeat customers. You can find a nice deal out here versus the city center.

Resting in the Shade
Amsterdam West

COFFEESHOPS

SHOP FEATURES

SHOP HOURS:

Daily:
9:00am-1:00am

THE SAINT

ADDRESS: Regulierssteeg 2, Amsterdam (Centrum)

MAP IT

The Saint Coffeeshop and Juicebar is found on Reguliersteeg, a small side street of Amstel, in the city's southern canal belt. It is close to the Bloemenmarkt, Amsterdam's famous floating Flower Market. This area of the city is also host to Rembrandtplein (Rembrandt Square), which is just a couple of blocks to the southeast. You will find an abundance of restaurants and shopping options here, which also makes it a very popular part of the city among travelers.

The Shop

The inside of this coffeeshop is fairly small. To accommodate a sufficient number of visitors, guests are focused around small circular tables. Tall, thin stools and long benches provide seating. The décor in here would be best described as jungle themed. There is a great deal of mural art on the walls to that effect. Outside, you will also find a long row of tables and chairs, if you prefer some fresh city air. The Saint would best be described as a traditional Dutch establishment. There are not a lot of frills, but there is a discernible focus on efficiency and service.

This shop does have a noteworthy tradition. Like a few others, it is a place where notes from visitors around the world are proudly displayed, whether they are written on rolling papers, stickers, or just small pieces of paper. Unusual here though is most are affixed to the overhead ceiling. You must have to stand on one of the stools to do it. Not sure who does it or how safe that is, but you might want to ask even if you have good balance.

The Menu

The cannabis menu is robust at The Saint. On the weed-side they usually have close to a dozen strains, mainly old-school genetics. This shop is more about hashish, though. This section of the menu usually hosts a dozen or more varieties, pressed imports from traditional source countries like Morocco, Lebanon, and Afghanistan. They also make decent edibles here. Where as many shops just list a poorly defined "space cake", they usually have different flavors of muffins and brownies on offer.

Aside from cannabis, do not forget that this is also a juice bar. If you are interested in some fresh squeezed orange juice or a strawberry smoothie, you are in the right place. They also make good coffee here, along with milkshakes, and a standard selection of other basic drinks and snacks.

COFFEESHOPS

COFFEESHOPS

SHOP FEATURES

SHOP HOURS:
Daily:
12:00pm-1:00am

THE SPIRIT

ADDRESS: Westerstraat 121, Amsterdam (Centrum)

  MAP IT

The Spirit Coffeeshop is found in the Jordaan area of Amsterdam, known for being a more peaceful section of the busy city center. Over the years the Jordaan has become one of the most desirable (and expensive) areas of the city to live in. Consequently, this neighborhood has experienced a great deal of economic growth and has attracted many new businesses. There is no shortage of small restaurants, cafés, trendy boutiques, and art galleries. These of course fit comfortably alongside plenty of old Dutch residential buildings, making this both a fun and beautiful part of the city.

The Shop

The Spirit is an establishment that would be best described as a cross between a traditional Dutch coffeeshop and a retro amusement center. Its interior is traditional with a lot of wood, and not a lot of frills. Not the place you will find granite tile floors, leather couches, and a full menu.

The above is not to say The Spirit Coffeeshop is boring. To the contrary, its "retro amusement center" side makes this one of the most interesting coffeeshops in the city. While many boast an old video game or pinball machine, The Spirit is like an old-school arcade. There is no other establishment like it in Amsterdam. Inside you will find a full wall of pinball machines (eight in total), a retro multi-arcade, and even a dual cockpit car racing game. If you enjoy playing old video games and/or pinball while consuming cannabis products, The Spirt is without question the place for you!

The Menu

The retro arcade aspect of The Spirit aside, this is a fairly traditional Dutch coffeeshop. The cannabis menu usually reflects a mix of old-school weed strains, along with imported varieties of hashish. They tend not to chase the latest award-winning genetics. The pricing is a bit more reasonable here than many shops in the city center as well. This is probably owing to the strong local clientele. Though The Spirit Coffeeshop is frequented by tourists (incidentally, some just looking for the retro games), the bulk of the visitors seem to be from the area.

It is also of note that they serve coffee, tea, soft drinks, juices, and some basic snacks here. Not a full service restaurant, but has more than enough to keep the munchies at bay, and you tapping away on the buttons.

COFFEESHOPS

COFFEESHOPS

SHOP FEATURES

SHOP HOURS:
Daily:
10:00am-12:00am

THE STORE

ADDRESS: Singel 14, Amsterdam (Centrum)

MAP IT

The Store Coffeeshop is a small shop on the north end of the Singel canal. This is a very busy area of the city center, which sees a great deal of tourist traffic. Understandably, the beautiful architecture and ample businesses in the area is a major draw.

The Shop

This is a rock 'n' roll themed shop. As expected, they play a lot of 60's and 70's classic rock in here. The main focus of the décor also reflects this era of music. For a long time this shop was actually known as "The Doors Coffeeshop", though they recently rebranded. Jim Morrison and The Doors photographs, as well as other memorabilia, still line the walls.

The inside has not changed much. Aside from this, the interior is fairly traditional for a Dutch coffeeshop. There is a lot of wood, and not a lot of frills. Outside you will find two picnic-style benches, once custom painted with an early likeness of Morrison (sadly, now just plain). These are prime seats on a sunny afternoon, probably more so due to the location than the art. This is a busy area of the city, as well as the Singel canal. The corner often draws quite a crowd at times. Presumably, the benches contribute to this. Sitting waterside here with a good smoke can make for a pleasant time.

The Menu

The cannabis menu at The Store Coffeeshop is a bit unique. Instead of using a standard printed or digital product list, they keep a "dark box". You will find it on the left side of the counter. Next to the box sits a large red button. When you hold it down, the inside of the box lights up, revealing physical samples and prices of their offerings. There is a mix of hashish and weed strains, generally more traditional varieties (old-school Amsterdam weed strains and imported pressed hashish).

Aside from cannabis, they also offer coffee and some standard drinks and snacks. However, this is far from a full service shop. They have the basics, if they are needed.

COFFEESHOPS

SHOP FEATURES

SHOP HOURS:
Daily:
7:00am-1:00am

THE STUD

ADDRESS: Molukkenstraat 581, Amsterdam (Oost)

MAP IT

The Stud Coffeeshop sits near the eastern edge of Amsterdam-Oost (Amsterdam East) in the Indische Buurt neighborhood. This translates into "Indies Neighborhood". You will notice many of the streets are named after islands and other parts of the former Dutch East Indies colonies. This shop is close to Flevopark, a large park with plenty of walking trails, tennis courts, and even an outdoor swimming pool.

The Shop

There is a seating area behind the counter here, which also serves as a smoking room. It is not very large, however, but comfortable and well appointed. They also have a television and a Volcano vaporizer. With vaporization becoming increasingly popular with cannabis connoisseurs, it is a good addition. They serve coffee, drinks, and some snacks here. There is enough here to keep you comfortable. More commonly though, The Stud Coffeeshop functions as a take-away establishment. A lot of people come in just to pick up some bits for the week. This is surely a testament to the cannabis quality here.

As you might expect being so far out of the city center, The Stud Coffeeshop caters mainly to Amsterdam locals. While they are welcoming to all, this is not an area of the city that is dense with tourists. The upside to this is that prices are much more competitive here than in Amsterdam Centrum. Expect a nice savings if you take a trip out here.

The Menu

Interesting for a smaller local shop, The Stud has invested in a full interactive digital menu with touch screen capability. Just touch a strain on the list, and a screen will open explaining its pedigree and unique properties. The system even has language options, ensuring that no communication barrier can prevent you from making the right purchase.

The cannabis menu itself is fairly large, with more than a dozen weed options. These include many established local favorites, as well as some of the more contemporary strains in the city. They work with Amsterdam Genetics, so expect some quality genetics from the USA (think Kush, Diesel). There are nearly as many options on the hash-side of the menu; all traditional imported varieties. The quality here is highly noteworthy. They also serve space cakes and pre-rolled joints. Pricing is mainly based on common bank notes. So you will find bags of various weights selling for 5€, 10€, and 20€, which makes for fast and easy transactions.

COFFEESHOPS

THE STUD

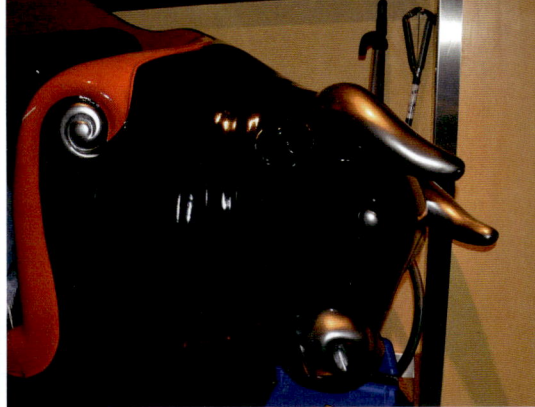

CONNOISSEUR GUIDE: AMSTERDAM

COFFEESHOPS

SHOP FEATURES

SHOP HOURS:

Daily
10:00am-12:00am

TOPWEAZLE

ADDRESS: Vechtstraat 63, Amsterdam (Zuid)

MAP IT

Topweazle Coffeeshop is found in the Rijnbuurt neighborhood of Amsterdam-Zuid (South). It is close to the Amstel River, and just a short walk from Martin Luther King Park. Aside from being a beautiful green area, every summer this park hosts the De Parade Theatre Festival; an event best described as a cross between a traditional carnival and a traveling theatre. With games, small rides, food vendors, and performers galore, it is both a bit unusual, and incredibly fun. We highly suggest a visit if you are in the city during the festival.

The Shop

Topweazle is a locals' gathering place, with a roomy smoking lounge. There is an African theme in this establishment. You will notice giant zebra and lion paintings on the walls, and various related bits of artwork and sculpture around the shop. The lounge is comfortable, especially its two-deep leather sofas. They also have ample extra amenities including WiFi, television, a dartboard, chess, and a table football (foosball) table. The vibe is generally upbeat and friendly in this coffeeshop, so do not worry if you are not a local. Note that they do prefer a slightly more mature crowd. This shop has a policy barring those under the age of 21, as opposed to the usual age of 18, from entry.

The Menu

The cannabis menu at Topweazle Coffeeshop is modest in size. The weed side of the menu is dominated by old-school favorites. Amsterdam is known for many specific strains, and you will likely find some of the more popular ones right here. For hashish, they have a small selection of imported pressed varieties. Pre-rolled joints are also available, if preferred to rolling your own.

Aside from cannabis, they also have a fair selection of coffees, teas, drinks, and basic snacks here.

De Reikermolen Windmill (circa 1636)

COFFEESHOPS

SHOP FEATURES

SHOP HOURS:
Daily:
9:00am-1:00am

TREFPUNT

ADDRESS: Zeeburgerdijk 33, Amsterdam (Oost)

MAP IT

Trefpunt Coffeeshop is found on Zeeburgerdijk, in the Oost (East) section of Amsterdam. The neighborhood here is largely residential, and a nice change of pace from the busy centrum. While there is not much to do on the immediate street here, Trefpunt is just around the corner from De Gooyer. This is Amsterdam's tallest wooden windmill, built back in 1814. It is an impressive iconic landmark. This is a perfect place for a photo, and the associated restaurant also has great food and an impressive beer selection.

The Shop

Trefpunt translates into "meeting point" in English. To that end, this shop does seem to live up to its name. Trefpunt Coffeeshop is a popular gathering place for locals. The interior is decidedly contemporary in appearance. Exposed brick and tiling on the walls provide a sense of contrast with the shop's polished hardwood floors and dark furniture. With its added green accent lighting, we would describe the whole vibe as urban-abstract-industrial.

This place is not just aesthetically pleasing. It is quite functional. There is usually ample room in the shop's smoking lounge areas. Seating is mainly in the form of cushy leather benches. Though it is not large, the place is definitely open, clean, and inviting. The shop seems to work hard to make sure it remains a comfortable place to hang out. If you prefer being outside, there is also a small fenced-in patio area out back.

The Menu

The cannabis menu at Trefpunt Coffeeshop is small. This is expected being that it is mainly a locals' place. In our experience, these shops usually keep a small, tight menu of familiar items. Often, pricing is more reasonable too. The weed-side will generally list several old-school varieties, with an occasional bit of imported genetics. For hashish, we have always noted this shop as strictly focusing on imported pressed varieties. Again, this is quite common outside the centrum. They also have pre-rolled joints, and a basic space cake for edibles.

CONNOISSEUR GUIDE: AMSTERDAM

COFFEESHOPS

CONNOISSEUR GUIDE: AMSTERDAM 307

COFFEESHOPS

SHOP FEATURES

SHOP HOURS:
Daily:
10:00am-1:00am

TWEEDE KAMER

ADDRESS: Heisteeg 6, Amsterdam (Centrum)

MAP IT

Tweede Kamer Coffeeshop is located on Heisteeg (Health Alley), a small side street on the edge of Spui square. This is a busy area for foot traffic, and among the more popular tourist destinations. Most people actually miss it, but this is the heart of the Amsterdam book scene. In addition to a nearly endless selection of small boutiques and cafés, if you look around the area you will find a high density of independent bookstores. This is a mecca for bookworms; the place in Amsterdam you want to go when searching for that first edition of something special. It is charming, even if you are not a bookworm.

The Shop

The name of this shop translates into "second room" in English. There is political meaning in this phrase. Tweede Kamer is the Dutch House of Representatives, a main branch of their elected government. The owners of this coffeeshop are not politicians, however. Actually, they are rooted in the coffeeshop industry, and have another famous shop to their credit: Coffeeshop Amsterdam. It may be a passive, thumbing of the nose at authorities. Whatever it is, it is memorable. We like it.

This shop first opened its doors in 1985. In the time since, Tweede Kamer has built itself up to be one of the more recognized coffeeshops in the city center. The décor in this shop is "modernized traditional." It is elegant, without the flash. The interior has an upscale pub or brown bar feel to it. There is a great deal of beautiful polished wood throughout - the bar counter, tables, booths, trim on the walls. This is accompanied by an ample collection of framed old pictures, artwork, and high-end fixtures.

This place is not big, which perhaps adds to its distinct warm and cozy atmosphere. This shop would actually make an excellent bar of a coffeeshop, had the city not banned such establishments years ago. No matter. Tweed Kamer is in a busy area of the city center, and is a long established brand here. Even without the draw of serving alcohol, this place does great business, as evidenced by how crowded it can get on most afternoons.

The Menu

Tweede Kamer is noted for its quality cannabis menu, not surprising given the owners. They offer a diverse variety of weed (flower) and hashish (concentrate) options here. The imported hashes, in particular, tend to be exceptional here. Many options are rich and flavorful in our experience. They also serve great coffee, along with teas, juices, drinks, and a selection of small snacks.

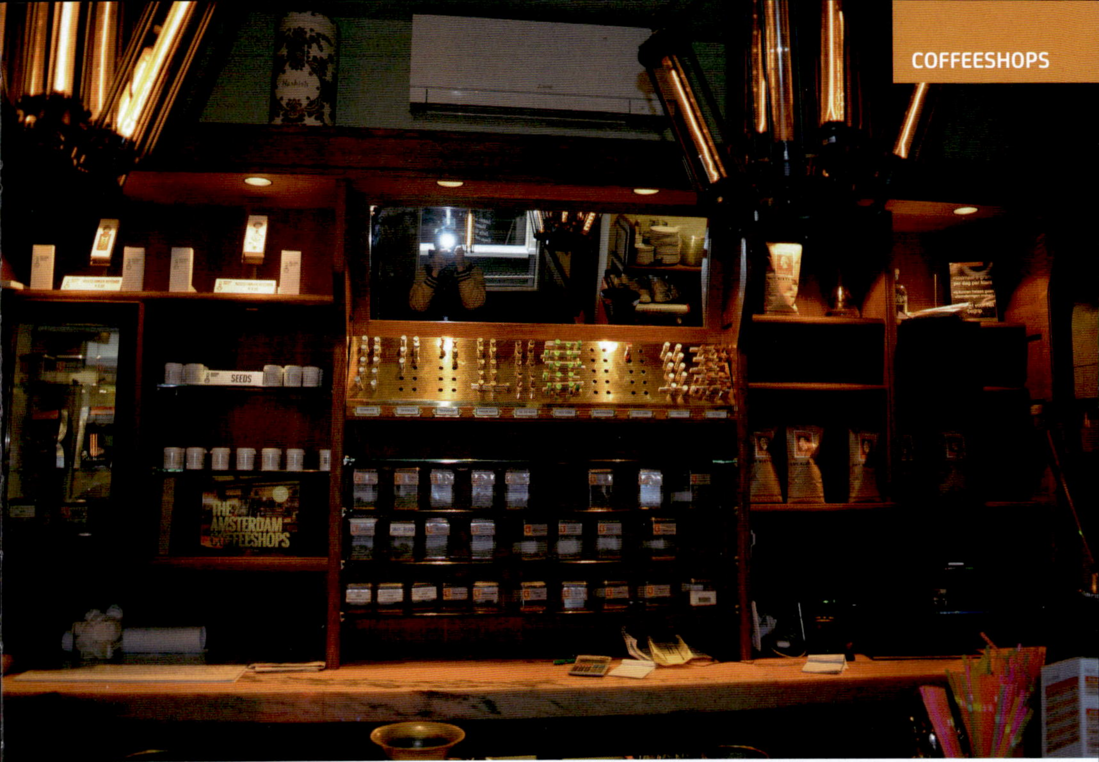
THE AMSTERDAM COFFEESHOPS
SEEDS

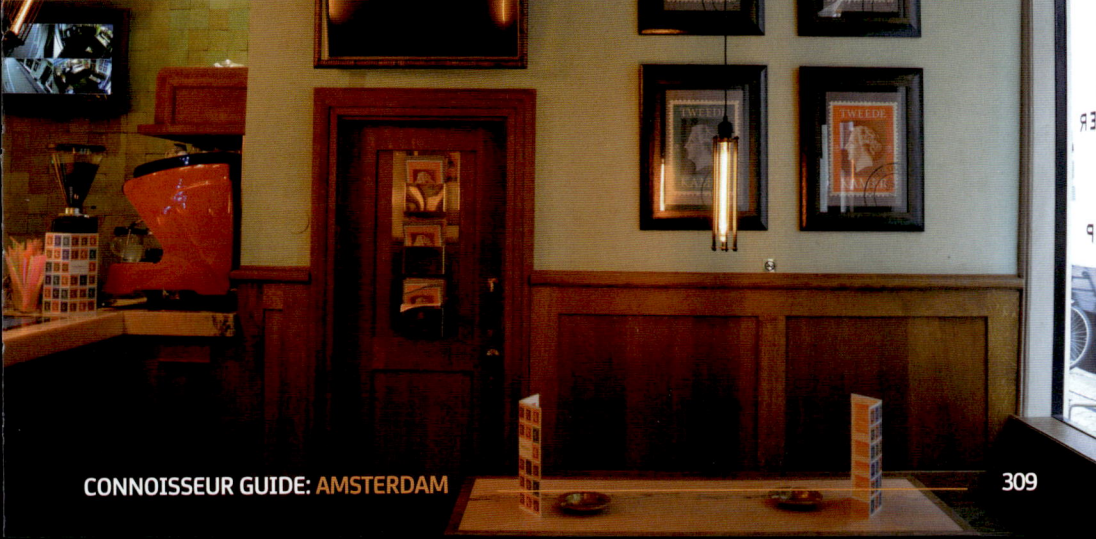

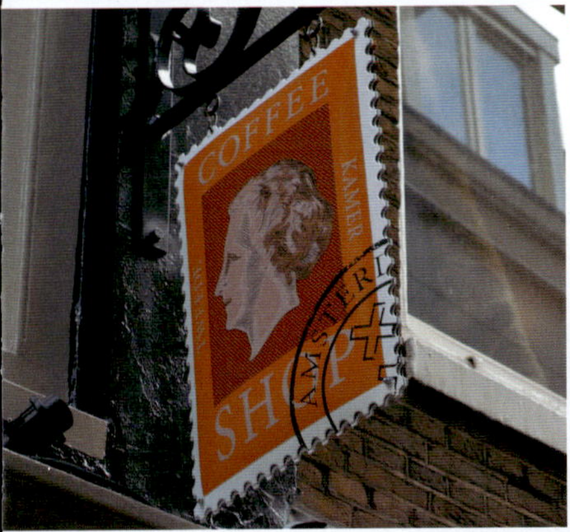
COFFEE
KAMER
SHOP
AMSTERDAM

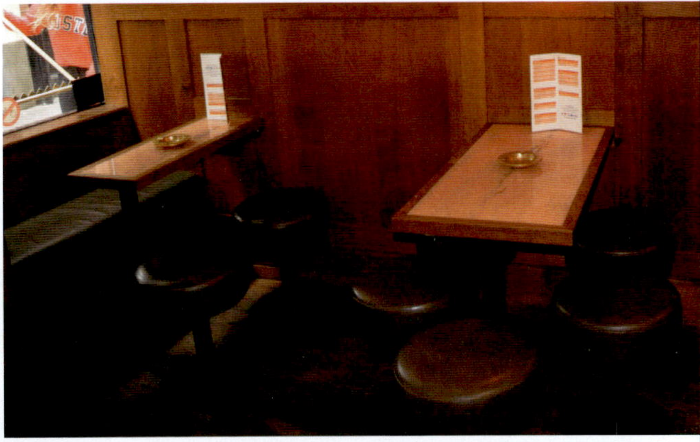

TWEEDE
KAMER

COFFEESHOPS

SHOP FEATURES

SHOP HOURS:
Daily:
10:00am-1:00am

VONDEL

ADDRESS: Overtoom 451, Amsterdam (West)

MAP IT

Vondel Coffeeshop is located on the main road of Overtoom, and sits just to the north of Vondelpark. The neighborhood here is largely residential, and decidedly upscale. The architecture, modern classic and beautiful, with many stunning buildings immediately bordering the park. Vondel coffeeshop fits in well with the surrounding area.

The Shop

As seen immediately when approaching this shop, this is quite an upscale location. The façade is made of polished dark wood, and runs the entire stretch, top to bottom, of this street-level shop. That is, barring the large bay window and sections of ornate stained-glass that allows an ample amount of light in.

Inside Vondel you will find a split-level floor plan. It is fairly roomy. There is a bar-like area for ordering on the main floor. Upstairs and downstairs you will find an enclosed tobacco room and a lounge, respectively. Both have large screen TV's, and are quite comfortable. The location is furnished with plush leather benches and stools, and has large wood tables to stretch out at. The bright rooms, recessed lighting, and bit of exposed brick also make this place feel like a modern loft or small city nightclub. In short, the interior matches the polish and sophistication of the exterior very well.

The Menu

This coffeeshop has a moderately sized cannabis menu. The selections favors weed (flower). Expect to find some old school favorite strains, mixed with more modern varieties. There are typically decent hash offerings as well, along with edibles in the form of traditional space cakes. Aside from this, they also have a drink menu (sodas/juices), some basic snacks, and frankly, some pretty good coffee.

As nice as Vondel Coffeeshop is, staying inside can be difficult on a warm sunny day. Vondelpark is one of the most popular parks in Amsterdam. It is beautifully maintained, lush with greenery, and peppered with a series of connected ponds and creeks. It is a serene respite from the busy city, and we highly recommend a visit before/after a stop here. Note that although Vondelpark is in Amsterdam-Zuid, Vondel Coffeeshop is technically over the line in Amsterdam-West.

COFFEESHOPS

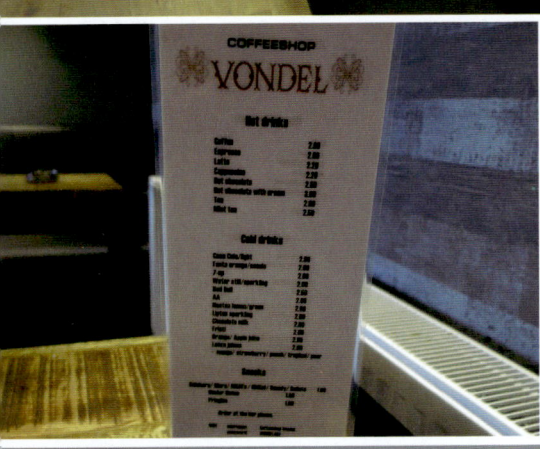

CONNOISSEUR GUIDE: AMSTERDAM

COFFEESHOPS

SHOP FEATURES

SHOP HOURS:
Daily:
10:00am-11:00pm

VOYAGERS

ADDRESS: Geldersekade 2, Amsterdam (Centrum)

MAP IT

Voyagers Coffeeshop is located just to the southeast of the main entrance to Centraal Station. This is an especially high trafficked part of Amsterdam given that Centraal Station is the entry and exodus point to the city for a large number of its visitors each and every day. Maybe so, but Voyagers sits on a less busy street corner at the northern tip of the Geldersekade canal. This location offers a respite from the hustle and bustle. It is quite nice.

The Shop

Voyagers coffeeshop is part of the budget smoker-friendly Voyagers hotel. It is found at the front of the building, and consequently the budtender also functions as the hotel receptionist. The entrance to the hotel is on the side, however, so the main entrance here is devoted principally to the coffeeshop. This hotel is quite popular with smokers. Many of those that book here undoubtedly do so to take advantage of its proximity to the downstairs coffeeshop.

The coffeeshop itself is not large by most standards. The tall narrow construction common to old city buildings is apparent here. Voyagers exists only on one level, on the main floor of the building. There is an open room in the front, with sufficient seating on most afternoons. Also, you will find an enclosed smoking lounge to the side. The décor is sparse, but the space is comfortable and down-to-earth. Further, there is clearly a "retro arcade" theme to its branding, as evidenced by the Space Invaders character that serves as the shop mascot. The gaming geeks in us just wish they would make good on it with an arcade. But we digress.

The vibe inside Voyagers tends to be chill, and highly accommodating to serious connoisseurs. This is reflected in the ready-access to quality glassware as well as a Volcano vaporizer in the shop. Let's face it. This is a requirement these days if you want your coffeeshop to be taken seriously by connoisseurs. And that is exactly what Voyagers aims to be, by our observation.

The Menu

As for the cannabis menu, it is another reflection of Voyagers' focus on connoisseur level product. While the selection is not extensive, this establishment does receive a great deal of attention for its quality. They mainly sell weed, often contemporary genetics from the USA. The coffeeshop has definitely been partnering with quality breeders. Likewise, they often have a menu with competition-winning selections on it. We recognize this shop as a connoisseur establishment; a distinction well deserved.

COFFEESHOPS

SHOP FEATURES

SHOP HOURS:

Daily:
8:00am-1:00am

WARDA 1

ADDRESS: Van Woustraat 147, Amsterdam (Zuid)

MAP IT

Warda 1 Coffeeshop is located on Van Woustraat, in the De Pijp section of Amsterdam Zuid (South). The immediate neighborhood around Warda is a fairly good mix of residential and commercial. While we would say this is a more "locals" corner of the city, there is most certainly plenty to do here if you find yourself visiting. It can be quite lively, and there is no shortage of restaurants, bars, cafés, and boutique shops in the area.

The Shop

The interior of Warda 1 feels more like a nightclub than a traditional Dutch coffeeshop. This is most notable in the shop's smoking lounge in the back. Here, you will find comfortable Moroccan couches paired with neon lighting and trendy wood accents. The vibe is "abstract", but quite agreeable, and certainly much more lavish than you will find in your average coffeeshop. You will also notice a second enclosed smoking lounge in here. The area is separated from the rest of the shop in order to comply with EU smoking regulations. This allows for the consumption of tobacco products (or mixed weed/tobacco) on premises.

The Menu

This shop has the identical menu as their other location. The cannabis selection is moderate in size. You will probably find roughly a half dozen varieties on the weed-side. The strains here are largely old-school varieties. Think Hazes and White Widow. They have roughly the same number of options on the hashish-side, which holds mainly traditional pressed Moroccan imports.

Pricing on both sides of the menu tends to be quite reasonable compared to more tourist-focused shops in the centrum. This is expected of shops that mainly service locals. If you want to maximize savings, they also offer discounts for five-gram purchases on most items.

CONNOISSEUR GUIDE: AMSTERDAM

SHOP FEATURES

COFFEESHOPS

SHOP HOURS:
Daily:
8:00am-1:00am

MAP IT

WARDA 2

Javastraat 104, Amsterdam (Oost) :**ADDRESS**

Warda 2 Coffeeshop is located on Javastraat, in the Indische Buurt section of Amsterdam Oost (East). Javastraat is probably the most popular shopping street in this part of the city. There is an ample selection of trendy, independent restaurants, bars, cafés, bakeries, and boutiques. While this is not regarded as a tourist-heavy neighborhood, it is a beautiful part of the city to visit, and definitely worth putting on your destination list.

The Shop

There is a fairly large smoking lounge at Warda 2 Coffeeshop. The décor inside is modern. Seating is basic, but comfortable. Around the shop you will find plenty of contemporary-styled tables and chairs. The lounge is open and bright, and generally kept clean. They also have several extra amenities including a table football (foosball) game, billiards, and flat screen TV's. The shop can be quite popular with local residents, often attracting a lively crowd in the evenings.

The Menu

The cannabis selection at Warda 2 is moderate in size. Similar to their other location, you will find roughly a half dozen varieties of weed here. Expect to find old-school genetics, almost exclusively. This means items like the Hazes, White Widow, Bubble Gum. The hashish menu is usually a bit smaller, and tends to be stocked with traditional Moroccan imported pressed varieties. Like Warda 1, pricing is reasonable here in our experience, and they offer quantity discounts on most items.

They also offer a large selection of soda and other drinks, along with some basic snacks, if needed.

CONNOISSEUR GUIDE: AMSTERDAM

COFFEESHOPS

SHOP FEATURES

SHOP HOURS:

Daily:
8:00am-1:00am

WAUW SHOP

ADDRESS: Spaarndammerdijk 9, Amsterdam (Centrum)

MAP IT

The Wauw Shop ("The Wow Shop") coffeeshop is found a bit to the north of Westerpark, at the edge of the Spaarndammerbuurt neighborhood. Immediately to the north is the Houthavens, where you will find docks, and a lot of industrial activity. To the south, however, Spaarndammerbuurt is largely residential. If you head here, perhaps you will find the quiet streets a nice change of pace from the hustle and bustle of Amsterdam centrum.

The Shop

As you enter The Wauw Shop, you approach a large security counter. It is the kind with a bulletproof partition to protect employees from robbery. Not that this is a bad neighborhood by any stretch, but these businesses handle a lot of cash and weed. As such, they can become targets, especially being in a less popular (Read as: "quieter with less people watching") location. You simply slide your money into the small window, and the budtender will slide back your purchase.

The Wauw Shop is largely frequented by locals. They do see tourists from time-to-time, though, being somewhat near the city center. Regardless, if you are a regular or a first time guest, this is not a "hangout" coffeeshop. You cannot smoke here. It is a strictly take-and-go location. There is, however, a small table in the corner, if you need to take a minute or two to roll a joint before heading out the door.

The Menu

The cannabis menu here is modest in size. On the weed side you should find several strains, typically old-school varieties, which are more recognized by the locals. They have a decent selection of traditional imported pressed hashish here as well.

Pricing on both sides of the menu tends to be much lower per gram than many of the shops in the center, given the local customer base. In addition to the basic products, The Wauw Shop also sells pre-rolled joint packs and a space cake (pound cake) or two.

SHOP FEATURES

COFFEESHOPS

SHOP HOURS:

Daily:
10:00am-1:00am

MAP IT

YIN-YANG

Knollendamstraat 5, Amsterdam (West) **:ADDRESS**

Yin Yang Coffeeshop is located in the Spaarndammer neighborhood of Amsterdam West. This is a largely residential area, with wider streets and more trees than you tend to see in the city centrum. It is just far out enough that it runs at a slower pace, and sees a much smaller tourist crowd. Yin-Yang sits just a few blocks to the north of Westerpark, one of the city's most notable green areas. It is definitely worth a stop if you are walking around this neighborhood on a sunny day.

The Shop

Yin-Yang Coffeeshop is a take-and-go establishment. There is no smoking lounge here. There is only a small shelf for rolling up your purchase before leaving. It mainly services locals, who stop in for a quick purchase. Even so, this shop has an open-arms policy for all visitors which one may feel is apparent by the very name of the shop. Yin and Yang, represents how nature allows opposing forces to work together in unison to the benefit of one another. But a sign displayed inside describes the attitude and karma-based philosophy of the shop perfectly: "Life is balance, you get what you give". We could not agree more.

The Menu

The cannabis menu is moderate in size here. Their stock seems to rotate quite a bit, with items frequently selling out. As such, expect to see little tags covering up out-of-stock or discontinued items. There is a fairly good balance of weed and hash options here, though the shop tends to favor hashish. The weed is quite traditional; Amsterdam old-school strains. The hashish options are traditional imported items, mainly Moroccan. Pricing tends to be reasonable, given the local clientele and focus on repeat business.

COFFEESHOPS

SHOP FEATURES

SHOP HOURS:

Sun-Thurs:
12:00pm-7:00pm
Fri-Sat:
12:00pm-8:00pm

YO-YO

ADDRESS: Tweede Jan van der Heijdenstraat 79/HS, Amsterdam (Zuid)

MAP IT

Yo-Yo Coffeeshop is located in the Oude Pijp (Old Pipe) section of Amsterdam South (Zuid). It sits on the eastern edge of this neighborhood, just a block from the Amstel river. This is a highly desirable residential part of Amsterdam; popular with young professionals. Though the immediate streets here can be a bit quiet, the De Pijp has no shortage of trendy bars, restaurants, cafés, and boutiques.

The Shop

This is an impressive coffeeshop on several levels. First, the shop itself. The décor at Yo-Yo Coffeeshop leans towards contemporary with an open and spacious layout that is awash with natural light. Spotless polished hardwood floors, deep comfortable couches, and beautifully crafted café tables make the shop's two rooms feel like a perfect city apartment, or small local café. This place is warm and welcoming, at times feeling as cozy as your own living room. Hospitality is usually off the charts, too.

Yo-Yo is officially described as a "gallery" ("galerie") coffeeshop. True to form, it also serves as an art gallery. Beautiful works of art by local artists is on display throughout the shop, and is rotated often. If you like something, be sure to ask about it. They even offer art classes here. To further the "home" feeling of this place, Yo-Yo sometimes also serves hot food. While the selection may not be extensive, they will fix you up with a deliciously satisfying meal. This is a rare feature in the Amsterdam coffeeshop scene.

The Menu

The cannabis menu is robust at Yo-Yo Coffeeshop. The weed-side of the menu typically has a dozen options, give or take. They seem to specialize in outdoor organically grown weed. There are fewer options on the hashish-side, though they still have several types of imported pressed varieties. These are mainly from Morocco and Afghanistan. They also serve great coffee here, as well as tea, and a large selection of sodas and juices.

COFFEESHOPS

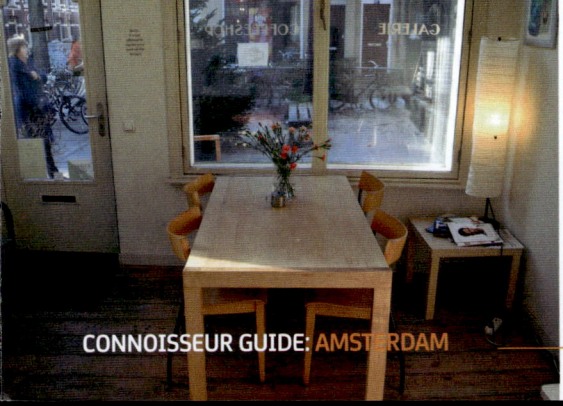

COFFEESHOPS

SHOP FEATURES

SHOP HOURS:

Daily:
7:00am-1:00am

1E HULP

ADDRESS: Marnixstraat 194, Amsterdam (Centrum)

MAP IT

1e Hulp Coffeeshop is located on Marnixstraat, at the western edge of Amsterdam Centrum. Just across the canal to the west is the s100 ring, a busy street that wraps around the city center and serves as a border for many neighborhoods. To the west is the section of the city known, appropriately, as Amsterdam-West. 1e Hulp is far enough out from the hustle and bustle of the centre that it is more commonly frequented by locals than tourists, though it gets its fair share of both. A reputation for quality cannabis, and some history of participating in marijuana competitions, has likely increased interest among tourists, who often make a special trip to see this interesting coffeeshop.

The Shop

The name of this shop literally translates into "First Aid". Perhaps they are referring to the palliative or medicinal benefits of cannabis. Either way, 1e Hulp is a shop of interest for a couple of reasons. The first and most obvious; the décor and atmosphere. This coffeeshop is quite nicely appointed, with an ornate Arabian theme throughout. It is also somewhat roomy, existing on three separate levels. You enter on the main floor, where you will find the cannabis serving counter. Upstairs is the shop's largest seating room. Though perhaps not expansive, it is quite comfortable, with plush couches and intricate wood-carved furniture. 1e Hulp is one of several shops in the city that has a resident cat. This one is quite friendly, and often found chilling out in the upstairs lounge.

Downstairs you will find an additional room for seating; perhaps the shop's most notable. There are couches, stools, and small tables here. Like the upstairs, everything is beautiful and plush. In the back, however, you will find something a bit extra on this floor... what would aptly be described as a "grand" seating area. Here, there is a small open section of room, elevated by a step-up platform. The section hosts a large plush U-shaped couch, and dark wood-carved coffee table. If you are with a group of people, be sure to check it out.

The Menu

The cannabis menu at 1e Hulp is fairly robust. The larger selection is on the weed-side, where you are likely to find over two dozen strains. These are some traditional Amsterdam favorites, but more so contemporary strains, many with USA genetics. The hash-side of the menu is also quite rich. These are mainly imported sieved press hashes, though they also usually stock some more potent isolator varieties. The edibles are also quite good. Where as the norm is one style space cake, this shop usually has several flavors and styles of muffins and cakes. Lastly, their pre-rolled joints selection is also quite good.

COFFEESHOPS

SHOP FEATURES

SHOP HOURS:

Daily:
9:00am-1:00am

3 FLOORS LOUNGE

ADDRESS: Halvemaansteeg 1, Amsterdam (Centrum)

MAP IT

3 Floors Lounge, formerly Andalucia Lounge, is located on the south side of the Amstel canal, adjacent to Rembrandtplein (Rembrandt Square).

The Shop

Though a fairly narrow building, common of architecture in the city center, this shop actually has three levels. This makes it quite roomy inside. The décor would be best described as simple, but contemporary. As you walk in on the first floor you will notice grey tiles under your feet, and green mood lighting all around. Here there is also a large counter for purchasing cannabis, as well as hot and cold drinks.

You will also find a row of stools and a long narrow table against one wall, if you need a place to sit and quickly roll a joint. If you plan to stay a while, it is recommended to take your purchase upstairs. Here you will find the two smoking lounge rooms that 3 Floors Lounge is named for. Both of these rooms have essentially the same layout.

There is modern bench seating that runs along three of the walls. In the center of the room are small tables with an ashtray on each, and large windows facing the street. You might find a stool or two, but the rooms are designed to encourage people to situate themselves along the walls. There are also TVs in both lounges. Note that on the second floor, the bench is uncovered (bare wood). The lounge is plusher on the top floor. Here, the seating has soft leather backing and cushions.

The Menu

The cannabis menu at 3 Floors Lounge is quite similar to many Dutch coffeeshops. There is a mix of weed strains, mainly recognized old-school favorites (think Amnesia, Cheese, Silver Haze). There are more options on the hash-side here. Most are traditional pressed hashes from places like Lebanon, Nepal, Morocco, and Afghanistan. They are also likely to have a higher potency isolator hash as well. In addition, they offer pre-rolled weed and hash joints, and the odd edible or two. They also offer free WiFi to their guests. If you are looking for a respite from the crowds of the Rembrandtplein, 3 Floors Lounge is a pretty good option.

COFFEESHOPS

CONNOISSEUR GUIDE: AMSTERDAM

COFFEESHOPS

SHOP FEATURES

SHOP HOURS:

Daily:
7:00am-1:00am

96

ADDRESS: Jan Pieter Heijestraat 96, Amsterdam (West)

MAP IT

Coffeeshop 96 is located on Jan Pieter Heijestraat, in the Oud-West (Old West) section of Amsterdam. It is a bit to the north of Vondelpark, one of the most notable green areas in the city. The neighborhood around here is largely residential. The streets are a bit quieter than in the city center. They can make for some quality sightseeing, if you are inclined to venture outside of the usual tourist spots. Being outside of central Amsterdam this shop caters largely to locals but, like most coffeeshops, is also welcoming to all visitors.

The Shop

Coffeeshop 96 is a hangout spot for locals. From the outside, it looks like a buy-and-fly spot with its unassuming appearance. The interior is small and has an enclosed smoking room, so that the shop is in compliance with EU regulations, and may permit tobacco consumption on site. There is also seating by the ordering counter. The shop is not focused on the décor or aesthetics. It is simply practical and functional.

Coffeeshop 96 has a few extras on the inside to keep guests entertained. The most notable, at least to us, is a retro arcade machine called "Super Zola Pac Gal". As its name suggests, it is a multi-machine that plays a list of classic arcade games like Pac-Man, Galaga, and Space Invaders. Granted, this shop is not a retro game haven, but the feature is an interesting distraction nonetheless.

The Menu

The cannabis menu is moderate in size at 96. On the weed-side, they have roughly a dozen items. These are usually a mix of Amsterdam old-school strains, along with a few lower cost imports such as Thai and Jamaican outdoor. The hashish selection is much smaller. The options here are limited to traditional pressed imports from Morocco and other regions.

SHOP FEATURES

SHOP HOURS:

Mon-Sat:
10:00am-1:00am

Sun:
12:00pm-12:00am

COFFEESHOPS

MAP IT

137

Brouwersgracht 137, Amsterdam (Centrum) **:ADDRESS**

Coffeeshop 137 is close to Haarlemmerstraat, a busy tourist street noted for its trendy cafés, craft businesses, and high-end coffee shops. In spite of its proximity to this bustling location, 137 is a bit set to the side. You will find it in a more residential neighborhood just to the southwest. It is not quite as popular or well-known as some of its neighbors to the east. As such, it is less busy with tourists than many of the other shops in the immediate area. This is probably a plus for the locals so not to deal with the throngs of tourists. However, 137 draws its fair share of travelers so one should not view this as a "locals" place.

The Shop

Coffeeshop 137 exists on one level. While perhaps not expansive in its size, the interior is quite comfortable and welcoming. The one-room shop has sufficient seating for visitors on most afternoons. While it looks like a traditional Dutch shop by the exterior, its décor leans towards contemporary. Seating consists of comfortable couch seating which lines the walls, as well as pull-out leather stools and benches. The best seating, however, is perhaps found on the benches outside. They are not quite as plush as the seating inside, but does provide a perfect location to light a joint or bowl, and soak in the wonder of the Brouwersgracht Canal.

The Menu

The cannabis menu at 137 is moderate in size. For weed, they usually stock close to a dozen items. They like contemporary genetics here. Expect to see some USA strains such as the OG and Kush hybrids. Being a shop with a lot of local business, they also stock some traditional items. You are likely to find several Amnesia and White Widow type options here. The hash menu is roughly the same size. Again, they feature both old and new. Potent Dutch isolator (Nederhasj) is found side-by-side with traditional pressed imports from Morocco, Nepal, and Afghanistan. There is a large pre-roll menu here, and there are plenty of glass bongs found throughout for customer use.

COFFEESHOPS

SHOP FEATURES

SHOP HOURS:

Daily:
10:00am-11:00pm

156

ADDRESS: Hudsonstraat 156, Amsterdam (West)

MAP IT

Coffeeshop 156 is found in the Hoofdweg en omgeving neighborhood of Amsterdam West. This translates roughly as "Main Road and Surroundings" in English. The name is probably too generic, as it does a poor job of describing the tranquil old streets that make up this predominantly residential neighborhood. Coffeeshop 156 is also close to Rembrandtpark (Rembrandt Park), one of the most beautiful parks in the city. While this area is far enough from Amsterdam Centrum that you see fewer tourists here, it is every bit as worthy of a visit.

The Shop

Like many of the other numbered establishments, this coffeeshop gets its name from its address: 156 Hudsonstraat. While not very imaginative, it works. Like its name, the shop itself is also best described as low-key. As you enter this establishment, you will find a small ordering desk. It is very basic, and glass-encased as if it were in a rough part of the city - something we would not describe this neighborhood as. Visible from the entryway and lobby, there appears to be a small seating area (enough for four or five people) in the back. Although this would be a sufficient amount of space, albeit a small one, for a smoking lounge, it goes unused as it is for employees only. Likewise, this place serves as a take-and-go establishment only at this time.

The Menu

The cannabis selection at 156 is moderate in size. For weed, expect maybe a dozen options. These are mainly long-established local strains. The hashish menu is much smaller, with less than a half dozen options on most visits. These are exclusively traditional pressed imports.

Even down to their name, Coffeeshop 156 appears to value simplicity and the simple art of providing their community a quality cannabis selection. Likewise, no extra amenities are offered here such as food or drink.

SHOP FEATURES

COFFEESHOPS

SHOP HOURS:
Daily:
10am-8:00pm

MAP IT

420 CAFÉ

Oudebrugsteeg 27, Amsterdam (Centrum) **:ADDRESS**

420 Café is found on Oudebrugsteeg, or in English, Old Bridge Alley. This is a small side street off of the Damrak, a main artery into the city center. The immediate area around this coffeeshop is amongst the busiest in Amsterdam. Likewise, it often gets packed with tourists; hustling in and out of Dam Square and the local high-end shopping district that runs between Kalverstraat and Nieuwendijk. If you can find a seat in here though, 420 can be a nice place to take a break from the crowds.

The Shop

This coffeeshop is also known by another name, De Kuil. This translates into "The Pit". In stark contrast to this name, 420 has a beautiful hardwood interior - the floors, trim, exposed ceilings, and especially the large ornate bar counter with glass-enclosed shelving behind it. The tables, chairs and stools are also wood, and traditional in style. This all makes the place look more like an upscale café or brew house, than a traditional Dutch coffeeshop.

The Menu

The cannabis menu at 420 Café is not very large. On the weed-side, there are usually about half a dozen items. The genetics here are mainly old-school. You should find things like Blueberry, White Widow, and Haze hybrids. However, you are also likely to find a contemporary strain or two. This is a popular shop that sees a lot of tourist traffic, many of whom are looking for USA strains these days. For hashish, the options are fewer, but they tend to be quality imports. 420 also makes some good edibles, usually in a couple of varieties.

Aside from cannabis, this shop also makes pretty good coffee. There is also a decent selection of sodas and other drinks, as well as some basic snacks to keep you comfortable.

CONNOISSEUR GUIDE: AMSTERDAM

COFFEESHOPS

SHOP FEATURES

SHOP HOURS:

Sun-Thurs:
12:00pm-8:00pm

Fri-Sat:
10:00am-1:00am

420 COFFEESHOP

ADDRESS: Singel 387, Amsterdam (Centrum)

MAP IT

420 Coffeeshop is a canal-side shop, resting on the corner of Singel and Heisteeg. It is just outside Spui Square, regarded as a main cultural center for the city. Spui is home to many trendy cafés, restaurants, and in particular, bookshops, some of the largest in the city. 420 Café is just to the west of this square, and provides a very nice view of one of Amsterdam's main canals. There is also a great deal of foot traffic, for those that enjoy people watching. If you do wander around the Spui area and pick up a book, 420 Coffeeshop just might be an ideal place to grab a smoke, cup of coffee, and settle in to read.

The Shop

This small coffeeshop would be best described as a cross between a neighborhood café, and an artsy coffee house. On the one hand, the interior has a lot of wood... dark wood floors, trim, café tables, and pull-up stools. In the back corner, you will even find two rows of old fold down seats, presumably from a movie theatre. These features seem in contrast with the shop's modern lighting fixtures and counter. It is worth noting that 420 Coffeeshop was once named Dutch Flowers. Now it serves as sister shop to 420 Café, a popular establishment closer to Centraal Station.

420 has a nice chill vibe and welcoming atmosphere. It also has a very open feel to it, much of which is attributed to the large windows, which let in an ample amount of natural light. A large double-paneled window in front even opens up, which they take full advantage of on warm sunny days. You can be seated inside, but feel like you are practically on the canal. They usually have tables and chairs out front too.

The Menu

The cannabis menu at 420 coffeeshop is modest in size. On the weed-side, they usually carry a half dozen items or so. The selection tends to consist of recognized old-school favorites, along with a strain or two of their own. Hashish seems more of their specialty. While the selection is smaller on this side of the menu, they tend to stock some quality imports from Morocco and other regions. They also offer a few pre-rolled joint options, as well as a couple different space cakes. We recommend the Lemon Cake, if they have it.

CONNOISSEUR GUIDE: AMSTERDAM

COFFEESHOPS

CONNOISSEUR GUIDE: AMSTERDAM

2nd floor seating area
CoffeeshopAmsterdam (Centrum)

BEST COFFEESHOPS

Amsterdam is home to 168 coffeeshops. This is a large number of businesses, with great diversity in terms of products, services, and amenities offered. In this book we have worked hard not only to compile information on all of these shops, but also to let you know, after many years of visiting them, which we feel are the best. We have broken them down into six categories. Our first list covers the fifteen Best Coffeeshops, overall. We have found them all to provide a great experience. The cannabis menu is a big part of it, but so are other factors, such as the comfort and vibe of the place, and how much we like to spend time there. In short, these are our favorite hangout spots. They are presented in no particular order.

CoffeeshopAmsterdam

This shop has been under new management in recent years, and has undergone a lot of renovation. Under its new name, CoffeeshopAmsterdam has emerged as one of the nicest coffeeshops in the city. It exists on three levels. The décor and atmosphere are modern, relaxed, and welcoming. Further, the cannabis menu reflects a lot of items from Amsterdam Genetics, which supplies a fair portion of the city's connoisseur shops. We love the menu and vibe, and spend a lot of time here.

Dampkring

Dutch for "The Atmosphere", De Dampkring is one of the most beautiful shops in the city. Just look at the hand carved wood façade, and stained glass windows. Inside is no less impressive, and one of the city's most distinct "theme" shops (if the theme is abstract trippy art). It is also a home to connoisseur cannabis, on both the weed and hash-sides of the menu. Not a ton of room in here, and Dampkring is very popular. That means crowds. We recommend that you plan the timing of your visit carefully, lest you will be waiting for a seat.

Katsu

This popular artsy coffeeshop is found in the De Pijp (The Pipe) neighborhood. Katsu is probably most well known for its colorful abstract exterior. However, this shop also has a long established reputation for cannabis. We would describe the place as unpretentious and chill. It is also a popular meeting point for travelers from all over the world. For whatever reason, the atmosphere is highly conducive to conversation here. We almost always meet someone new.

Green House United

This is another of Amsterdam's most noteworthy "full service" coffeeshops. Green House United has a nightclub or lounge feel too it, with beautiful leather trim and cool mood lighting. The weed is exceptional here, as the many trophies are a testament to. But this list is about the shops, and here they deliver. Green House is lush, expansive, and full-service: Burgers, steak sandwiches, eggs, pancakes, salads… you can get it all here. And it is really good!

The Stud

On the east side of Amsterdam you will find The Stud. This part of the city is more residential, so you will find more locals and better pricing here. But The Stud is more than that. There is just something about it. We really love this place. It is cool, real, chill. Whenever we are in the area, we make sure to include The Stud as a resting and re-energizing point. Further, we like the menu as much as the lounge. The quality is excellent for both weed and hashish.

1e Hulp

There is a lot we really love about 1e Hulp. For years this shop has cultivated a quality menu… always looking to improve the weed and hash offerings. We know we will find something nice here. But we rarely just buy and go. We love to hang out at 1e Hulp. This shop has one of the nicest smoking lounges in the city. The place is roomy and artistic, and they place a major emphasis on comfort. The vibe is also upbeat and positive. Frankly, this place can be hard to leave.

Green Place

This is a fun coffeeshop. Green Place is right in the Nieuwmarkt, which happens to be one of the busiest destinations in the city center. There are usually a lot of people around here to begin with. Add to that, a long-standing reputation for quality cannabis. We can see why this shop draws crowds, especially during peak hours. That is fine. This is a place to mingle. The vibe inside is, quite appropriately, more nightclub than the average coffeeshop. It works well.

Abraxas

Looking for even more funkiness? Abraxas is a full-on theme coffeeshop, with its décor modeled after the famous children's story The Little Witch. The inside of this shop is downright cool. It would make a good movie set for something like Harry Potter or Lord of the Rings. But we like it for more than just aesthetics. They have created a comfortable and fun environment here, with an emphasis on customer service. They usually have something nice on the menu too. We always have a good time when we visit Abraxas.

Smoke Palace

This coffeeshop is part sports bar, part sidewalk café. Smoke Palace is a bit out of the city center, so it has more room than many other shops. With it, they have created a spacious lounge, filled with polished wood and comfortable leather-topped benches. Outside, there is a separate seating area, with an "al fresco" vibe we really dig. They have great drinks and desserts here too, and even a few hot food options on the menu. It is the type of place you can wind up staying for hours.

Het Ballonnetje

Het Ballonnetje is an historic shop, dating all the way back to 1978. The building it sits in, much older than that; an impressive bit of classic Amsterdam architecture. The long-established operator here is serious about cannabis quality. You will also find them on our best weed list, deservedly. Further, they foster a very welcoming and friendly environment. This shop is just plain cool; and a pleasure to hang out in. We always find ourselves back here, and recommend it highly to others.

Club Media

The inside of the shop is open, bright, and comfortable. Club Media feels like a small restaurant, with an artistic mix of modern and classic elements. We find the décor quite nice, and the vibe chill and friendly. They are also pretty serious about cannabis here. We have especially found favor with their hashish, but would never criticize the weed menu. This establishment seems to have cultivated a good reputation on many fronts, and gets a lot of repeat business.

Amnesia (2)

The single room smoking lounge here is far from expansive. Even so, they manage to offer guests a great selection of coffees and teas, delectable milkshakes and desserts, a trio of Volcano vaporizers, and frankly, a cannabis menu marked by quality and diversity. This shop is run by the same group that operates the Barney's brand, which is known for higher-end products and service. Amnesia does all this with a super cool and chill urban vibe too. This is one of the shops we really like to hang out at.

Easy Times (25)

This establishment would probably be best described as half nightclub, half coffeeshop. Easy Times has become an increasingly popular destination in the Leidseplein area. Likewise, this place can get crowded, especially on weekends and evenings. The shop is strong on many fronts; cannabis (flower), amenities, vibe. Though we would say it is far from a quiet chill spot. This is the type of place you come to when you want to meet new people, and have a more energetic night out.

Siberië (51)

This coffeeshop is just an all-around chill hangout spot. The place is artsy, without being pretentious. The furniture is mainly tables and chairs. Decorating the walls is a variety of event posters, and paintings from local artists. We would describe the whole vibe as cool, comfortable, and inviting. They are big into coffee too, and have a nice selection of snacks and other things to nibble on. The cannabis menu is usually pretty impressive as well, the weed-side especially. We find ourselves back here often.

Bulldog Palace (16)

Talk about cool coffeeshop history. Bulldog Palace used to be a police station. Years ago the Bulldog team bought the historic building, and turned it into one of the city's largest and most famous coffeeshops. They did preserve some of the original holding cells in the basement, which they turned into an Al-Capone-era museum. What better place for them to sell cannabis products? Upstairs, spend time in the enormous Grand Café.

use your head

discover how to enjoy cannabis at coffeeshopamsterdam.com

coffeeshopamsterdam

amsterdam café

Gorilla Glue #4
Voyagers (Centrum)

BEST WEED (FLOWER)

Amsterdam has long been a global center for cannabis genetics. You can find some of the best cannabis flower (weed) in the world here. It would not be true to say that everything is world class, however. Like any canna-friendly city, quality will vary from one shop to the next. When you spend as much time here as we do, you begin to figure out which establishments are working with the top growers. While a true definitive best weed list might be hard to come by, we do believe these fifteen shops carry some of the best flower in the city. These are all great spots for weed. They are listed in no special order.

1e Hulp (61)

Eerste Hulp ("First Aid") is a favorite shop for many locals and visitors alike. They are much more low key than some of the other connoisseur coffeeshops in Amsterdam. They are a modest independent local shop, with a reputation for high quality cannabis. Most people learn about them, first and foremost, through word-of-mouth. That speaks to the quality here. We are regular visitors ourselves, and cannot recall being disappointed.

Siberië (51)

A short walk to the south of Centraal Station, this is another great place for cannabis flower. They mainly offer the more contemporary strains here. The product is well cultivated; most of the bud here is very potent and quite flavorful. The shop also offers independent lab testing on their product, which is rare in Amsterdam. Note that this is one of four shops under the same management (see also: De Supermarkt, De Republiek, and LoFt). The same high quality cannabis can be found at all of them.

Boerejongens (12) (13) (14) (15)

The name of this shop translates into "Farmer Boys" in English, speaking to this shop's focus on the craft of cultivation. Boerejongens' cannabis stock is grown from Amsterdam Genetics seed, a well-known breeder with numerous awards to its name. They tend to develop a lot of contemporary West Coast USA hybrid strains including some solid Kush varieties. In recent years their shops have earned a reputation for stocking a wide variety of top shelf flower.

FAVORITES

Green House   ㉛

Green House is world-renowned for its focus on cannabis genetics. The vast majority of breeders are content cross-breeding common strains. We celebrate that work, don't get us wrong. However, the team at Green House is at a whole other level. They travel the globe looking for land-race strains: the root genetics, if you will. That is some pretty serious dedication. This shop has produced many award-winning strains. As you might have guessed, they have their own seed line.

Voyagers

This is essentially a take-and-go shop, though there is some limited seating here. They reside at the north-end of the city center, and see a lot of foot traffic from people coming into the city. But the popularity of this shop is unquestionably due to one thing: cannabis quality. Voyagers works with some solid breeders on their strains. The selection is not extensive. Expect to find maybe 6-10 strains on the menu. However, the quality tends to be really on point here. This shop has become a first-stop for many a visiting cannabis connoisseur.

Grey Area

You cannot make a best weed list without including this shop. Like Voyagers, Grey Area is not much to speak of with regard to size, seating, or amenities. There are a few chairs, some stools, and a few corners to squeeze into. Otherwise, this place is a take-and go. Their reputation for weed, however, is nothing short of legendary. This shop used to specialize in American "eighths" complete with traditional sandwich bags. Now you will find regular gram bags, and the pricing is not quite as reasonable as it once was. However, the inventory has remained top notch.

Barney's

Like Green House, the people behind Barney's have done a solid job cultivating a reputation for quality cannabis and delivering a high-end experience. They have been breeding their own strains for a long time now, and have won numerous awards for their genetics. You can find many of their trophies encased in the wall here. Sometimes Barney's can be a victim of its own success – the choicest strains sometimes move too fast. But we always recommend checking out the stock when you are near.

CONNOISSEUR GUIDE: AMSTERDAM

De Kade

People that live in Amsterdam, no doubt, have an advantage over visitors when it comes to sniffing out quality cannabis. You are less distracted by the flash, and eventually find the shops that serve the best quality or value. De Kade is that kind of shop...a locals' favorite. Presently, they are working with an awesome grower. They have a good mix of genetics as well, including some stand out contemporary hybrids. We have no hesitation recommending this shop.

Mr. K & Co.

Another locals' favorite shop. Mr. K & Co. is currently working with Devil's Harvest and Lady Sativa Genetics for their flower stock. The quality has been pretty outstanding. While they do carry an old-school variety or two, think Thai or White Widow, this shop is really known for contemporary strains. They try to stock rare strains, so the inventory is not just "more of the same" when you come here. You can always expect to see an unusual item or two on the menu.

Het Ballonnetje

Coffeeshop "The Balloon" also makes our Best Weed in Amsterdam list. This is an iconic Amsterdam shop, with a long-standing presence in the city (since 1978). In recent years, they have really been focusing on their cannabis inventory, and putting out some great flower in particular. We often find ourselves back here, and always look forward to seeing what is new on the menu. This is a great shop for weed! It is also an uber cool hangout place.

Bagheera

A shop with two cup wins recently for flower also makes our Best Weed list. Bagheera is fairly new on our radar, but certainly a shop we will keep an eye on moving forward. The inventory has been of remarkably high quality as of late, and we have not been disappointed with anything we have purchased on the weed or hashish-side. We suspect you will not be either. If we had to choose one though, we would focus on the flower. They often have some seriously tasty strains.

CoffeeshopAmsterdam

Situated in a busy section of Haarlemmerstraat, CoffeeshopAmsterdam is undoubtedly one of the nicer shops in the area. This large establishment has been rebuilt in recent years, and now boasts a contemporary new interior and vibe. They have three floors of seating, separate cannabis and drink bars, cool accent lighting, and a wonderful view of the crowds from upstairs. The cannabis offerings have steadily improved, especially the flower. You should find some great contemporary genetics.

Solo

They have been paying a lot of attention to the cannabis menu at Solo. Weed and hashish have both been exceptional as of late. Not all that long ago, this shop was mainly about Amsterdam old-school favorite strains. Today, you will find a menu that is also robust with contemporary genetics. Regardless if it is classic or new, you will tend to see some amazingly well-cared-for cannabis at this shop. We would be shocked if you are unable to walk out of here with something aromatic, and glistening with trichomes.

The Plug

If you have been to Barcelona, you might be familiar with The Plug. This is a popular cannabis social club in that city, we would say well known for quality product. The owner has since struck a deal to take over the former Utopia Coffeeshop location here in Amsterdam. The quality here has been excellent, for sure. The Plug is big into "Cali" weed, in particular. That is, product (or genetics) originating from West Coast USA. Expensive? Usually, yes. Worth it? That all depends on how you value these strains. You will find them here though, if looking.

Green Place

We have long been fans of Green Place. This coffeeshop is comfortable, lively, and fun, and never feels like a tourist trap. You can quickly see that they are serious about cannabis here. Lately, the contemporary genetics and connoisseur flower (weed) have been exemplary. The stock rotates often, and they are always bringing in something new, potent, and flavorful. The quality and selection here have put Green Place on our list of go-to shops for flower.

BOEREJONGENS

The Best Amsterdam Coffeeshop
'Where Quality Meets Excellence'

'High Quality Cannabis Seeds'

amsterdamgenetics.com

boerejongens.com

White Choco-Block Hash
Boerejongens West

FAVORITES

BEST HASHISH

Hashish is quite popular in Europe, and a staple at every single coffeeshop in the city. As with cannabis flower, there can be a lot of variation in quality from one shop to the next. The range can be from outrageously delectable, to downright scary. The fact that the supply-side of the market is unregulated in Amsterdam certainly does not help. Like flower, there are some coffeeshops that take its hash much more seriously than others. While it would be impossible to produce a true definitive list, we have found these shops to be among the very best currently for high quality hashish. As with all of our favorite shop lists, these are presented in no special order.

Tweede Kamer

This shop is old school. In the heart of Amsterdam Centrum, they are in a great location, and people make their way here. However, the shop has never seemed to be complacent about this. They care about cannabis, and have long cultivated a solid reputation for their menu, especially with hashish. Tweede Kamer works with a few well-established brands, and stocks a nice variety of high quality items. You will find great Moroccan imports here, and domestic waterworks. This is one of those "must do" places if you are big on hash.

Solo

This down-to-earth establishment is quite comfortable, and uber chill. Solo is big into music. In recent years, this shop has become really serious about their cannabis menu too. The hashish is no exception. Solo has had some of the more delectable imports we have seen as of late. The stock is usually soft, flavorful, and highly potent. If hashish is your thing, we highly recommend a visit here. This is a quality establishment that carries quality product.

El Marssa

This is largely a neighborhood place. As one might expect from a more locals establishment, they do not offer a large selection of cannabis products here. The menu is moderate in size, even on the hashish-side, which they do seem to specialize in. They are big on Moroccan pressed imports, in particular. What products they do have on the menu tend to be quite consistent in quality though, in our experience. Their love of hashish shows.

CONNOISSEUR GUIDE: AMSTERDAM

Boerejongens

Farmerboy seems to love his hashish. This chain of coffeeshops is growing in Amsterdam, largely based on its reputation for product quality. The hashish is no exception. They specialize in something called "block hash" - a specialized type of hash production that is utilized by some growers in Morocco. It involves partitioning sections of farmland into "blocks", so that strains can be segmented off. When done correctly, it is a way to maintain a much higher quality and variety. The quality of the Boerejongens product has been exceptional as of late.

Family First

A new player in Amsterdam is Family First, which appeared on the scene in 2018. It took over the old Bushdocter location on Amstel. So far, they appear to be working hard to stand out from the competition (not an easy task with over 160 competitors). One of the ways they are attempting to do this is by going strong on new genetics. Especially noteworthy, you will usually find some hot USA strains used in traditional pressed hashish products. They also have some higher potency items like Nederhasj (Isolator).

Rusland

After the close of Mellow Yellow, Rusland is now the oldest coffeeshop in the city. Historically, it tended to operate as a low-key type of place. You either knew about them or you did not. They did not promote themselves as a tourist attraction. Time will tell if that changes given their unique position now. Until then, old school Amsterdammers will keep coming here, mostly for the hashish, which they seem to specialize in. They have slowly improved the shop over the years. The place is now quite luxurious, and comfortable to hang out in.

Bluebird

This shop has an extensive hashish menu. Bluebird has a lot of imported pressed hashish; many classic varieties. The product is usually pre-bagged, which is not our favorite practice. There is something about watching a big chunk of hash being taken out, and having a sliver sliced off with a fat knife right in front of you. However, we will not give them too much flack for their effort to be efficient. The hash is quite good here, in our experience. They are nothing if not very consistent with the quality.

Roxy

This shop is found in the trendy De Pijp (The Pipe) section of Amsterdam-Zuid. The cannabis menu is noteworthy here. It is substantial in size. And while it is particularly heavy on the flower (weed) side of things, they are more well known for their hashish. Most notable is their Moroccan Tidghine, which they always seem to feature on the menu. This soft blond hash has won multiple awards in local cannabis competitions. It is potent and flavorful; excellent quality.

Dampkring

Do not let the Ocean's 12 movie appearance and incredible popularity of this place with tourists fool you. Dampkring is old school. They have long been very serious about their cannabis here. The quality of the inventory shows it. We find great options on both sides, but give a slight nod to their hashish. This place does get crowded, but the cannabis (not the fame) is still the draw for most visitors. We are among them, and always enjoy checking out the large menu.

1e Hulp 61

"First Aid" also makes our list of best shops for hashish connoisseurs. This large and cozy coffeeshop generally has a very strong menu on both the flower and hash-side. As we understand it, the owner works hard to secure their supply, often traveling away from the business to do so. At 1e Hulp you will find both imported traditional hashish options, as well as more exotic higher potency products like Jelly Hash, Nederhasj (Isolator), and moonrocks. Such diverse selection alone makes this shop standout from most competitors.

The Stud 57

This coffeeshop is a bit out of the way, over in Amsterdam Oost (East). It is more a locals place, and does not see big crowds of tourists. Consequently, it is often overlooked when people talk about great shops. That is a mistake. Not only is this place pretty darn nice, but the hash menu in quite strong. They have been working with quality suppliers on the stock. The champagne hash has been particularly noteworthy during recent visits, though you will probably find several excellent options if you drop in.

De Kroon

We are also pretty big fans of this shop. Dutch for "The Crown," De Kroon is not expansive. This coffeeshop is, however, quite warm and cozy. The interior is funky and modern, and the furniture extremely comfortable. They are pretty big into cannabis here too. The weed has been great, though we might give them a slight edge on the hashish. The stock tends to be exceptional. Plus, we are pretty sure they were the first shop in Amsterdam to add a rosin press. Customers are free to make their own dabs, if they wish.

Johnny

This shop has evolved over the years, and now has a very "dispensary" type feel. The interior is clean and clinical; the focus squarely on the cannabis inventory. Johnny has been stocking the shop with great product as of late. We have taken an especially strong liking to the hashish. They always seem to have highly potent domestic isolators, and super flavorful Moroccan "block" hashes. Like many favorites on the hash list, they also tend to have top-shelf weed here. We just like the hash a little better on most days.

Bagheera

They usually have a nice selection of both imports and higher potency Isolator (Nederhasj) at Bagheera. The latter is more difficult to come by in Amsterdam, in spite of its local origin. Isolator is a more complicated process, and one with a lower yield. But the potency can be much higher than traditional imports. With both types of hashish though, the quality at this coffeeshop has been excellent, and consistent. We doubt you will be disappointed with anything you end up buying.

Katsu

This is another great shop. Katsu has a long-established reputation for quality cannabis, particularly hashish. They usually sell pre-weighed bags here. While that is not our favorite practice, we will not give them any flack about the quality. It is usually excellent. The products are mainly traditional. This is not the place to come if you are looking to torch dabs. However, if you want some soft, oily, flavorful hashish, Katsu should be right up your alley. Plus, it is a really chill place to hang out at.

TWEEDE KAMER
1985

COFFEE SHOP ❌❌❌ **AMSTERDAM**

One of
THE OLDEST COFFEESHOPS
in town.

Colorful cakes
Kooi (Centrum)

BEST EDIBLES

Looking for marijuana infused edibles? Barring the occasional standout (who remembers the Bonbons from Café Chocolata?) Amsterdam used to be a pretty bleak place for it. That has been changing in a big way in recent years. A good number of coffeeshops now have great edibles; far improved from the basic space cakes (granted, often good) we lived with for so many years. We have thoroughly enjoyed the change, and have done our best to keep up with all the new inventory. Right now, we believe these shops are among the very best for edibles.

DNA (24)

DNA is mainly a takeaway place. With not much of a lounge to speak of, they focus on their menu for recognition. We have really liked their edibles lately. Their selection is quite large most days. More importantly though, the products are quite a step above the traditional "space cake". Just look at some of their items: Brownie Oreo, White Chocolate Cake, Brownie KitKat. Their cakes are so delicious but remember, these are potent marijuana edibles. You may not want to go overboard.

Basjoe (7)

This coffeeshop has a cool and relaxed vibe that makes it feel somewhat like a café or bakery. The edibles suggest this may have been intentional. Whereas many shops are content with just a simple weed brownie, Basjoe delivers a wide selection of muffins and cakes. Most have between .4 and .5 gram of weed in each. The weed is a Kush strain too. These are quite potent. Do not let the fractions fool you. Between the excellent edibles, great coffee, and wide range of other basic drinks and snacks, this place really does feel like a small weed café.

Best Friends

While it is impossible to know what something tastes like from a photograph, we suspect this one of Best Friends' weed cupcakes might offer a pretty good idea. They have a nice range of edibles, and they do them right. Honestly, we have not tasted them all yet. We would like to, but it is hard to get passed the cupcakes. These gooey fluffy cakes are quite potent, and even more delicious than the photo lets on.

Bagheera

The cannabis products have been solid at Bagheera. The weed, the hash - we like this shop across the board. Their selection of edibles is no exception. They usually have a decent variety of cakes and brownies to choose from. Flavors often go far beyond the standard chocolate and vanilla. If you cannot find something you like, you are probably going to be in trouble. These edibles are really delicious, and as we have come to expect of Bagheera, quite strong too.

Boerejongens

Boerejongens has definitely upped their game with edibles. Their "Spacetry" line of products includes a wide variety of cakes, muffins, and other delectables. It was created by a Michelin Star chef, clearly much more gourmet than you typically find at a coffeeshop. Likewise, they are taking edibles to a level of quality usually reserved for top-shelf brands from Colorado or Las Vegas. These products are simply amazing, which has earned the Boerejongens shops a definite spot on our list of best places for edibles.

Greenhouse Effect

This shop is kind of low on the radar for most people. They have a similar name to the famous Green House brand of Amsterdam, though not related. It can be easy to overlook these guys, but that would be a mistake. Locals know Greenhouse Effect has a long-established reputation for quality edibles. While their line might not be quite as large as some other shops, their cakes are great. Like all shops on our list, they do not seem to cut corners on ingredients (including the cannabis).

Paradox

They do not make a lot when it comes to edibles. However, Paradox unquestionably has a reputation for their homemade pound cake. This has been earned by robust use of potent ingredients. By that we mean they put a FULL GRAM of cannabis in each cake. This shop tends to have good weed too, so this is no joke. It will flatten you if you are not experienced with edible products. They recommend you start with a quarter slice and wait two hours. Good advice.

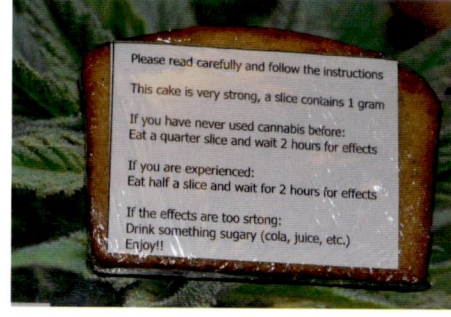

1e Hulp

One of the best all-around coffeeshops in the city, 1e Hulp is also one of our favorite places to go for edibles. They have a delicious line here, mainly a variety of cake squares and muffins. You almost always have several options. The different flavors should all be very good. Though these products are potent, they do a good job of masking the cannabis taste. Keep this in mind. Some space cakes you have to choke down. These you have to remind yourself to stop eating.

Rookies

This is a hip chill place, which is popular with locals and city visitors alike. Rookies is pretty down-to-earth, even after its recent renovation, which was extensive. The "real" vibe of this place has endured the new leather seats and plush décor. The cannabis offerings are generally very good here. If we had to put a finger on just one that makes them stand out, it is probably the "Happy Cake." Their signature edible is delicious, and also quite potent.

La Tertulia

We would have regretted leaving La Tertulia off the list of best coffeeshops for edibles. This shop is one of those places that seem to do it right when it comes to coffee and food. They are not the biggest, and the selection is not always the largest. But their chef is really good, and when they do an edible, it is usually spot on scrumptious. These brownies during a recent visit were no joke.

Kooi

Kooi is one of the new players on the Amsterdam coffeeshop scene. They took over the spot for Old Amsterdam, and completely remodeled the place. With new management came new, well, just about everything. The cannabis menu is quite decent here, and we have taken a special interest in the edibles. They usually do not have a big variety, but whatever cake they have on offer should be tasty, and quite removed from a standard weed brownie.

CONNOISSEUR GUIDE: AMSTERDAM

Relax

The Relax shops are pretty strong with the locals. As such, they tend to have a menu that is more reasonable in price. They also need to keep the inventory pretty tight if they are going to keep their regular business coming in. On that front, they have been doing a good job. They usually have some solid offerings when it comes to their weed and hash. The edibles, however, have been a knockout. Made with a hefty dose of weed or hash, the taste still seems to be well masked. Delicious. We are impressed. Thumbs up.

Siberië

They do not offer a wide variety of edibles here. Actually, they usually just carry one option at Siberië. It is a walnut brownie, made with a mix of white and dark chocolate. The rest of the ingredients are equally simple and natural. No artificial colors, flavors, or sweeteners. It tastes really good. And they make each with .5 gram of cannabis. The weed here is very good, and the brownie will pack a punch. Take it easy. Thankfully, if you get too stoned to leave you will be stuck in one of our favorite coffeeshops.

Easy Times

There is usually a good variety of edibles here; various muffins, brownies, and/or cakes. This makes Easy Times stand out quite a bit. Most shops only focus on their flower and hash. The edibles are an afterthought. Here, they seem to take them seriously. We would not say these are the most potent in our experience. They are good, but not over the top. As such, this is a great place to bring someone new to cannabis, and looking for an edible they are not going to overdo it on.

„YO-YO"
GALERIE COFFEESHOP

"More Like a Living Room Than a Coffeeshop."

Yo-Yo is a unique experience. Local art, an impressive organic menu, and warm community feel make this one of the most comfortable and welcoming shops in the city.

MONDAY TO THURSDAY	FRIDAY AND SATURDAY	SUNDAY
12:00 – 19:00	12:00 - 20:00	12:00 - 19:00

2e Jan van der Heijdenstraat 79
Amsterdam, Oud Zuid

Row of Verdampers
Happy Feelings (Centrum)

BEST VAPOR LOUNGES

Vaporization is the practice of consuming cannabis by heating it to where key cannabinoids boil (and vaporize) off the plant, but below the point of combustion. With it, much of the plant matter is left behind, with no charring or ash. Given proper temperature and device, you can produce an almost pure mist of cannabinoid/terpene vapor, which many regard as potentially less harmful to your health than smoking. Vapor can also be more flavorful than smoke, and at least by some accounts, more economically efficient. Whether you are a serious vaporist, or are interested in trying it for the first time, Amsterdam has a nice collection of coffeeshops with vaporizers available for your use. These are our picks for the best.

Barney's

This shop gets the first spot on our list. Why? How about a Volcano vaporizer unit at every table? Barney's has long been serious about vaping, and installs numerous Volcano units (which are top of the line) in all of their establishments. Barney's gets crowded, so it can be hard to find a spot. However, if you do get one, you can chill comfortably. You will never have to leave your seat to fill a balloon with vapor, unless you run out of weed.

Barney's Lounge

Like we said, they are big on vaping at Barney's. The Lounge is in second place for total number of Volcano units in Amsterdam, behind only to their flagship coffeeshop. Depending on where you sit, you might need to get up to fill your balloon. Frankly though, it will be a very short walk at best. They have Volcano units in practically every corner of the shop here. Finding an open one has never been a problem for us. This is a very comfortable and chill coffeeshop beyond the vapes too; highly rated.

Amnesia

This coffeeshop is operated by the same people that run the Barney's shops. Not surprisingly, Amnesia is another big destination for vaporists. Though this coffeeshop is fairly small, you will find a trio of Volcano Digit units sitting on a small shelf against the side wall. We have never seen more than two in use at any given time, which means you are pretty much guaranteed an open spot if you come here. Plus, the coffee and desserts are great, and the vibe is pretty cool.

Happy Feelings

Coffeeshop Happy Feelings has a nice collection of Verdamper vaporizers. The Verdamper is a Dutch invention, and one of the first commercial vaporizers available. Truth be told, we do not like these as much as the Volcano units. They just aren't quite as user friendly, or as aesthetically pleasing. But they do work well, and are bong-attached, so these units are great if you love the higher density (albeit with less flavor) when water-filtering your vapor.

Paradox

One of Amsterdam's more funky and artistic shops also makes our list for Best Vapor Lounges. With one room, Paradox is not a very large shop. Still, they host two Volcano units here. Like Amnesia, this makes it a popular city destination for visiting vaporists. It is also a really cool place, generally speaking, so you would probably wind up here at some point anyway. The Volcano units are just icing on the cake.

Abraxas

We love the lounge at Abraxas. This is a great hangout spot for any cannabis enthusiast. But it can be an especially great shop for vaporists. They have multiple Volcano units here. They keep them on the main floor, not far from the cannabis and drink counters. While the units may not be at every table, serious vaporists should have no problem accessing one. You might just want to find a close seat downstairs, however. The narrow winding staircase may be a bit much to go up and down for every fill.

Easy Times

This cross between a nightclub and a coffeeshop is uber chill, and located in a prime location behind the Leidseplein. It gets very busy, especially in the evenings. If you can shoulder through the crowds, you will find two Volcano units at a vape station in the middle of the shop. Even with this nice setup, Easy Times is low on the vaporist's radar. It should not be. The units are well maintained, and usually open… at least one of them.

Bluebird

Bluebird was recently renovated. The new lounge is quite impressive. It is clean and contemporary... chill and comfortable. They have long been supportive of vaporists here at Bluebird. Presently, you will find two Volcano units on the coffeeshop floor for customer use. Just ask for a chamber and bag. Note: this is a well-known hash shop, but you probably do not want to vape hash in a Volcano. It can work, but also makes quite a mess.

Green House United

Of the vapor lounges on our list, this is the first that has only one vaporizer unit available for use. How then does it make our list? First, the shop is not extremely large. There is not usually an issue using the Volcano when needed. Worst case, you may have a small wait. Second, Green House tends to be really good about maintaining the unit and its accessories. Nine times out of ten, a coffeeshop will hand you a crusty well-used chamber and a leaky old balloon. At GH, everything is usually fairly new, clean, and ready to go.

Smoke Palace

We love this coffeeshop for many reasons; one being that it can be a great spot if you like to vape. They usually keep their Volcano unit at the counter. Simply ask to take it to the back. There are several power outlets spaced out against the wall, under the leather benches. Just find one not being used to charge a cellphone. Plug the Volcano in and take a seat. You can usually have the unit to yourself for a while. This place is more of a local's hangout, and does not see many serious vaporists.

Baba

Baba used to be in the Red Light District. The place got very crowded. It was definitely not a vape hangout. The shop was forced to move though, this time to a less popular area. You will find the new shop quite an improvement over the old one if you are a vaporist. They now have a pair of Verdampers set up on one of the lounge tables. While we prefer the Volcano, these units do work very well. Plus, the Verdampers are water cooled, which adds a different element to the experience; thick vapor bong hits.

CONNOISSEUR GUIDE: AMSTERDAM

Katsu

Another highly artsy coffeeshop, Katsu has long been accommodating to vaporists. They have a dedicated Verdamper station here. The unit is usually well-kept, with clean water. The dedicated area helps keep the unit safe, but you should still be careful with fragile glass. Like the sign says here, "Breaking = Paying." Katsu is one of our favorite shops in Amsterdam overall. While it is not on the top of our list of best vapor lounges, we feel it is still worthy of inclusion.

The Stud

We won't say The Stud is the most serious vapor lounge. They have a single Volcano unit at this coffeeshop, that is about it. No wall of Volcanoes; no neon-lit Verdamper station. But this is a great coffeeshop, with exceptional weed and hashish. And there is a chill vibe in here too. This shop tends to be less crowded than some of popular places in the city center as well, another bonus. The fact that they have a proper vaporizer unit makes it even more desirable as a hangout spot.

De Supermarkt

This coffeeshop is part of the same group that runs Siberië, LoFt, and De Republiek. They have a dedicated Volcano vaporizer station here at De Supermarkt. They not only make the unit available, but promote the health benefits of the practice, as well as the general information and review site vaporizerblog.com. We celebrate the fact that they are passionate about vaping. De Supermarkt can be a really chill and down-to-earth place to hang out. We happily recommend it to others.

The CoffeeShops.com

Quality and Excellence
Since 1984

Siberië
Brouwersgracht 11

Monday - Thursday
09:00 - 23:00

Friday & Saturday
09:00 - 00:00

Sunday 10:00 - 23:00

LoFt
Jan van Galenstraat 285

Monday - Thursday
09:00 - 23:00

Friday & Saturday
09:00 - 00:00

Sunday 10:00 - 23:00

De Republiek
Tweede Nassaustraat 1B

Monday - Thursday
09:00 - 23:00

Friday & Saturday
09:00 - 00:00

Sunday 10:00 - 23:00

De Supermarkt
Frederik Hendrikstraat 69HS

All Week
11:00 - 23:00

Pinball Museum
The Spirit (Centrum)

SPECIAL INTEREST

There are many great coffeeshops in Amsterdam. It can be a challenge to narrow down our favorites at times. Certainly, there are some shops we would regret not mentioning. This section covers those places not featured in our other specific favorites lists, yet we still recommend seeing. Some are historic. Others are just really cool places to hang out. Whatever the reason, we recommend giving this list a scan before ending any trip to this city. You might come across something you really don't want to miss.

Bulldog 90

Bulldog was one of the first coffeeshops in Amsterdam. It is also one of the longest running, having stood in this same exact spot since opening in 1975. Cannabis sales still take place in the basement, as they did before tolerance. They have a lot of history on display here. Check out the "orange alarm", which was once used for warning staff downstairs when the police were coming in, for one of their frequent raids. Our biggest complaint about this place is that it gets too crowded. But it is really famous. We get it.

The Spirit

Love pinball? How about retro arcade games? If you answer yes to either question, than The Spirit is for you. This coffeeshop has a FULL WALL of pinball machines in the back, along with some other video arcade games. It is practically a museum. These bits of history are scarce these days. You usually only find them being maintained by collectors that really love them. And love them they do here. This place is known for it. In fact, many non-smokers come in here just to play the games.

Kashmir

This shop has a super comfortable, artistic, and funky vibe. The menu is great, especially for hashish. But it is not the coffeeshop, but the Kashmir Café/Lounge across the street, which really makes this brand stand out. This large cannabis-friendly restaurant serves hot food and cold beer. The vibe in here is equally cool, making this a great hangout spot. Were the coffeeshop connected to the lounge, we would undoubtedly have this on the Best Coffeeshop list. But technically speaking, we would be listing a non-coffeeshop in this case.

CONNOISSEUR GUIDE: AMSTERDAM

Yo-Yo

This is a truly unique establishment. Yo-Yo does not feel like a coffeeshop at all. Rather, it feels like you have been invited to a friend's house to smoke and hang out. Grab a comfortable spot in the living room, order some coffee (at times, even hot food!), and just soak up this place. The management here is real, and extremely welcoming. It is rarely crowded too, providing an intimate setting for those that pay a visit. Yo-Yo also serves as an art gallery for local talent. This is definitely a neighborhood place with an uber cool vibe.

Resin

The lounge is what we like most about Resin. The smoking area past the main counter is both artistic, and really cool. Funky green stools and tiered benches provide ample seating in this place. Behind them are walls with giant murals of cultural figures like Snoop and Bob Marley. These are stunning. Add a green playground swing and a cozy balcony that overlooks the room, and you have a place that is uniquely Amsterdam. This place is quite popular, and we can understand why.

The Noon

This coffeeshop is not big, but it is chill and artsy. Its one-room smoking lounge is open, and comfortable. We would not describe the décor as luxurious, but then again The Noon is not on the list for its décor or amenities. We like it because it is down-to-earth, and just plain cool to hang out at. We also like the menu. This shop has a history of entering cannabis competitions, at least off and on, and was probably placed on the map for its award-winning Blueberry strain. You will find that this shop is quite popular with locals.

Prix D'Ami

This place is MASSIVE. Prix d'Ami is the largest coffeeshop in Amsterdam, and has some impressive amenities. How about the only 3D movie lounge in the city? Check the top floor. Pool tables, DJ booth, hot food. It is all here. Prix D'Ami is an experience in and of itself. This shop of closer to a mega nightclub than a quiet down-to-earth Dutch coffeeshop. If you are looking for a loud, fun, wild night in a packed-to-the-gills coffeeshop, come on by.

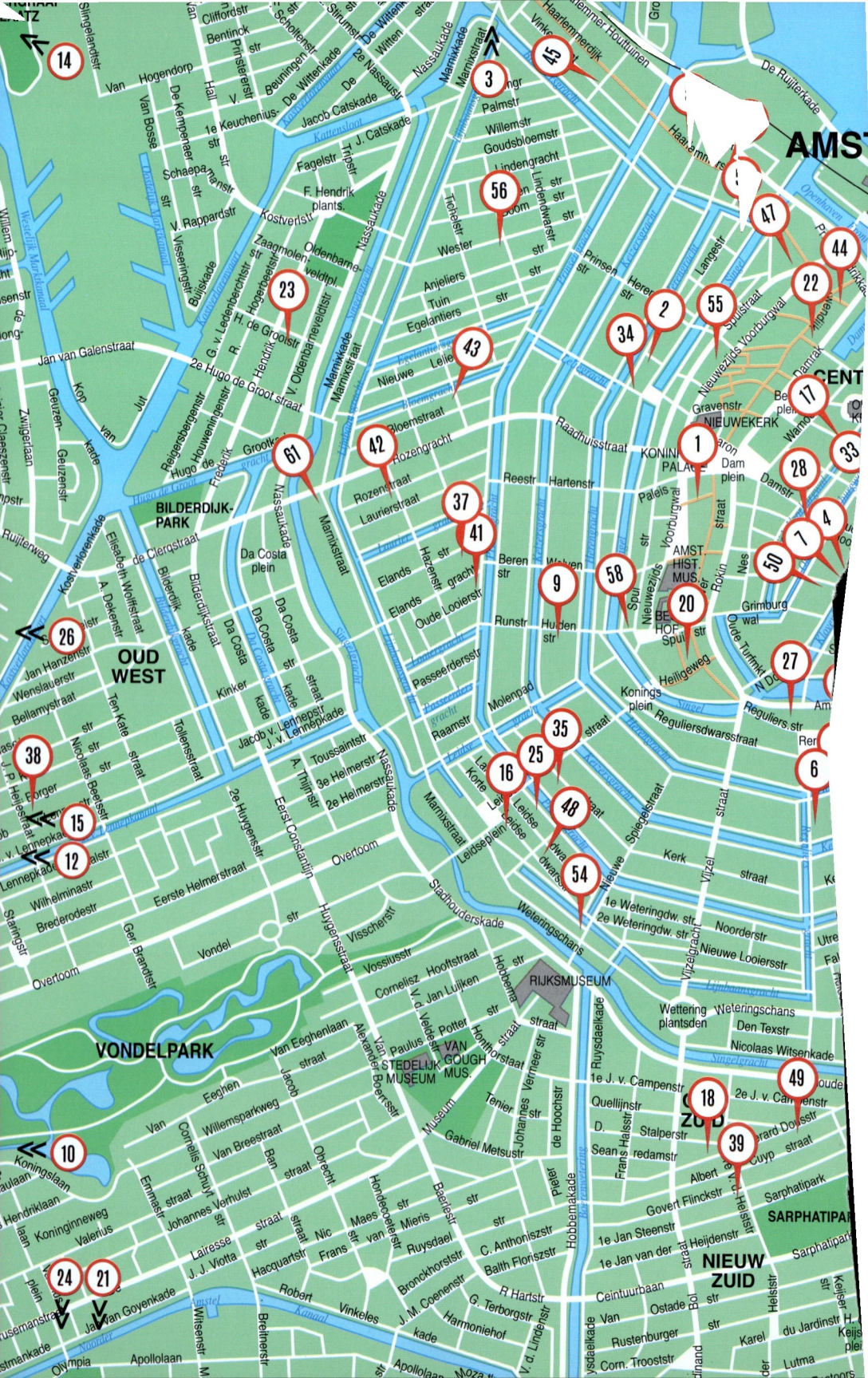

OUR FAVORITES
COFFEESHOP MAP

1. Abraxas
2. Amnesia
3. Baba *
4. Bagheera
5. Barney's
6. Barney's Lounge
7. Basjoe
8. Best Friends *
9. Best Friends II
10. Best Friends III *
11. Bluebird
12. Boerejongens Bij *
13. Boerejongens Center
14. Boerejongens Sloterdijk *
15. Boerejongens West *
16. Bulldog Palace
17. Bulldog 90
18. Club Media
19. Coffeeshop Amsterdam
20. Dampkring
21. De Kade *
22. De Kroon
23. De Supermarkt
24. DNA *
25. Easy Times
26. El Marssa
27. Family First
28. Green House Centrum
29. Green House Namaste
30. Green House Pijp
31. Green House United
32. Greenhouse Effect
33. Green Place
34. Grey Area
35. Happy Feelings
36. Het Ballonnetje
37. Johnny
38. Kashmir
39. Katsu
40. Kooi
41. La Tertulia
42. Mr. K & Co.
43. Paradox
44. Prix D'Ami
45. Relax
46. Relax Zuid *
47. Resin
48. Rookies
49. Roxy
50. Rusland
51. Siberië
52. Smoke Palace
53. Solo
54. The Noon
55. The Plug
56. The Spirit
57. The Stud *
58. Tweede Kamer
59. Voyagers
60. Yo-Yo
61. 1e Hulp

* Outside Map Area >>